INTERNATIONAL DEVELOPMENT IN FOCUS

Youth Employment in Nepal

Dhushyanth Raju and Jasmine Rajbhandary, Editors

WORLD BANK GROUP

Contents

Tables

Acknowledgments

This book was edited by Dhushyanth Raju and Jasmine Rajbhandary. Chapter authors include Scott Abrahams, Laurent Loic Yves Bossavie, Anastasiya Denisova, and Jyoti Maya Pandey. Sailesh Tiwari served as a member of the team. Pradeep Singh provided research assistance in the early stages of the work, and Rajshree Karki provided administrative support.

The team would like to thank the following World Bank Group colleagues: Pablo Gottret, Takuya Kamata, Stefano Paternostro, and Martin Rama, who provided guidance and support from management; Johannes Koettl and David Newhouse, who served as peer reviewers at the concept and decision review stages for the book; and Taneem Ahad, Mohan Prasad Aryal, Roshan Bajracharya, Manav Bhattarai, Purna Chhetri, Damir Cosic, Sangeeta Goyal, Markus Kitzmuller, Gladys Lopez-Acevedo, Yasuhiko Matsuda, Elliot Mghenyi, Bigyan Pradhan, Maya Sherpa, Bandita Sijapati, Jayakrishna Upadhya, and Thomas Walker, who provided input, feedback, and support at various points during the book's preparation.

The team would like to express its appreciation to external stakeholders who provided feedback and assistance at different points during the book preparation process. From the government of Nepal (in alphabetical order): Jayanath Acharya, Baikuntha Aryal, Dilli Bastola, Surya Bhandari, Rama Bhattarai, Govinda Mani Bhurtel, Lok Nath Bhusal, Prasad Gautam, Tulasi Prasad Gautam Bhojraj Kafle, Raghuraj Kafle, Badri Karki, Laxman Prasad Mainali, Umesh Kumar Mishra, Yuga Raj Pandey, Nabaraj Paudel, Khagaraj Paudyal, Shivaram Pokharel, Bhumishwor Pokhrel, Jiwan Kumar Rai, and Gyan Raj Subedi. From the government of the Republic of Korea: Ki-Wook Kim. From academic, civil society, international development, nongovernmental, and private-sector organizations: Meena Acharya, Bal Gopal Baidya, Hridaya Ratna Bajracharya, Sunila Baniya, Cecilia Banks, Sukriti Bashyal, Punya Bhandari, Usha Bhandari, Rita Bhandary, Anil Chaudhary, Rajju Malla Dhakal, Ram Chandra Dhakal, Anna Engblom, Hiramani Ghimire, Sita Ghimire, Ganesh Gurung, Manju Gurung, Pravina Gurung, Meenu Hada, Avinash Karna, Shaleen Khanal, Brabim Kumar, Andrew J. Nelson, Baburam Pant, Bishnu Dev Pant, Meena Poudel, Uddhav Raj Poudyal, Bina Pradhan, Kaajal Pradhan, Priti Prajapati, Vidhan Rana,

Dipendra Sharma, Neelam Kumar Sharma, Sarojini Sherchan, Dipanker Shrestha, Mangesh Shrestha, Prativa Shrestha, Subas Subedi, Deepak Thapa, Gaurav Thapa, Labisha Uprety, and Mio Yokota.

The team sincerely apologizes to any individuals or organizations omitted inadvertently from this list, and expresses its gratitude to all who provided guidance and assistance for this book.

About the Contributors

EDITORS

Dhushyanth Raju is a Lead Economist in the Office of the Chief Economist, South Asia Region, of the World Bank. Currently, he provides policy advice to client countries and conducts economic research on human development in South Asia. He holds a doctorate in economics from Cornell University.

Jasmine Rajbhandary was born in Lesotho, and grew up as a "UN child" in various parts of Africa and the United States. She completed her bachelor's in economics and sociology at Binghamton University in New York. After completing her master's in international development at American University in Washington, DC, she returned to Nepal in 1997. Since then, she has worked for Save the Children, the UK Department for International Development, and now the World Bank. Her career has focused on working with vulnerable communities, women, and children, and on developing processes and services to improve their life outcomes and inclusion in development.

At the World Bank, Rajbhandary is a Senior Social Protection Specialist and leads on projects that help the governments of Bhutan, India, and Nepal provide more efficient social protection services.

AUTHORS

Scott Abrahams is a doctoral student studying labor and development economics at Duke University. Previously, he worked as a research consultant at the World Bank and the Inter-American Development Bank, and taught at the Johns Hopkins University School of Advanced International Studies, where he also completed his master's in international economics and China studies.

Laurent Bossavie is an Economist (Young Professionals Program) in the Social Protection and Jobs Global Practice of the World Bank. His primary specialization is in applied labor economics and the economics of education. At the World Bank, he has been conducting research and providing policy advice on those topics for the South Asia and Europe and Central Asia regions. Prior to joining the World Bank, he was a researcher at the Department of Economics of the European University Institute, and a research consultant at the Inter-American Development Bank. He holds a doctorate and master's in economics from the European University in Florence, Italy.

Anastasiya Denisova is an Economist in the Social Protection and Jobs Global Practice, South Asia Region, of the World Bank. Her work focuses primarily on labor market issues, and on social protection systems. Prior to joining the World Bank through the Young Professionals Program, Denisova worked with the International Finance Corporation. She holds a doctorate in economics from Georgetown University.

Jyoti Pandey is a Social Protection Specialist at the World Bank country office in Nepal. Her work focuses on safety net systems and adaptive social protection. Prior to joining the World Bank, she worked on local governance with the German development agency, GIZ. Pandey has a master's degree in public policy from the Hertie School of Governance in Berlin.

Abbreviations

ADB	Asian Development Bank
AME	average marginal effect
ANTUF	All Nepal Trade Union Federation
CTEVT	Council for Technical Education and Vocational Training
DOFE	Department of Foreign Employment
EPF	Employees Provident Fund
FEA	Foreign Employment Act
FEPB	Foreign Employment Promotion Board
FET	Foreign Employment Tribunal
FEWF	Foreign Employment Welfare Fund
GDP	gross domestic product
GEFONT	General Federation of the Nepalese Trade Unions
HDI	Human Development Index
ILO	International Labour Organization
KNOMAD	World Bank Global Knowledge Partnership on Migration and Development
MOYS	Ministry of Youth and Sports
NAHS	Nepal Annual Household Surveys
NEP	National Employment Policy
NLEP	National Labor and Employment Policy
NLFS	Nepal Labour Force Survey
NLSS	Nepal Living Standards Survey
NMS	Nepal Migration Survey
NSTB	National Skills Testing Board
NTUC	National Trade Union Congress
OLS	ordinary least squares
PSC	Public Service Commission
PSU	primary sampling unit
SDC	Swiss Agency for Development and Cooperation
SLC	School Leaving Certificate

SSF	Social Security Fund
SWTS	School-to-Work Transition Survey
TSLC	Technical School Leaving Certificate
VDC	Village Development Committee
VIF	variance inflation factor
VSDTC	Vocation and Skills Development Training Center

1 Overview

DHUSHYANTH RAJU AND JASMINE RAJBHANDARY

INTRODUCTION

Promoting the smooth integration of workers into the labor market and ensuring their early success has increasingly emerged as an important economic and social development goal around the globe. This is exemplified by the 2030 United Nations Sustainable Development Goals 4 and 8, which explicitly refer to youth and their employment (United Nations 2015). Many low-income countries, including Nepal, are in the middle of a youth bulge—and an expanding one at that—in their demographic structure. In addition, today's youth are, on average, more educated than past generations. These dynamics present real opportunities for Nepal's economic growth and development.

Nepal also faces risks from failing to provide sufficient, suitable employment that is productive and remunerative for the country's youth, potentially resulting in substantial, lasting economic and social costs—not just for the affected youth but also for their families and communities. A particularly relevant issue for Nepal, given its recent history, is the interplay between poor labor market conditions and prospects for youth and social unrest.

International evidence suggests that the labor market opportunities, challenges, and behaviors of youth can differ in important ways from those of older individuals. For example, youth labor outcomes are more likely to be adversely affected, and youth are more likely to migrate out of their communities, when local economic conditions are weak or when such conditions worsen. Youth can face additional barriers to labor market integration because of their relative lack of labor market experience and lack of access to social, financial, and physical capital to establish their own income-generating activities. Youth's exposure to weak labor market conditions—even if such conditions are short-lived—can lead to long-lasting, adverse labor market and economic outcomes over their working lives (ILO 2017; World Bank 2006, 2012).

The Nepal government sees addressing the social and economic challenges of youth, and leveraging their social and economic prospects, as critical for the country's economic growth and development. This priority is reflected, for example, in the government's latest national economic program blueprint, the *14th Periodic Plan*, released in 2017 (Government of Nepal 2017), and the *Youth Vision 2025 and Ten-Year Strategic Plan* and *National Youth Policy*, both issued in 2015 (Government of Nepal 2015a, 2015b). The development research and practice communities in Nepal share the same perspectives regarding the relationship between youth labor and livelihoods and the country's economic growth and development.

There has been limited systematic, policy-oriented empirical research conducted on labor and livelihoods in Nepal. Dedicated examinations of Nepalese youth labor are rarer still. The literature tends to be composed of sociological studies of Nepal's labor history, intertwined with the country's social and political history; labor market statistical profiles and survey reports; and qualitative and empirical studies of international migration by Nepalese workers, its determinants, and its effects. These studies paint a relatively distinct picture of the nature and evolution of Nepal's labor market. However, with a few exceptions, existing studies are largely nonempirical, weak in statistical rigor, biased in terms of the representativeness of the data, or partial in terms of what aspects of the labor market or what issues are covered.

This book aims to improve our understanding of the labor conditions, behaviors, and outcomes of Nepalese youth. It examines these aspects of Nepal's domestic labor market, as well as in relation to labor migration to India and other countries, including the temporary "foreign employment" of Nepalese workers under bilateral labor agreements between Nepal and destination countries. In so doing, the book seeks to present insights and implications for research and public policy, with the goal of improving the labor prospects of Nepalese youth.

In the book, youth are defined as individuals ages 16–34 years. This definition largely overlaps with Nepal's official definition (ages 15–40 years); it is consistent with the "extended youth" definition applied in other research internationally; and it is appropriate, given that sizable shares of men and women ages 15–24 years (24 percent and 17 percent, respectively, in 2010–11) are still attending education institutions. Because Nepalese law considers individuals as children at age 15 (Government of Nepal 2000), this book sets the minimum age for youth at 16.

The book mainly uses four data sources for the various empirical analyses: (1) the 2008 Nepal Labour Force Survey (NLFS), (2) the 2003–04 and 2010–11 Nepal Living Standards Surveys (NLSSs), (3) the 2013 School-to-Work Transition Survey (SWTS), and (4) foreign employment permit data from the Nepal government's Department of Foreign Employment (DOFE). These data sources are summarized in annex 1A. Data are analyzed by applying statistical methods that mostly are standard in microeconometric research. The book also synthesizes existing literature for Nepal and draws on published statistics for the country, as relevant.

One limitation of the book is that it does not analyze youth labor demand by firms. Although the country has surveys of certain types of firms, those surveys gather firm-level information on workers in general, and not on youth workers specifically.[1]

COUNTRY BACKGROUND

Nepal is a landlocked country situated between China and India. It is composed of three main ecological regions that run east to west: the Mountains, the Hills, and the Terai (lowlands). The country's population totaled 26.5 million in 2011, with an annualized growth rate of 1.4 percent between 2001 and 2011. Four-fifths of the population resided in rural areas in 2011 (Government of Nepal 2012).

The World Bank classifies Nepal as a low-income country, with an estimated per capita gross domestic product (GDP) of US$685 (in constant 2010 U.S. dollars) in 2016. The country has experienced weak economic growth, especially compared to other South Asian countries, some of which rank among the fastest-growing in the world. Since the 1990s, the country's annual economic growth rate has averaged about 2.5 percent. In 2016, the real annual GDP growth rate was 0.4 percent (World Bank 2017).

In contrast to its weak economic growth performance, Nepal's record in reducing consumption-based poverty has been impressive. Measured using the World Bank's US$1.90 per day per person line, the country's national poverty rate declined from 45.7 percent in 1995–96, to 34.8 percent in 2003–04, and to 15 percent in 2010–11 (World Bank 2018).[2] Over this period, income inequality appeared to increase and then to decrease: the national income–based Gini coefficient rose from 0.34 in 1995–96 to 0.41 in 2003–04, and then declined to 0.33 in 2010–11 (World Bank 2014).

The United Nations classifies Nepal as a "medium human development" country, ranking it 144 out of 188 countries in the Human Development Index (HDI) for 2015, with a life expectancy of 70 years, average years of schooling of 4.1, and expected years of schooling for a child at entry into school of 12.2. The country's 2015 HDI value is higher than that for least-developed countries, but lower than for South Asia overall. Although the country's HDI value increased by roughly 150 percent from 1990 to 2015, its international ranking has changed little (UNDP 2016).[3]

Agriculture and services are the mainstays of Nepal's economy, with the two sectors jointly accounting for 85 percent of GDP in 2016. The relative contribution of agriculture to GDP has fallen over time (from 42 in 1990 to 32 percent in 2016), whereas that of services has increased (from 32 percent to 52 percent over the same period) (see figure 1.1). Industry (manufacturing),

FIGURE 1.1

Sectoral distribution of GDP, 1990–2016

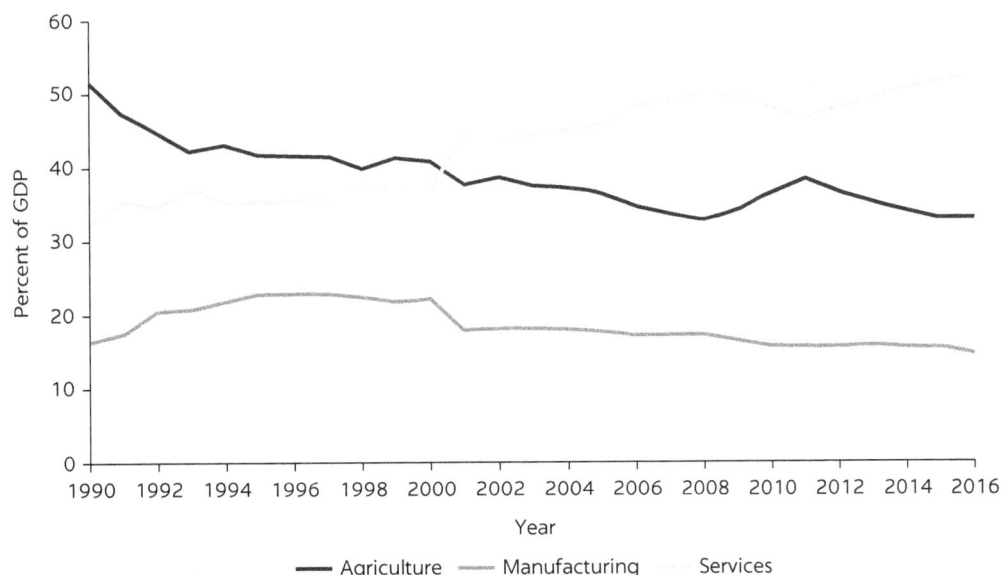

Source: Statistics obtained from World Bank 2017.
Note: GDP = gross domestic product.

which accounted for 15 percent of output in 2016, is mainly composed of agro-processing. Its contribution to output has remained relatively stable, at about 15 percent, since the early 2000s (World Bank 2017).

The size and dynamism of Nepal's economy are considered to have suffered from violent civil conflict from 1996 to 2006, political instability and deadlock over the 2000s, a severe earthquake in May 2015, and a trade and supply disruption from September 2015 to February 2016.

MAIN CHAPTERS

This book comprises five main chapters. Chapter 2, titled "Youth Sensitivity of Labor Laws and Policies," examines Nepal's labor laws and policies in terms of whether and to what extent they cover youth labor issues and interests. The chapter mainly reviews official documents and the small number of available review studies of labor regulation. It describes labor laws, policies, and institutions that cover workers irrespective of age, but highlights those that specifically aim to promote the labor interests of youth. Note that the chapter reviews relevant government institutions prior to the recent reorganization of Nepal's government into a federal structure. However, we expect the conclusions drawn from the review to remain relevant.

The chapter argues that Nepal's labor laws and policies have largely failed to influence the labor decisions and outcomes of youth or older individuals because of poor implementation, stemming from weak government commitment and capacity. With the exception of civil and armed services recruitment rules, labor laws generally do not include special provisions for youth. Government policies on domestic employment, foreign employment, and training tend to focus on or prioritize youth. The policies set ambitious targets for youth employment, but these targets often are not based on sound estimations or predictions using suitable data. The government also does not have in place the organizational arrangements, operational plans, or resources needed to meet these targets.

Chapter 3, titled "A Profile of Youth in the Domestic Labor Market," examines how youth fare in the domestic labor market, mainly on the basis of 2010–11 NLSS data. The chapter finds that youth unemployment and time-related underemployment rates tend to be low. An analysis of trends between 2003–04 and 2010–11 indicates two major shifts in labor patterns for youth in general: (1) an increase in the share of youth attending school, which indicates more years of schooling and thus later entry into the labor market, and (2) a decline in the share of workers who are self-employed in agriculture and an increase in the shares of workers who are self- or wage-employed in nonagriculture. The chapter also documents three major shifts in labor patterns among rural youth: (1) a decline in the employment rate for women, (2) a decline in average hours worked by female and male workers, and (3) an increase in real hourly earnings for rural male wage workers in agriculture.

Annual wage statistics corroborate the labor earnings trends for Nepal, showing that agricultural workers have experienced the largest real gains in wages, whereas salaried workers essentially have experienced no real gains. Given that salaried workers tend to be more educated than wage workers, labor-earnings returns to education appear to be declining. The evidence suggests that the demand for more-educated workers is not keeping up with the increase in the supply of such workers.

Chapter 4, titled "Labor Market Perceptions and Sentiments among Youth Workers," examines the views that employed and unemployed workers ages 16–29 years report in relation to their labor decisions and outcomes, on the basis of SWTS data. With respect to employed workers, the chapter finds that most found employment by either joining their family's income-generating activity or asking friends or family for assistance. The majority of workers say that their qualifications are relevant, but a sizable minority believe that they need additional education or training.

Most employed workers report that their main difficulty in finding employment is either insufficient employment opportunities or inadequate qualifications. In rural areas, wage workers are more likely to report insufficient employment opportunities were the main difficulty, whereas unpaid family workers are more likely to report inadequate qualifications were the main difficulty. Most workers are dissatisfied with their employment, at a rate that is much higher than for workers in other SWTS-surveyed countries. A large share of workers desire to change employment, mainly to find employment that has better working conditions, offers more work hours, or better matches their qualifications.

With respect to unemployed workers, the chapter finds they had longer employment searches and are more likely than employed workers to have refused employment offers. The main reason unemployed workers give for turning down an offer is low wages.

Similar to employed workers, most unemployed workers report that the main difficulty they face in finding employment is either insufficient employment opportunities or inadequate qualifications. Nepalese unemployed workers are more likely to report insufficient employment opportunities are the main difficulty than their counterparts in other SWTS-surveyed countries. Within Nepal, more-educated unemployed workers are more likely to report insufficient employment opportunities are the main difficulty.

Chapter 5, titled "Youth Labor Migration," uses NLSS and DOFE foreign employment permit data to examine internal and external labor migration by Nepalese youth. External labor migration is separated into the flow to India, which is unregulated, and the flow to other countries, which typically takes the form of temporary contract migration to countries with bilateral labor agreements with Nepal (referred to in Nepal as "foreign employment").

The chapter finds that youth labor migration is extensive in Nepal, and that it is male dominated. Male youth labor out-migration rates are highest from the rural Terai, rural Hills, and the Mountains. Most female youth labor migrants move within Nepal, whereas most male youth labor migrants go to other countries. Irrespective of gender, most youth migrants appear to be wage-employed, particularly when they go to other countries, and to engage in services. The chapter also examines the correlates of youth labor migration, by gender and by destination type. It finds, for example, that labor migration is positively associated with education attainment for women, but negatively associated for men. Labor migration is also positively associated with household economic status for women.

Foreign employment permit data indicate that foreign employment workers from Nepal primarily go to Malaysia, Qatar, Saudi Arabia, and the United Arab Emirates. Foreign employment outflow appears to be mainly influenced by economic and other forces in destination countries, rather than in Nepal. Nepal's foreign employment system faces several challenges, including implementation shortcomings in the government's institutional arrangements for workers, and the substantial market power in Nepal of private recruitment agencies over workers.

The chapter examines the effects that male youth labor migration has on the labor outcomes of youth household members, and the home labor outcomes of returned youth labor migrants compared to youth nonmigrants. Male youth labor migration appears to have a negative effect on the likelihood of employment and hours worked for both female and male youth household members. Returned youth labor migrants from external destinations other than India appear to have poorer labor outcomes than youth nonmigrants.

Chapter 6, titled "Youth Labor Skill Training," examines formal off-the-job training by youth, mainly on the basis of NLFS data. Such training involves short courses or vocational education tracks that confer a Technical School Leaving Certificate (TSLC) or a technical diploma. The chapter finds that, measured in 2008, 10 percent of youth had received training at some point in the past—a relatively high rate among South Asian countries.

Training rates are higher for urban residents than for rural residents, and for individuals who have obtained at least a School Leaving Certificate. Differences in training rates are small between genders, but large between regions in Nepal. Training tends to be short-term, with basic computing and dressmaking and tailoring the most popular fields for women, and basic computing the most popular for men. Youth training recipients tend to be on the older end of the 16–34 years age range, better educated, and more likely to be attending school. They also tend to come from wealthier households and traditionally advantaged ethnic or caste communities, especially for those who received training in basic computing.

Training is associated with higher likelihoods of employment, wage work, and nonfarm work for women. Whether such effects are statistically significant varies by selected sociodemographic and training subgroups, namely schooling status, education attainment, rural versus urban residence, short training versus TSLC or technical diploma programs, and basic computing versus other fields. For men, training does not appear to be associated with the likelihood of employment, wage work, or nonfarm work; and the effects on these outcomes vary little by the examined sociodemographic and training subgroups. In general, the chapter does not find that training is associated with wage earnings for either gender.

The chapter also examines interest in training among Nepalese youth. In 2008, 40 percent said they would like to obtain training, with interest especially high among youth outside the Kathmandu Valley. Women express the most interest in training in the fields of dressmaking and tailoring and basic computing, whereas men are mostly interested in basic computing. Although wealthier youth tend to have higher rates of training, interest in training is higher among less wealthy youth. Interest in training is also higher among those who have previously received training and among those who are already employed.

RESEARCH AND POLICY DIRECTIONS

The analysis and findings in the book point to several potential areas for further data collection and research on Nepal's youth labor market. These include the evolution of female labor force participation in rural areas; the employment search and worker–employment match process; labor productivity; worker preferences for employment, measured more rigorously, such as through preference elicitation experiments; the gains and costs of internal and external migration; the organization and functioning of the foreign-employment recruitment market; the structure and functioning of training programs, including on-the-job training; and the interplay between public and private labor markets.

The collective findings in the book point to three directions for orienting public policies and programs. First is raising rural labor productivity, urban labor demand, and urban worker–job matching efficiency. The youth labor market patterns and trends documented in the book suggest (1) large adjustments in rural labor markets produced by labor supply shifts and (2) depressed labor demand in urban labor markets, particularly for more-educated workers. In rural labor markets, rising wage earnings appear to mainly reflect falling labor supply rather than rising labor productivity. Strategies are needed to (1) raise labor productivity in agriculture and rural agribusiness, (2) improve the employment search and matching process for workers, and (3) spur labor demand by employers—for example, by addressing any policy distortions that depress firm output and employment.

Second is supporting the labor market integration of rural youth migrating to urban parts of Nepal and of youth labor migrants returning from India and other countries. Although rural–urban labor migration is also important, there is, however, little government support to help prospective labor migrants from rural areas find suitable employment in the Kathmandu Valley and other urban areas. At present, such labor migrants find employment through informal personal networks or chance breaks. In addition, there is little government support to help labor migrants returning from other countries integrate into Nepal's labor market so as to generate not only significant private labor returns for returning migrants but also positive labor market spillovers (that is, employment creation or earnings gains for other individuals). Evidence suggests that returning youth labor migrants are more likely than youth nonmigrants to engage in agriculture. Thus, returning youth labor migrants may be an important target group for the government's intent to modernize agriculture. Strategies are needed to help both rural–urban and returning labor migrants integrate into the labor market in a way that is more efficient and effective.

Third is improving the orientation and efficacy of labor skill training. Strategies are needed to widen and enhance the potential labor market gains from skill training, and to strengthen the quality and relevance of training delivered by private and public providers. Evidence suggests strong demand for skill upgrading. Workers who are already employed—specifically, women in all sectors and men in agriculture—express a higher desire for training. Past training recipients express a higher desire for further training in the same fields. Relatively poorer households and households in regions outside the Kathmandu Valley also express a higher desire for training. In line with this evidence, strategies are needed to better match training supply to demand.

ANNEX 1A: MAIN DATA SOURCES

Nepal Living Standards Survey: 2003–04 and 2010–11

Administered by the Central Bureau of Statistics, the NLSS is a national household sample survey based on the World Bank's Living Standards Measurement Survey instrument and approach. The 2003–04 survey round, administered between April 2003 and April 2004, is representative at the level of six strata or regions: (1) the Mountains (rural), (2) the Kathmandu Valley (urban), (3) urban Hills, (4) rural Hills, (5) urban Terai, and (6) rural Terai. The survey consisted of a panel sample and a cross-sectional sample. The original panel sample was 1,232 households from 100 primary sampling units (PSUs) drawn from the 1995–96 NLSS, of which 1,160 households from 95 PSUs were successfully interviewed. The original cross-sectional sample was 4,008 households from 334 PSUs, of which 3,921 households in 326 PSUs were successfully interviewed.

The 2010–11 survey round, administered between February 2010 and February 2011, is representative at the level of twelve analytical domains: (1) the Mountains (rural), (2) the Kathmandu Valley (urban), (3) urban Hills—Other, (4) urban Terai, (5) rural Hills—Eastern, (6) rural Hills—Central, (7) rural Hills—Western, (8) rural Hills—Mid- and Far Western, (9) rural Terai—Eastern, (10) rural Terai—Central, (11) rural Terai—Western, and (12) rural Terai—Mid- and Far Western. The sample consisted of a panel sample and a cross-sectional sample. The original panel sample was 1,200 households from 100 PSUs drawn from the 2003–04 NLSS, of which 1,032 households from 100 PSUs were successfully interviewed. The original cross-sectional sample was 6,000 households from 500 PSUs, of which 5,988 households in 499 PSUs were successfully interviewed.

The 2003–04 and 2010–11 survey rounds contain information on housing, access to facilities, literacy and education, health, marriage and maternity history, employment and earnings, home production, assets and expenditures, farming and livestock, nonfarm enterprises and activities, credit and savings, and migration and remittances, transfers, and social assistance. See Government of Nepal (2004, 2011) for survey design details.

Nepal Labour Force Survey: 2008

Administered by the Central Bureau of Statistics, the NLFS is a household sample survey based on the International Labour Organization's Labour Force Survey instrument and approach. The survey round was administered between January and December 2008. It is representative at the level of six strata (regions): (1) the Mountains (rural), (2) rural Hills, (3) rural Terai, (4) the Kathmandu Valley (urban), (5) urban Hills, and (6) urban Terai. The original sample was 16,000 households in 800 PSUs, of which 15,976 households in 799 PSUs were successfully interviewed. The NLFS contains information on demographics, education, current and past economic activities, current noneconomic activities, unemployment, underemployment, absentees, and remittances. See Government of Nepal (2009) for survey design details.

Nepal School-to-Work Transition Survey: 2013

SWTSs are an effort coordinated by the International Labour Organization as part of the Work4Youth Project financed by Mastercard Foundation. Surveys were conducted in 28 low- and middle-income countries between 2012 and 2015. The Nepal SWTS was administered by the Centre for Economic Development and Administration (CEDA). Tribhuvan University, Kathmandu. The survey is representative at the level of six strata: (1) the Mountains (rural), (2) rural Hills, (3) rural Terai, (4) the Kathmandu Valley (urban), (5) urban Hills, and (6) urban Terai. The original sample was 3,020 households from 151 primary sampling units. Only individuals 15–29 years of age were to be interviewed. The SWTS successfully interviewed 3,584 individuals in this age group from 2,652 households. The survey contains information on demographics, education, training, aspirations, activity history, and nonworking young adults. See Serriere and CEDA (2014) for survey design details.

Department of Foreign Employment Permit Data: January 2010–May 2016

The employment permit data cover January 2010 to May 2016 for foreign employment workers who used private recruitment agencies (referred to in the book as agency-based foreign employment workers) and from September 2011 to May 2016 for foreign employment workers who did not use recruitment agencies (referred to in the book as individual foreign employment workers). The data contain information on the worker's age, gender, district of origin, destination country, date of permit issue, recruitment agency, foreign employer, occupation, and wage.

NOTES

1. In addition, the available firm surveys from Nepal suffer from issues regarding coverage and representativeness, which are not uncommon for such surveys in low- and middle-income countries.
2. Unofficial poverty estimates based on data from the national Nepal Annual Household Survey rounds from 2013–14 and 2014–15 indicate that the poverty rate has continued to fall.
3. When the country's 2015 HDI value is adjusted for inequality in human development outcomes, the value falls by 27 percent—roughly in line with the declines in HDI values for least-developed countries and South Asia when the same adjustment is made.

REFERENCES

Government of Nepal. 2000. Child Labor (Prohibition and Regulation) Act, 2056 (2000). Government of Nepal, Kathmandu.

——. 2004. *Nepal Living Standards Survey 2003/04: Statistical Report—Volume One.* Kathmandu: Central Bureau of Statistics, Government of Nepal.

——. 2009. *Nepal Labour Force Survey 2008: Statistical Report.* Kathmandu: Central Bureau of Statistics, Government of Nepal.

——. 2011. *Nepal Living Standards Survey 2010/11: Statistical Report—Volume 1.* Kathmandu: Central Bureau of Statistics, Government of Nepal.

——. 2012. *National Population and Housing Census 2011 (National Report).* Kathmandu: Central Bureau of Statistics, National Planning Commission Secretariat.

——. 2015a. *Youth Vision—2025 and Ten-Year Strategic Plan.* Kathmandu: Ministry of Youth and Sports, Government of Nepal.

——. 2015b. *National Youth Policy 2072 (2015).* Kathmandu: Ministry of Youth and Sports, Government of Nepal.

——. 2017. *14th Periodic Plan.* Kathmandu: National Planning Commission, Government of Nepal.

ILO (International Labour Organization). 2017. *Global Employment Trends for Youth 2017: Path to a Better Working Future.* Geneva: International Labour Office.

Serriere, Nicolas, and CEDA (Centre for Economic Development and Administration). 2014. *Labour Market Transitions of Young Women and Men in Nepal.* Work4Youth Publication 12. Geneva: International Labour Office.

United Nations. 2015. *Transforming Our World: The 2030 Agenda for Sustainable Development.* A/RES/70/1. New York: United Nations.

UNDP (United Nations Development Programme). 2016. *Human Development Report 2016: Human Development for Everyone.* New York: United Nations Development Programme.

World Bank. 2006. *World Development Report 2007: Development and the Next Generation.* Washington, DC: World Bank.

——. 2012. *World Development Report 2013: Jobs.* Washington, DC: World Bank.

——. 2014. *Nepal–Country Partnership Strategy for the Period FY 2014–2018.* Washington, DC: World Bank.

——. 2017. *World Development Indicators 2017.* Washington, DC: World Bank.

——. 2018. *Nepal: Systematic Country Diagnostic.* 114659-NP. Washington, DC: World Bank.

2 Youth Sensitivity of Labor Laws and Policies

JYOTI PANDEY

INTRODUCTION

Nepal has several laws and policies that aim to regulate the labor market.[1] These laws and policies mainly focus on employment in private enterprises, public employment, and the temporary, contract-based private employment of Nepalese workers in other countries under labor agreements (this form of labor migration is referred to in Nepal as "foreign employment").

Do Nepal's labor laws and policies shape youth labor decisions and outcomes? This chapter reviews sensitivity of various labor laws and policies with respect to youth, using mainly a review of official documents and the small number of available review studies of labor regulation in the country. Although summarizing labor laws and policies that cover workers irrespective of age, the chapter highlights labor laws and policies, or provisions within them, that specifically aim to promote the labor interests and outcomes of youth. Note that the chapter reviews government institutions before the Nepal government was recently organized into a federal structure. Nevertheless, we expect the review findings to remain relevant.

Most labor laws do not have provisions specifically related to youth. The areas where laws particularly affect youth are public employment, where entry is generally restricted to those below age 35, and foreign employment, which is dominated by youth. Motivated by growing concerns over the large scale, and low-skilled nature, of foreign employment by youth, the government has recently introduced policies that aspire to promote domestic employment and higher-skilled foreign employment for youth.

Arguably, with the exception of public sector and foreign employment regulations, labor laws and policies are poorly enforced or implemented and thus have little bearing on the labor decisions and outcomes of workers in general. Implementation failures are considered to arise from a lack of government commitment and capacity. The problem is, however, not unique to labor regulations but afflicts the country's public policy and action in general. In addition to policies, the government has administered labor projects, mainly in labor skill training, supported by international donors with the aim of influencing the labor outcomes of youth and older workers. These projects tend to be piecemeal and small in scale.

The remainder of the chapter is organized as follows. The next section discusses the adoption and application of international labor standards by the Nepal government. The following section discusses labor laws and youth-related policies. The fourth section, "National Development Plans," discusses the government's economic plans and their coverage of youth employment issues. "Donor Engagement" discusses labor projects supported by international donors. The chapter concludes with a summary.

INTERNATIONAL LABOR STANDARDS

International labor standards, specifically conventions and recommendations developed by the International Labour Organization (ILO), aim to promote opportunities for women and men to obtain decent and productive work in conditions of freedom, equity, security, and dignity. The Nepal government has ratified all but one of the eight fundamental conventions. The exception is Convention 87 on Freedom of Association and the Protection of the Right to Organize. In addition, the government has ratified 1 of the 4 ILO governance conventions, and 3 of the 177 ILO technical conventions. Ratification of a convention signifies that the government has committed to applying the convention in practice, and regularly reporting to ILO on the application of the convention, with technical assistance from ILO if needed.

The government's application of the conventions in national law and practice often falls short. For example, the government ratified fundamental Convention 182 on the Worst Forms of Child Labor in 1997 and passed relevant legislation, including the Child Labor (Prohibition and Regulation) Act in 2000.[2] The incidence of child labor is estimated at 28 percent, on the basis of 2010–11 Nepal Living Standards Survey data (Government of Nepal 2011a). The initial National Master Plan on Child Labor (2004–14) was reviewed in 2010. Following the review, the National Master Plan on the Elimination of Child Labor in Nepal (2011–20) was drafted but not approved by the government. The plan aimed to eliminate the worst forms of child labor by 2016, and all forms of child labor by 2020.

Likewise, the government ratified fundamental Convention 29 on Forced or Compulsory Labor in 2002 and fundamental Convention 105 on the Abolition of Forced Labor in 2007, and passed the Bonded Labor (prohibition) Act in 2002. The act contains provisions for the freedom of *kamaiyas* (a form of traditional bonded labor), penalties for employers that use bonded labor, and rehabilitation for freed *kamaiyas*, and prescribes the formation of Freed Bonded Laborer Rehabilitation and Monitoring Committees in relevant districts.[3] The *haliya* bonded labor system was prohibited in 2008. However, many of the traditional bonded labor systems continue to exist.

The 2015 Constitution of Nepal guarantees fundamental rights and duties related to labor, such as the right to employment, the right to proper work practices and social security, and the right to form labor unions and associations. The Constitution also has provisions against discrimination and forced and bonded labor, specifying them as acts punishable by law. It also calls for the rehabilitation of *kamaiyas, kamlaris, haruwas, charuwas,* and *haliyas,* by providing them with land and livelihoods.

LABOR AND YOUTH POLICIES

Labor

The Labor Act of 1992 was the main legislation that regulated employment until September 2017, when the Labor Act ("New Labor Act") of 2017 was approved by the government. The two acts specify rules regarding (1) employment and job security, (2) working hours, (3) pay, (4) benefits, and (5) occupational health and safety, among others. The Labor Act of 2017 seeks to address concerns regarding stringent hiring and dismissal procedures and inadequate social security provisions.

Whereas the previous act applied only to private enterprises with 10 or more workers, the New Labor Act applies to all enterprises, irrespective of their size.[4] However, specific provisions—such as collective bargaining and the requirement to establish a labor relations committee—apply only to employers with 10 or more workers. Employers with 20 or more workers are also required to establish a health and safety committee. The Labor Act of 1992 mandated that all positions be advertised prior to appointing workers, that appointment letters be provided to selected workers, and that the Labor office be notified of new appointments. Upon hiring, a worker was to be placed on probation and then appointed permanently after one year of continuous service if considered to demonstrate efficiency, sincerity, and discipline.[5] The New Labor Act requires the existence of an employment agreement between the employer and the worker prior to commencement of work. In the case of casual employment, this agreement can be verbal. The New Labor Act has reduced the probation period to six months and waived the requirement to notify the Labor Office of any new appointments. The New Labor Act has also introduced provisions for internships and traineeships.

Dismissal regulations in Nepal were considered to be among the most stringent in the world for permanent staff. Nepal was among 33 countries, including India and Sri Lanka (out of 187 countries), where not only prior notice to, but also prior approval by the government were required for dismissal (World Bank 2016). The only acceptable grounds for dismissal were misconduct and redundancy. Poor worker performance could not be grounds for dismissal. The New Labor Act allows for dismissal of workers if work performance is found to be unsatisfactory in three or more consecutive performance appraisals.

Severance pay remains one of the most generous, with pay of one month of salary per year of service. For workers with 10 years of service, this equals 43 weeks of salary—well above the average of 24 weeks in low-income countries (World Bank 2017). The New Labor Act states that employees who receive unemployment allowance as per the Social Security Act will not be eligible for severance pay. According to the 1992 act, the social security provisions—including contributions to the provident fund, gratuity, and health and accident insurance—applied only to permanent workers; these provisions now apply to all workers, irrespective of their employment type—regular, work-based, time-based, casual, or part-time.[6]

Along with the New Labor Act, the Social Security Act of 2017 has been approved. The Social Security Act seeks to provide contributory social security to workers, including the self-employed, in both formal and informal sectors. The act governs the establishment of the Social Security Fund (SSF), which will implement the schemes, including (1) medical treatment and health security,

(2) maternity security, (3) accident security, (4) disability security, (5) old age security, (6) dependent family security, (7) unemployment assistance, and (8) others as defined by SSF. The act requires employers to enlist their existing workers in SSF within six months and new workers within three months of the act's going into effect. The act authorizes SSF to take actions against employers that either do not enlist their workers or do not pay the contributions into SSF. The rate of contribution to SSF by the worker and the employer is to be recommended by a committee formed per the act. In the case of self-employed and informal-sector workers, the government will contribute a specified amount to SSF, based on the worker's contribution. In the case of part-time workers, the New Labor Act states that each employer has to contribute on the basis of the basic salary paid to the worker. SSF will operate as a revolving fund, funded by contributions from workers and employers, the mandatory 1 percent tax on the salary of all formal sector workers levied beginning in fiscal 2011/12, grants from the government and other donors, and income from its investments.

The two recently approved acts governing labor and social security are expected to improve industrial relations. Effective labor market regulations strike a balance between incentivizing employers to create jobs and protecting workers. Nepal's labor regulations, similar to those of other low-income countries in South Asia, were criticized for being stringent and more protective of employers than of workers (World Bank 2012). However, labor regulations are not reported to be a major obstacle to doing business in Nepal, according to the 2013 Nepal Enterprise Survey (World Bank 2013a). Only 2.7 percent of the employers in Nepal see labor regulations as a significant obstacle to their operation, compared to 11.2 percent of employers in India (World Bank 2014a). Private enterprises in Nepal report political instability as the main obstacle, followed by inadequate electric power availability and access to finance. Among 15 types of obstacles to doing business, labor regulations ranked 12th in Nepal. In comparison, labor regulations ranked 6th on the list of obstacles to doing business in India, and 14th in Bangladesh (World Bank 2013b, 2014a).

Although labor market regulations may not be the major constraint on employment growth, they were seen to have failed in protecting workers because of past regulations' limited coverage of employers (they applied only to employers with 10 or more workers) and because of noncompliance (World Bank 2012). Job vacancies are not always advertised, working hours are not fixed, and minimum wages are not enforced. Pay, benefits, and working conditions for workers are generally poor, and worker absenteeism and tardiness are widespread and acute (Sijapati 2014). Employers experience frequent, crippling industrial strikes, in addition to other disruptions such as political instability and electric power shortages. In 2013, labor issues such as trade union action (much of it led by labor unions affiliated with political parties), civil unrest, or employee absenteeism were considered to have led to an estimated loss in productive activity of 21 days (World Bank 2014b).

Low government capacity is considered to be a binding constraint on the effective implementation of the provisions of the New Labor Act. For example, safety and health provisions of this act are to be enforced by factory inspectors. Although the Department of Labor has provisions for 10 factory inspectors to be placed in the 10 labor offices across the country, there were only 5 in fiscal 2015/16. The budget speech for fiscal 2016/17 noted mandatory factory inspections and plans to mobilize the needed number of inspectors. The ILO recommends 1 labor inspector for 40,000 workers in low-income countries, which would imply the need for over 60 labor inspectors to cover wage workers in Nepal.[7] The act also has provisions for labor officers, who are to be responsible for coordinating between workers and employers to promote the rights and interests of workers. The government has not appointed any labor officers to date. Labor regulations often do not take into account enforcement capacity. Stringent labor regulations coupled with weak enforcement capacity tend to mean poor compliance. As regulations become costlier to implement, employers seek to circumvent them (World Bank 2012; Sapkal 2015). A recent study has also shown stringency of labor regulations to be negatively correlated with enforcement: the more stringent the law, the weaker the enforcement (Ronconi and Kanbur 2016).

Low enforcement capacity is not unique to Nepal in South Asia. The factory inspection regime in Bangladesh is similarly plagued by an acute shortage of inspectors, limited resources, and ineffective inspection services, which has meant that even core labor standards are not met (Chowdhury 2017). Enforcement is weakened by the complexity of the regulations (India), collusion between employers and inspectors (India and Pakistan), and inadequate dispute resolution mechanisms (India, Pakistan, and Sri Lanka) (World Bank 2012).

To improve labor market outcomes, the Nepal government needs to strengthen its enforcement capacity. It should also benefit from less stringent labor laws, improved social security, and active labor market programs, as recommended for low-income countries with similarly stringent regulations but poor enforcement and compliance (World Bank 2012).

Following the Labor Act of 1992, the government introduced the Labor Policy in 1999. This policy has been updated twice, first as the National Labor and Employment Policy (NLEP) in 2005 and second as the National Employment Policy (NEP) in 2015. The 2005 NLEP focused on promoting labor standards, such as eliminating forced labor, child labor, and discrimination; establishing a social security system; increasing the efficiency of labor; investing in skills; and creating a business-friendly environment. The 2015 NEP focuses on coordination across sectors including agriculture, energy, and tourism for employment creation; skill training suited to labor market demand; regulation of foreign employment; development and use of a labor market information system; and prioritization of youth-focused employment creation.

However, the policies are neither based on evidence nor backed by resources for effective implementation. Actual coordination across sectoral policies and government agencies for employment creation is poor or absent, and there has been little investment in developing a labor market information system. Under the Department of Labor, there are 14 employment information centers across the country with the mandate to manage labor market information, maintain a register of unemployed workers, and match unemployed workers with employment vacancies. The centers are barely functional, not only because of limited resources but also because employers do not provide information on employment vacancies.

Despite prominent mention in the policy documents, the state of public employment policies and services—including career counseling, job-search, and job-matching support, and labor market information—is similarly poor in many low-income countries (ILO 2015). A large proportion of young people in Nepal, Bangladesh, Cambodia, and Vietnam find their jobs through personal connections (ILO 2015).

Trade unions

Trade unions are governed by the Trade Union Act of 1992, which was amended in 1999 (Trade Union [First Amendment] Act 1999). The act mandates that unions have to register with the government, and that a worker can be a member of only one firm-level trade union at a time. To qualify for registration, a firm-level trade union must have at least 25 percent of the workers in the firm as members. Registration of an association of trade unions requires a membership of at least 50 firm-level trade unions, whereas registration of a federation of trade unions requires a membership of at least 10 trade union associations. Civil service employees can form trade unions, but armed forces and police officers are not allowed to unionize.

The Trade Union Act calls for trade unions to work to improve working conditions for workers, establish good relations between workers and management, and support worker discipline and productivity in the firm. The objectives of the trade union associations and federations, as stated in the Trade Union Act, are to disseminate information beneficial to workers, establish relations with international institutions for the benefit of workers, advise the government in the design of labor policies, and negotiate with the government and take other steps to protect and promote the rights and interests of workers (Sijapati 2014). The Trade Union Act has no provisions specific to youth workers.

The history of trade union activity is linked with the history of political movements in Nepal. The first trade union, the National Trade Union Congress (NTUC), was established by the Nepalese Congress Party in 1947. The Communist Party of Nepal founded its trade union wing in the 1950s, and it was later renamed the General Federation of the Nepalese Trade Unions (GEFONT).The Maoist-affiliated All Nepal Trade Union Federation (ANTUF) was established in 2007. In terms of membership, ANTUF is the largest trade union, with over 600,000 members (Sijapati 2014). GEFONT and NTUC both claim memberships of over 400,000 workers.[8] The Joint Trade Union Coordination Center is the umbrella body of trade unions, composed of the above three unions and others.

Documentation on the role of trade unions in promoting the rights and interests of youth workers is unavailable. According to 2013 School-to-Work Transition Survey (SWTS) data, 12 percent of employed youth workers (19 percent of wage-employed youth workers) were trade union members. Common responses provided by workers in the SWTS as to why they did not join trade unions indicated a lack of awareness, a lack of interest, and limited trade union activity.

Public employment

The civil service is governed by the Civil Service Act of 1993 and Civil Service Regulations. The fourth amendment in 2015 to the act is the latest. The Public Service Commission (PSC) is responsible for civil service recruitment. The Ministry of General Administration is responsible for civil service personnel and human resource management, including placement, professional development, promotion, transfer, retirement and postretirement services, and recording and information systems. Public health workers are recruited through the PSC, whereas public school teachers are recruited through a separate teaching service commission.

The second amendment (in 2007) to the Civil Service Act has provisions that promote inclusion. Of the vacancies to be filled through open competition (instead of internal competition and promotion), 45 percent are reserved for specific categories of individuals. Of the reserved positions, 33 percent are reserved for women, 27 percent for Adivasi/Janajati, 5 percent for Madhesi, 9 percent for Dalit, 5 percent for those with a physical disability, and 4 percent for people from backward regions. The number of vacancies per category is announced when the vacancies are published. For example, if there are 20 vacancies, 9 vacancies are to be reserved for specific groups. Of the nine vacancies, three vacancies are to be reserved for women, two each for Adivasi/Janajati and Madhesi, and one each for Dalit and those with a physical disability. At least 13 vacancies have to be open for a vacancy to be reserved for people from backward regions. Applicants can be eligible under more than one category. Table 2.1 reports the number of vacancies, applicants, and candidates recommended for appointment by the PSC for vacancies in fiscal 2015/16 and 2016/17.

Civil service candidates have to be above age 18 for nongazetted and classless job vacancies and above age 21 for gazetted job vacancies. Men must be below age 35 and women and those with disabilities must be below age 40. The probation period after job appointment is set at six months for women and one year for men. The retirement age is set at age 58 for both genders.

Quotas are fixed for recruitment into Nepal's police and armed forces. Of the positions to be filled through open competition (as opposed to internal competition or promotion), 45 percent are reserved for women, Dalits, those with physical disabilities, Madheshi, indigenous peoples, and people from backward regions. Candidates for the police and armed forces have to be above age 18,

TABLE 2.1 **Number of vacancies, applicants, and candidates recommended for appointment, based on open competition**

	FY 2015–16				FY 2016–17			
	VACANCIES	APPLICANTS	RATIO OF APPLICANTS TO VACANCIES	RECOMMENDED FOR APPT.	VACANCIES	APPLICANTS	RATIO OF APPLICANTS TO VACANCIES	RECOMMENDED FOR APPT.
	(1)	(2)	(3)	(4)	(5)	(6)	(7)	(8)
Total	9,487	595,031	63	5,319	7,451	837,661	112	9,299
Open to all	5,210	317,074	61	2,981	4,041	475,505	118	5,273
Reserved for:								
All specific groups	4,277	272,085	64	2,338	3,410	362,156	106	4,026*
Women	1,406	127,858	91	797	1,136	157,222	138	1,383
Adivasi/ Janajati	1,143	61,637	54	629	890	81,342	91	1,026
Madhesi	942	53,196	56	503	751	74,941	100	901
Dalit	421	12,432	30	213	324	19,403	60	385
Physically disabled	221	5,598	25	101	170	7,001	41	189
Backward regions	144	11,364	79	95	139	22,247	160	142

Source: Statistics obtained from Public Service Commission Annual Report 2072–73 and 2073–74.
Note: FY = fiscal year. Some vacancies remain unfilled because of a lack of applications or suitable candidates.

except in case of police peons (low-ranking police/workers), where those above age 16 are eligible.

Civil servants and armed forces and police officers who have served at least 20 years receive a pension upon retirement. Those who have served at least 5 years but less than 20 years receive gratuities that are set as a function of their years of employment. In addition to pensions and gratuities, the government matches the employee contribution of 10 percent of salary deposited in the Employees Provident Fund (EPF).

Despite the age requirements for entry into public service and quotas for various groups, Nepal does not have recruitment quotas for youth, which some other countries do. For example, the public sector in the Republic of Korea aims to recruit youth so that they account for at least 3 percent of the total number of employees per year (ILO 2015).

On the basis of EPF membership figures for fiscal 2014/15 (EPF Annual Report 2071–72), the latest available at the time of writing, the civil service employed 93,000 individuals, the armed forces 101,000 individuals, and the police 103,000 individuals. Public teaching employed 91,000 (community and institutional) teachers, and public enterprises 112,000 individuals. In total, public employment comprised 500,000 individuals. According to 2013 SWTS data, 7 percent of employed youth workers were engaged in public employment.

Public employment appears to be a highly attractive option for youth workers. Also according to SWTS data, 52 percent of unemployed youth workers indicated that they prefer public employment. The number of applicants for public employment vacancies was more than 100 times the number of available positions in the last four fiscal years, except in fiscal 2015/16 (see table 2.1).

Foreign employment

Labor migration from Nepal on fixed-term contracts to international destinations other than India (referred to as "foreign employment") is a major phenomenon.[9] As one indication of current scale, in fiscal 2014/15, over 520,000 foreign employment permits were issued by the government, an average of about 1,400 per day, according to the Department of Foreign Employment (DOFE) (Government of Nepal 2014b). Foreign employment is dominated by youth: according to 2010–11 Nepal Living Standards Survey (NLSS) data, 75 percent of household absentees engaged in foreign employment were between the ages of 16 and 34.

The Foreign Employment Act of 1985 was the first legislation on foreign employment, and it focused on regulating and controlling migration for foreign employment. Recognizing the inexorability of the phenomenon, the Foreign Employment Act was amended in 2007 to focus on promoting the rights and interests of foreign employment workers. The changes in the act aim to facilitate the foreign employment process for workers, make foreign employment safe, and provide workers with relevant labor skills.

The 2007 act makes it compulsory for workers to undergo orientation from a government-recognized institution prior to departing for foreign employment. The act also mandated the establishment of the Foreign Employment Welfare Fund, the Foreign Employment Promotion Board (FEPB), DOFE, and the Foreign Employment Tribunal (FET).

The Welfare Fund was established to provide social security benefits to foreign employment workers. It raises funds from payments by foreign employment workers, interest accrued from deposited funds, and license fees (Government of Nepal 2007). The fund is managed by FEPB, which is responsible for providing predeparture information to workers and managing grievances of workers in relation to injuries, and fatalities in particular. The fund is to be used to provide training to workers, provide employment-oriented programs to returning workers, repatriate stranded workers, bring back unattended deceased workers, and provide compensation to the families of deceased workers (Government of Nepal 2011b).

DOFE is responsible for regulating foreign employment by licensing private recruitment agencies, approving applications submitted by private recruitment agencies for contracting workers, issuing foreign employment permits to workers, and managing grievances from migrant workers. It has an investigations office that receives complaints made by workers against private recruitment agencies and agents, conducts investigations and imposes penalties, and registers more serious cases with FET. FET is responsible for resolving more serious and criminal cases under the Foreign Employment Act, which fall outside the jurisdiction of DOFE.

In addition, the Foreign Employment Act requires Nepalese embassies in countries with more than 5,000 foreign employment workers to have a labor attaché. The labor attaché in the country is responsible for overseeing the rights and interests of foreign employment workers there.

The Foreign Employment Policy, adopted in 2012, aims to further promote skill acquisition of workers to meet the skill-related demands of foreign labor markets and ensure that foreign employment is safe. The policy focuses on all stages of migration: preemployment, predeparture, departure, on the job, and reintegration into the Nepalese labor market. The policy also aims to address the concerns of female migrants in the migration cycle, and to mobilize remittances for investments in human development and productive activities.

Despite what is commonly perceived to be a broad Foreign Employment Act and Foreign Employment Policy, the process of foreign employment is considered to be poorly governed. Government regulation of private recruitment agencies and individual recruitment agents, the major domestic players engaged in the process of foreign employment, is weak. Common violations by private recruitment intermediaries include misrepresentation of the nature of the job and remuneration, overcharging of fees, and failure to provide workers with receipts and contracts (Paoletti et al. 2014). Workers' access to justice is limited because they lack awareness of redressal mechanisms or lack documentation, and because of recruitment agencies' reliance on unregulated individual recruitment agents, the limited capacity of the responsible government agencies, and the centralization of the activities of the responsible government agencies in Kathmandu (Paoletti et al. 2014). Private recruitment intermediaries often control workers' access to information about foreign employment options and grievance redressal mechanisms (Helvetas 2013). In addition, DOFE has conflicting mandates because it has responsibility both for licensing the recruitment agencies and issuing employment permits and for investigating the recruitment agencies upon complaints from the workers.

DOFE and FET are considered to lack funds and staff to effectively perform their regulatory responsibilities. For example, DOFE does not have adequate staff to effectively review complaints from workers (Paoletti et al. 2014). According to its progress report, DOFE had six investigation officers to review 2,172 cases filed in fiscal 2015/16, and it resolved only 520 during the year.

DOFE is also responsible for regulating access to specific countries for foreign employment. Currently, DOFE has listed 110 countries as recognized destinations for foreign employment through private recruitment agencies. At times, the government has imposed foreign employment bans in certain countries, and additional restrictions on women going for domestic work; it has cited concerns regarding worker exploitation or security, but in a manner that appears ad hoc and reactive.

Youth

The government began to recognize youth as an important target group for public policy and action after the end of the Maoist insurgency in 2006 (World Bank 2013c). The creation of the Ministry of Youth and Sports (MOYS) in 2008, the launch of the Youth and Small Entrepreneur Self-Employment Fund (YSEF) in 2009, and the adoption of the National Youth Policy (NYP) in 2010 (updated in 2015) provide a basis for promoting youth labor interests.

Targeting unemployed individuals ages 18–50 years, YSEF provides collateral-free, low-interest loans of up to NPR 200,000 to serve as start-up capital for self-employment. YSEF also offers training in commercial farming, livestock management, agro- and forestry-based businesses, and traditional trades. YSEF prioritizes youth from conflict-affected communities, ethnic groups engaged in traditional trades, Dalits, and indigenous groups.

Defining youth as those ages 16–40 years, the 2015 NYP identifies three priority groups of youth: (1) women; (2) indigenous Janajati and Madheshi; and (3) special priority groups—conflict-affected, at risk/vulnerable youth, those with disabilities, marginalized, endangered, minorities, Dalits, Muslims, and those from Karnali and backward regions. It places importance on employment through skill and entrepreneurship training, access to finance, commercialization of agriculture, and domestic employment creation.

The government has also introduced the Youth Vision 2025. The Vision has five pillars: (1) quality and professional education; (2) employment, entrepreneurship, and skill development; (3) youth health and social security; (4) mobilization, participation, and leadership development; and (5) sports and entertainment. Each pillar is accompanied by a set of goals and indicators with ambitious targets for 2020 and 2025.

With respect to the Vision's pillar for employment and skill development, the government aims to reduce the daily number of departing foreign employment workers to 750 by 2020 and 375 by 2025. Concurrently, by 2025, the government aims to increase the share of foreign employment workers who are skilled to 50 percent and who are semiskilled to another 50 percent. Also by 2025, the government aims to create 325,000 wage jobs and 120,000 jobs in self-employment activities for youth. District Youth Committees under the National Youth Council, established by the National Youth Council Act of 2015, are expected to support the implementation of the Youth Vision activities. Such ambitious targets, which are not grounded in any analysis of demand for Nepali workers abroad and which have no clear implementation plan, will likely mean that the policy fails to influence youth labor market outcomes.

Labor skill training

Labor skill training is a key government objective, as reflected in different major policy documents. Technical and vocational education and training (TVET) in

Nepal is offered by both public and private training institutes. Constituted in 1989, the Council for Technical Education and Vocational Training (CTEVT) is the autonomous apex body for TVET, mandated with technical, regulatory, and provision functions through its constituent public training institutes and affiliated private training institutes. In addition, several government ministries, such as the Ministry of Commerce and Industries and Ministry of Labor and Employment (MOLE), also administer formal and informal training programs.

The TVET Policy 2012 aims to (1) expand the provision of training and make training accessible to all, (2) adjust training programs as needed to make provided skills relevant for the domestic labor market and foreign employment, (3) use the skills of returning foreign employment workers in the domestic labor market, and (4) promote training for prospective foreign employment workers. CTEVT also has a strategic plan for 2014–18 that seeks to support the implementation of the 2012 policy. Equitable access to skill training and better matching of the supply of skills through TVET to labor market demand are common interventions identified in TVET and employment policies in many countries (ILO 2015).

The government's Youth Vision sets specific targets for training. The government aims to increase the share of people who receive formal technical education to 25 percent by 2025 (from 5 percent in 2015), and increase the budget allocated to TVET to 15 percent by 2025 (from 2 percent to 3 percent). The government also aims to increase its annual provision of short-term training to 200,000 workers by 2025 (from 70,000), and provide training to prospective foreign employment workers. The Youth Vision, however, makes no reference to the 2012 TVET policy or to CTEVT's strategic plan.

At present, project documents of international donors have noted key problems in TVET, including inequitable access, poor quality, and low market relevance of supplied training. The government recognizes in its policy documents the need to better match the provision of training to the skills demanded in the domestic labor market and by foreign employers. To better coordinate the provision of training across the various public and private providers, the Youth Vision envisages the implementation of a "one-door policy."

Implementation

The policy and institutional framework for youth and employment is considered to be adequate. However, policy implementation falls short. One major factor is the lack of resources and capacity in responsible government ministries, among which MOLE and MOYS are key. Despite the rhetoric on youth employment, there has been little change in government commitment and action.

MOYS is a relatively new ministry, established in 2008. The ministry's mandate covers youth awareness and mobilization, skill training, research on issues related to youth and sports, organization of sports events, and capacity development of relevant government agencies. The ministry's main programs are the National Sports Council, the Sports Development Program, and the National Youth Mobilization Program (NYMP). Under the NYMP, youth information centers have been set up in every district. The primary objectives of the centers are to provide information and work on issues of youth capacity development, entrepreneurship and employment, and awareness about drug addiction and HIV/AIDS.

The Ministry of Labor and Employment was established in 2012. It evolved from the Ministry of Labor and Social Welfare, established in 1981, to the

Ministry of Labor, established in 1995, to the Ministry of Labor and Transport Management, established in 2000. The ministry's mandate covers, among other things, the formulation, implementation, and monitoring of labor and employment policies; collection and analysis of labor data; promotion of the welfare of workers; relations between workers and employers; employment services; coordination among relevant stakeholders on employment creation; skill training; regulation of trade unions and labor agencies; provision of worker social security benefits; foreign employment by Nepalese workers; and employment permits for foreign workers in Nepal.

MOYS and MOLE have small budgets. In fiscal 2014/15, MOLE's budget was less than 0.2 percent and MOYS's budget was about 0.3 percent of the total public budget (Government of Nepal 2015d).[10] Of the budget allocated to MOYS in fiscal 2016/17, about 70 percent was assigned to the National Sports Council, leaving scant resources for all other programs.

Although MOYS is responsible for coordinating the overall implementation of policies and programs for youth, many of these policies and programs fall under the purview of other ministries, such as MOLE or the Ministry of Education. There is no specific budget allocated by the government for the implementation of policies and programs. Policies and programs are meant to be implemented under the regular budgets of relevant ministries but not explicitly assigned as such, thus causing confusion and a lack of ownership and accountability.

Similarly, the National Employment and Foreign Employment policies are crosscutting policies to be adopted and implemented by various government ministries to promote employment, with MOLE responsible for overall coordination and monitoring and evaluation. However, no specific targets and no budget are identified in these policies.

NATIONAL DEVELOPMENT PLANS

The government has prepared 14 periodic plans in the last six decades. The National Planning Commission recently approved the three-year 14th Plan for the period fiscal 2016/17–2018/19. According to the 14th Plan, the government aims to lift Nepal from least-developed-country status by 2022, achieve the 2030 United Nations Sustainable Development Goals, and become a middle-income country by 2030.

On labor and employment, the 14th Plan sets an ambitious target of creating 400,000 jobs a year. The government aims to achieve this target by creating a business environment conducive to employment creation, expanding training opportunities, and improving worker-employer relations. Industry, tourism, and agriculture are identified as the main sectors for job creation. In terms of specific initiatives, the plan proposes to develop a labor management information system, gradually consolidate the various skill training centers, establish one training center in each federal province, and establish an integrated fund for investing in TVET (consistent with CTEVT's strategic plan). The plan also proposes to extend social protection by registering informal workers and providing work accident insurance to all workers. Given that the new Constitution of Nepal enshrines the right to employment, the plan proposes to guarantee 100 days of employment for each household below the poverty line defined by the Ministry of Cooperatives and Poverty Alleviation.

On foreign employment, the plan proposes that those concerned with its implementation better monitor foreign employment, keep records of returning foreign employment workers, sign bilateral labor agreements with more countries, and make arrangements to allow only workers with skill test certificates to undertake foreign employment.

With respect to youth, the plan envisages making youth more competent, entrepreneurial, and self-reliant through technical education and skill training. It proposes to improve the performance of youth information centers and the Youth and Small Entrepreneur Self-Employment Fund under the Ministry of Finance.

DONOR ENGAGEMENT

International donors have provided financial and technical support mainly for short-term training for wage- and self-employment, as well as capacity building for the TVET system. Other labor areas have received relatively little support. The major donor-funded training projects include the Asian Development Bank's (ADB) Skills for Employment Project (SEP) from 2006 to 2012; ADB's Skills Development Project (SDP) from 2013 to 2018; and the World Bank's Enhanced Vocational Education and Training (EVENT I) Project from 2011 to 2016 and EVENT II from 2017 to 2022. ADB's SEP and SDP focused on increasing access to quality skill training through support to the provision of skill training and strengthening CTEVT's capacity. SEP trained over 59,000 individuals, of whom 50 percent were women and 25 percent were Dalits. SDP aimed to provide basic-level short-term training courses for 45,000 people, and mid-level training courses for 1,000 people (ADB 2013a, 2013b).

The World Bank's EVENT project aimed to expand the supply of skilled labor by increasing access to quality training and by strengthening the TVET system. It provided short-term training to over 58,000 individuals and supported certification of skills acquired previously. The project targeted disadvantaged youth, mainly the poor, women, Dalit, Janajati, individuals from other marginalized communities, and individuals with disabilities. EVENT II aims to improve equitable access to skill training programs and strengthen TVET service delivery.

The UK Department for International Development, the Swiss Agency for Development and Cooperation (SDC), and the World Bank, in partnership with the Nepal government, supported an Employment Fund between 2007 and 2016. Implemented by Helvetas Swiss Intercooperation, an international nongovernmental organization, the fund offered short-term training and support to establish microenterprises. The latter included (1) support for business planning, (2) financial literacy training, (3) on-the-job training and exposure visits, (4) support for enterprise registration, (5) provision of a starter kit of occupation-related tools worth up to NPR 8,000 after the enterprise is operational, and (6) support to access financial services. The fund targeted unemployed youth ages 18–40 years, and prioritized poor women from disadvantaged groups.

The donor-funded projects also supported the institutional development of TVET institutions, particularly CTEVT. ADB's two projects supported the review of training curricula and provided training to CTEVT personnel in management, instructional skills, and curriculum development. In addition,

SDP supports the development of mid-level training programs in construction, manufacturing, and services; the refurbishment of selected TVET institutions; and strengthening the regulatory capacity of CTEVT. SDP also aims to support the establishment of a TVET fund, a key proposal in the TVET Policy, and the establishment of a TVET Sector Development Unit under the Ministry of Education, which will be responsible for overall coordination of the TVET sector. The World Bank's EVENT project supported capacity building for CTEVT in planning, management, quality assurance, review of curricula, and training of trainers and master trainers. The project also supported the National Skills Testing Board by reviewing skill-testing materials and training assessors.

Support in labor areas other than training comprises small, piecemeal initiatives. The ILO has provided support for strengthening the institutional capacity of SSF and the design of social security schemes under it; 5 of the 14 Employment Information Centers under the Department of Labor; capacity building for major trade unions (through a project that closed in 2015); and the drafting of the new labor bill, the Social Security bill, and national employment policies. The United Nations Entity for Gender Equality and the Empowerment of Women (UN Women) supported the government in the drafting of the Foreign Employment Act. Initiated in 2011, SDC's Safer Migration Project aims to promote safer foreign employment by seeking to prevent fraud and exploitation in the process of seeking, securing, and engaging in foreign employment through providing information and legal and psychosocial support. The project is being implemented by the government in 9 districts and by Helvetas Swiss Intercooperation in 10 districts.

CONCLUSION

Nepal's labor laws and policies have largely failed to influence the decisions and outcomes of youth and other workers because of poor implementation, stemming from weak government commitment and capacity. With the primary exception of civil and armed services recruitment rules, labor laws tend not to have youth-related provisions; however, government policies on domestic employment, foreign employment, and training tend to focus on or prioritize youth. The policies set ambitious targets that frequently fail to matter because the targets are not based on evidence, and because specific organizational arrangements, operational plans, and resources do not follow.

The two labor policy areas that appear to have the strongest influence on youth labor decisions and outcomes are training and foreign employment. Nevertheless, there are design and implementation shortcomings with laws and policies related to training and foreign employment—such as issues in the quality and relevance of training supply and fraudulent or exploitative practices of private recruitment agencies engaged in foreign employment—that may constrain how much youth benefit. Information on any issues regarding public employment recruitment is absent.

In 2017, the Nepal government approved two major pieces of legislation: the New Labor Act and the Social Security Act. The acts aim to improve industrial relations and ensure social security to workers. Whether these laws will potentially influence the labor decisions and outcomes of youth and other workers will again depend on how well the acts are implemented.

NOTES

1. This review was conducted prior to the reorganization of the federal ministries and, thus, may not fully reflect the changes carried out in early 2018.
2. According to the 2014–15 Nepal Annual Household Survey, 32 percent of children ages 5–14 were employed in economic activities (Government of Nepal 2016b).
3. Other forms include *kamlari, haliya, deuki, haruwa* and *charuwa, bhunde, badi,* and *balighare* (Sijapati, Limbu, and Khadka 2011).
4. The Labor Act 2074 does not apply to the Civil Service, the Police, Armed Police Force, and the Army.
5. One year of "continuous service" is defined as 240 days of work in a 12-month period.
6. Casual work is defined as work for a period of seven days or less.
7. The number of wage workers age 16 and above was estimated using data from the 2010–11 NLSS.
8. Data come from the GEFONT website, https://www.gefont.org/GG2303390.html, and the NTUC website, http://ntuc.org.np/?page_id=46 (last accessed on January 5, 2016).
9. The migration of Nepalese workers to India is not regulated. The only legal framework that governs the movement of people across the Nepal–India border is the 1950 Treaty of Peace and Friendship. The treaty seeks to strengthen the historical ties between Nepal and India and to maintain peace and harmony between the two countries. The treaty allows for free movement of people across the border while providing Nepalese workers in India with the same privileges as Indian citizens with regard to employment and ownership of property.
10. In comparison, in India, the Ministry of Labor and Employment was allocated 0.27 percent of the total budget in 2015–16 (see http://indiabudget.nic.in/vol1.asp). In Bhutan, the Ministry of Labor and Human Resources was allocated 0.84 percent of the total budget in 2014–15 (see http://www.mof.gov.bt/wp-content/uploads/2014/07/BudgetReport2016-17 -ENG.pdf). These ministries have similar portfolios to Nepal's MOLE.

REFERENCES

ADB (Asian Development Bank). 2013a. *Nepal: Skills for Employment Project—Completion Report.* Manila: Asian Development Bank.

——. 2013b. Skills Development Project, Grant Agreement between Nepal and Asian Development Bank, 12 July. Asian Development Bank, Manila.

Chowdhury, Muhammad Shaheen. 2017. "Compliance with Core International Labor Standards in National Jurisdiction: Evidence from Bangladesh." *Labor Law Journal,* Spring. http:// labourlawresearch.net/sites/default/files/papers/Chowdhury_Article%20copy_1.pdf.

Government of Nepal. 1985. *Foreign Employment Act 1985.* Kathmandu: Government of Nepal.

——. 1992. *Labor Act 1992.* Kathmandu: Government of Nepal.

——. 2000. *Child Labor (Prohibition and Regulation) Act.* Kathmandu: Government of Nepal.

——. 2005. *Labor and Employment Policy 2005.* Kathmandu: Ministry of Labor and Employment, Government of Nepal.

——. 2007. *Foreign Employment Act 2007.* Kathmandu: Ministry of Labor and Employment. Government of Nepal.

——. 2010. *National Youth Policy 2010.* Kathmandu: Ministry of Youth and Sports, Government of Nepal.

——. 2011a. *Nepal Living Standards Survey 2010–11: Statistical Report Volume II.* Kathmandu: Central Bureau of Statistics, Government of Nepal.

——. 2011b. *Foreign Employment Promotion Board, Operation Guidelines 2068.* Kathmandu: Foreign Employment Promotion Board, Government of Nepal.

——. 2012a. *Foreign Employment Policy 2012.* Kathmandu: Department of Foreign Employment. Government of Nepal.

——. 2012b. *Technical and Vocational Education and Training (TVET) Policy 2012.* Kathmandu: Council for Technical and Vocational Training, Government of Nepal.

——. 2014a. *CTEVT Strategic Plan 2014–2018*. Kathmandu: Council for Technical and Vocational Training, Government of Nepal.

——. 2014b. *Annual Report 2070–71*. Kathmandu: Department of Foreign Employment, Government of Nepal. http://dofe.gov.np/new/uploads/article/year2070-71.pdf

——. 2015a. *National Employment Policy 2014*. Kathmandu: Ministry of Labor and Employment, Government of Nepal.

——. 2015b. *National Youth Policy 2015*. Kathmandu: Ministry of Youth and Sports, Government of Nepal.

——. 2015c. *Youth Vision 2025*. Kathmandu: Ministry of Youth and Sports, Government of Nepal.

——. 2015d. *Red Book Fiscal Year 2016–17*. Kathmandu: Ministry of Finance, Government of Nepal.

——. 2016a. *Directives on Domestic Workers Going for Foreign Employment 2072*. Kathmandu: Ministry of Labor and Employment, Government of Nepal.

——. 2016b. *Economic Survey: Fiscal Year 2015/16*. Kathmandu: Ministry of Finance, Government of Nepal.

——. 2016c. *Budget Speech of Fiscal Year 2016/17*. Kathmandu: Ministry of Finance, Government of Nepal.

——. 2016d. *Monthly Progress Report of Asar 2071*. Kathmandu: Department of Foreign Employment, Government of Nepal.

——. 2016e. *Recognized Destination*. Kathmandu: Department of Foreign Employment. Government of Nepal. http://dofe.gov.np/new/pages/details/28.

——. 2016f. *Civil Service Act (Fourth Amendment) 2072*. Kathmandu. Government of Nepal.

——. 2016g. *57th Annual Report*. Kathmandu: Public Service Commission, Government of Nepal.

——. 2017a. *The Social Security Act*. Kathmandu: Ministry of Labor and Employment, Government of Nepal.

——. 2017b. *The Labor Act*. Kathmandu: Ministry of Labor and Employment, Government of Nepal.

——. 2017c. *58th Annual Report*. Kathmandu: Public Service Commission, Government of Nepal.

Helvetas. 2013. "Learning of SaMi Pilot Phase (1 Feb. 2011–15 July 2013)." Helvetas Swiss Intercooperation, Kathmandu. https://assets.helvetas.org/downloads/2013_12_13_sami _learning_of_pilot_phase.pdf.

ILO (International Labour Organization). 2006. "ILO Calls for Strengthening Labor Inspections Worldwide." Press release, November 16. http://www.ilo.org/global/about-the-ilo /newsroom/news/WCMS_077633/lang--en/index.htm.

——. 2011. "ILO/ACTRAV/ITUC AP/Trade Unions in Nepal National Trade Union Conference on Ratification and Implementation of ILO Core Labour Standards, Record of Decisions, 25 August 2011." ILO Nepal, Kathmandu. http://www.ilo.org/global/docs/WCMS_161683 /lang--en/index.htm.

——. 2015. *Comparative Analysis of Policies for Youth Employment*. Geneva: ILO.

Paoletti, Sarah, Eleanor Taylor-Nicholson, Bandita Sijapati, and Bassina Farbenblum. 2014. *Migrant Workers' Access to Justice at Home: Nepal*. New York: Open Society Foundations.

Ronconi, Lucas, and Ravi Kanbur. 2016. "Enforcement Matters: The Effective Regulation of Labor." Working Paper 2016–03, Charles H. Dyson School of Applied Economics and Management, Cornell University, Ithaca, NY. http://publications.dyson.cornell.edu /research/researchpdf/wp/2016/Cornell-Dyson-wp1603.pdf.

Sapkal, Rahul Suresh. 2015. "Labour Law, Enforcement and the Rise of Temporary Contract Workers: Empirical Evidence from India's Organised Manufacturing Sector." *European Journal of Law and Economics* 42:157–82.

Sijapati, Bandita. 2014. *Enhancing Employment-Centric Growth in Nepal: Situational Analysis for the Proposed Employment Policy*. Kathmandu: International Labour Organization.

Sijapati, Bandita, Amrita Limbu, and Manisha Khadka. 2011. *Trafficking and Forced Labor in Nepal: A Review of the Literature.* Kathmandu: Center for the Study of Labor and Mobility.

World Bank. 2012. *More and Better Jobs in South Asia.* Washington, DC: World Bank.

——. 2013a. *2013 Nepal Enterprise Survey.* Washington, DC: World Bank.

——. 2013b. *2013 Bangladesh Enterprise Survey.* Washington, DC: World Bank.

——. 2013c. *Migration and Entrepreneurship in Nepal with a Focus on Youth: An Initial Analysis.* Kathmandu: World Bank.

——. 2014a. *2014 India Enterprise Survey.* Washington, DC: World Bank.

——. 2014b. *A Vision for Nepal: Policy Notes for the Government—Volume II, Sector Notes.* Kathmandu: World Bank.

——. 2016. *Doing Business 2016: Measuring Regulatory Quality and Efficiency—Economy Profile 2016, Nepal.* Washington, DC: World Bank.

——. 2017. *Doing Business 2017: Equal Opportunity for All.* Washington, DC: World Bank.

3 A Profile of Youth in the Domestic Labor Market

DHUSHYANTH RAJU

INTRODUCTION

How do youth fare in the domestic labor market? As a first step toward answering this question, this chapter constructs a domestic labor profile for youth, where youth are broadly defined to be individuals ages 16–34 years. Existing labor profiles for Nepal tend to examine all working-age individuals, disaggregating labor statistics for youth and other age groups (Government of Nepal 2009). This profile goes farther by investigating (1) youth labor statistics additionally disaggregated by gender and by location (urban versus rural), as well as finer youth cohorts (a younger youth cohort ages 16–24 years and an older youth cohort ages 25–34 years); (2) the association of various youth labor indicators with an extensive set of potentially relevant individual, household, and community factors; and (3) youth wage earnings in greater depth.

The labor profile we construct is mainly cross-sectional, using data from the 2010–11 Nepal Living Standards Survey (NLSS). This multitopic survey is representative at the country, urban and rural, and regional levels. Using an earlier round of the same survey, the chapter also examines trends in labor statistics between 2003–04 and 2010–11.

The main questions asked in this chapter on youth labor are the following:

(1) What are the levels of unemployment, and what explains observed levels?
(2) What are the patterns and correlates of school attendance and employment activity status, sector and type of employment, hours worked, and wage earnings?
(3) How have patterns in activity status, sector and type of employment, hours worked, and wage earnings evolved over time?
(4) What are the levels of time-based underemployment, and what explains observed levels?
(5) How do labor and education statistics compare between youth and older individuals (nonyouth)?

Contrary to the common claim made in Nepal, we find that youth unemployment and time-related underemployment rates, based on either standard or relaxed definitions, tend to be low, consistent with rates typically found in other low-income countries. The main determining factor appears to be the unavailability of individuals for (more) work. The main self-reported reasons for this unavailability are school attendance and, in the case of women, engagement in noneconomic activities.

An individual's school attendance and employment activity status mainly differ by youth cohort and gender. Women are more likely than men to be neither attending school nor working, and the younger youth cohort is more likely than the older youth cohort to be attending school. Factors that tend to have the largest effects on activity status are age, marital status, engagement in noneconomic activities, and education attainment. A worker's type of employment mainly differs by gender and by location. Urban workers are more likely than rural workers to be engaged in nonagricultural employment and wage employment, and women are more likely than men to be engaged in agricultural employment and self-employment. Factors that tend to have the largest effects on type of employment are age, education attainment, and region of residence.

For both women and men, median hours worked tend to be higher for wage-employed workers than for self-employed workers, for the older youth cohort than for the younger youth cohort, and for urban workers than for rural workers. Regressions explain more of the variation in hours worked for men than women. Factors that tend to have the largest effects on hours worked are age, marital status, current school attendance, type of employment, and region of residence. For both women and men, median hourly earnings for wage-employed workers tend to be higher for nonagricultural workers than agricultural workers, for urban workers than rural workers, and for the older youth cohort than the younger youth cohort. Regressions explain the same extent of variation in wage earnings for women and men. Factors that tend to have the largest effects on wage earnings are education attainment and region of residence.

In terms of trends between 2003–04 and 2010–11, the share attending school has increased, indicating rising education attainment. Workers are shifting out of agriculture and into nonagriculture. Hours worked, and the employment rate in the case of women, are declining in rural areas. Real gains in earnings are largest for rural male workers who are wage-employed in agriculture.

Last, the older youth cohort, a group whose members have mostly completed their education, has a higher level of education attainment, a lower rural employment rate, and a higher unemployment rate than nonyouth, and accounts for a larger share of wage employment in nonagriculture.

The results suggest strong shifts in local rural labor markets. Rising real agricultural wages presumably reflect falling labor supply rather than rising labor productivity. An important factor behind the declining labor supply is the substantial out-migration of male youth from rural areas (discussed in chapter 5). The results suggest weak shifts in urban labor markets. An expanding supply of more-educated youth, along with restrained, real gains in wage earnings, indicates that urban areas in Nepal lack sufficient (growth in) demand for educated workers. In light of these issues, a two-pronged public policy agenda seems appropriate: the first focused on raising rural labor productivity and the second focused on strengthening urban labor demand for more-educated workers.

The rest of the chapter is organized as follows. The next section presents the data and sample, and the basic structure of the analysis. The following section presents the results. The final section concludes by discussing implications of the main results for research and policy.

DATA, SAMPLE, AND STRUCTURE OF THE ANALYSIS

Data and sample

We mainly use data from the 2010–11 NLSS (Government of Nepal 2011). The NLSS is representative at the national level, as well as for the country's 12 regions. The original sample consisted of 7,200 households from 600 primary sampling units (PSUs). Out of this total sample, 1,200 households from 100 PSUs were drawn from the previous NLSS round (the 2003–04 survey) to form a panel sample, and 6,000 households from 500 PSUs were drawn to form a new cross-section. We use the cross-sectional sample for our analysis.

The labor module in the 2010–11 NLSS captured information that allows us to construct all the main labor market indicators using standard definitions, such as on engagement in economic and noneconomic activities, hours worked in the reference week, availability for employment or for more work hours, active search for employment or for more work hours, type of employment (self-employed in agriculture, wage-employed in agriculture, self-employed in nonagriculture, and wage-employed in nonagriculture), occupation based on standard occupation codes, and cash and in-kind earnings for wage-employed workers. We also examine the evolution of labor outcomes since 2003–04, using data from the cross-sectional sample of the 2003–04 NLSS (Government of Nepal 2004).

Since the 2010–11 NLSS, the Nepal government has conducted household sample surveys—called the Nepal Annual Household Surveys (NAHS)—annually from 2012–13 onward.[1] The primary aim of the NAHS is to regularly gather consumption expenditure and employment data. Although the data from the NAHS are representative for the country and for rural and urban areas, the sample sizes are smaller than for the 2010–11 NLSS. For example, the original sample size for the 2014–15 NAHS was 4,500 households from 300 PSUs (compared to 6,000 households from 500 PSUs for the cross-sectional sample of the 2010–11 NLSS) (Government of Nepal 2011; Government of Nepal and UNDP 2016b). Data other than on consumption and labor are especially limited in the NAHS. Understanding the correlates of various labor outcomes is a key aim of the chapter, and we can construct a more extensive set of potentially relevant individual, household, and community factors using the NLSS than using the NAHS. In addition, the larger sample size for the NLSS provides us with higher statistical power for detecting correlates in regressions for specific population subgroups (such as female youth).

NAHS reports compare labor statistics across the survey years, and with labor statistics from the 2010–11 NLSS. The statistics are comparable across years (that is, confidence intervals for the statistics overlap). Thus, given the stability of the broad labor market structure over the period that is covered by these surveys, using data from 2010–11 does not appear to be a large disadvantage—at least not one that outweighs the noted advantages of the NLSS.

Labor force surveys offer another source of information. The Nepal Labour Force Survey (NLFS) has a larger set of labor questions and household sample size than the 2010–11 NLSS, but the last NLFS was administered in 2008. Apart from being more recent, the 2010–11 NLSS has more extensive data than the 2008 NLFS on potentially relevant factors.

In our analysis, youth is defined as those ages 16–34 years, and nonyouth as those ages 35–54 years. We further disaggregate youth into two cohorts: ages 16–24 years and 25–34 years. We mainly examine all youth, or those who are employed. We often disaggregate these groups by gender, youth cohort (ages 16–24, 25–34), and location (rural, urban). Depending on the subgroup, in the 2010–11 NLSS, the sample size ranges from 451 to 1,540 observations for youth, and from 238 to 1,047 observations for employed youth. In the 2003–04 NLSS, the sample size ranges from 647 to 1,777 observations for youth, and from 283 to 793 observations for employed youth.

Structure of the analysis

Using 2010–11 NLSS data, we construct univariate statistics for key labor indicators, and examine associations in bivariate and multiple-regression analyses. We also combine 2003–04 and 2010–11 NLSS data to examine time trends in key labor indicators. All estimates are adjusted for survey sampling weights.

We disaggregate the full set of analyses by gender. We also disaggregate the subset of univariate and bivariate analyses by location and youth cohort. Employed workers can engage in more than one employment activity. In such cases, we set the employment activity with the most hours worked in the reference week to be the main employment activity.

We estimate regressions for activity status, type of main employment, log hours worked, and log hourly wage earnings. In all these regressions, we examine the association between the outcome of interest and potentially relevant individual, household, and community factors. Individual factors include how old the person is (in quadratic form); whether the individual is, or has ever been, married; has a disability or chronic illness; has suffered from an illness or injury in the last month; is engaged in noneconomic activities, or is currently attending school; and what education level the individual has attained, specifically whether he or she completed some secondary education (grades 6–10), only passed the School Leaving Certificate (SLC), or completed at least higher-secondary education (grade 12 or higher) (the omitted category is primary education [up to grade 5] or no schooling).[2] In addition, for the hours and earning regressions, we include indicators for the sector and type of main employment.

Household factors comprise household size, the household's economic status (based on per capita household consumption expenditure information), and the household's caste or ethnicity (the reference category is Brahmin or Chhetri). Individuals who are from the Brahmin, Chhetri, Terai middle caste, or Newar are considered to be traditionally advantaged in Nepalese society, whereas individuals who are Dalit or Janajati are considered to be traditionally disadvantaged (DFID and World Bank 2006).

Community factors include the time taken to travel from the community to the nearest paved road (in log terms); whether the community experienced a natural disaster in the last five years; whether it is easier or more difficult to find employment in the community compared to five years ago (the reference category is no change in difficulty); whether the community experienced a net increase in population, a net decrease, or a movement of people without a net change in number over the last five years (the reference category is no movement of people); and whether the community has active user groups or associations (such as those related to farming, water, forestry, women, or credit). We also include indicators for five regions, namely rural Hills, urban Hills, rural Terai, urban Terai, and the Mountains (the reference region is the Kathmandu Valley). The Mountains are rural, and the Kathmandu Valley is urban.

For our categorical outcome variables, we estimate maximum-likelihood multinomial logit regressions, and transform the estimated coefficients into average marginal effects (AMEs), which we report. For our continuous outcome variables, we estimate ordinary least squares (OLS) regressions, and report the estimated coefficients (which are same as the AMEs). Before estimation, the continuous outcome variables are trimmed at the 1st and 99th percentiles to eliminate outliers. Inference is based on heteroscedasticity-robust standard errors, clustered at the PSU level to account for potential correlation in outcomes within the PSU.

Although we include a large number of covariates (factors) in the regressions, we do not find signs of severe multicollinearity. As a first test, we examine variance inflation factors (VIFs) after the OLS regression estimations and find that, apart from age, which is included in quadratic form, and two regions (rural Hills, rural Terai), which have VIFs between 3 and 4, the rest of the covariates have VIFs between 1 and 3. As a second test, estimated standard errors in the regressions are stable when we arbitrarily add or remove covariates.

UNEMPLOYMENT

Public officials and commentators in Nepal widely perceive that unemployment—specifically youth unemployment—is an acute problem in the country. Many believe that the large labor migration outflow of Nepalese workers to external markets are due to a high level of domestic unemployment or, alternatively, that the level of domestic unemployment would be substantially higher absent the high migration outflow.

In most low-income countries, open unemployment exists but represents a small share of the labor force irrespective of the rate of labor migration to other countries (ILO 2017a, 2017b). Consistent with this generally observed international pattern, the level of youth unemployment does not stand out for Nepal. According to the standard definition of unemployment—that is, the individual is not working, but is available for work and actively searching for work, all in the reference week—Nepal's youth unemployment rate ranges from 1 percent to 5 percent, depending on the gender and the youth cohort (table 3.1). Although the age groups do not perfectly match up, these statistics are comparable to unemployment rates of 2 percent to 7 percent for youth cohorts within the 15–34 age group reported in the 2014–15 NAHS report (Government of Nepal and UNDP 2016b).

Discouraged individuals—defined as those who are not working, are available to work, but are not actively looking for work—are excluded from the calculation of the unemployment rate. Table 3.1 also reports unemployment rates where we relax the active search condition, thereby bringing discouraged individuals into the calculation. Doing this raises the unemployment rate by 2 to 5 percentage points, depending on the gender and the youth cohort. The highest estimated unemployment rate based on the relaxed definition is 9 percent, for men in the 16–24 age group.

What explains the observed levels of youth unemployment in Nepal? One way to answer this question is to examine the share of individuals in each condition that defines unemployment: not working (which we further disaggregate by school attendance status given that schooling is a major activity of youth),

TABLE 3.1 **Unemployment among youth, 2010–11**

	FEMALE		MALE	
	16–24 YEARS	25–34 YEARS	16–24 YEARS	25–34 YEARS
	(1)	(2)	(3)	(4)
a. Rates				
Unemployment rate (%)	2	1	5	3
Unemployment rate (relaxed def.) (%)	7	4	9	5
b. Decomposition of unemployment conditions				
(1) Not employed, attending school (%)	26	2	36	1
(2) Not employed, not attending school (%)	34	45	14	20
(3) Of (1) and (2), available to work (%)	5	4	10	19
(4) Of (3), actively searched for work (%)	32	38	51	59

Source: Estimated using 2010–11 Nepal Living Standards Survey data.
Note: Under the relaxed definition, a worker is defined as unemployed if he or she is not employed and available to work, whether or not he or she actively searched for work. Estimates are adjusted for sampling weights.

available to work, and actively searching for work. Section b of table 3.1 reports the share of individuals in each condition.

A large share of individuals are not working. For those in the 16–24 age group, 60 percent of women and 50 percent of men are not working. However, as expected, a sizable share of these individuals who are not working are attending school. For those in the 25–34 age group, 47 percent of women and 21 percent of men are not working. The larger share of women than men who are not working is consistent with the well-recognized gender-based division of roles within and outside of the labor market.

Among those who are not working, the share who report being available to work is small. For example, in the 25–34 age group, 4 percent of such women and 19 percent of such men report that they are available to work. Among those who are not working and are available to work, the share of those who are actively searching for work is large. For example, in the 25–34 age group, 38 percent of such women and 59 percent of such men report that they searched for work. Thus, the evidence suggests that unavailability for work is driving the observed levels of unemployment among youth.

For individuals who are not working and are unavailable for work, the survey asks the reasons they are unavailable. Figure 3.1 shows the distribution of self-reported reasons. As expected, the majority of women report the reason as either that they are attending school or that they are engaged in noneconomic activities. Notwithstanding, 18 percent of those in the 16–24 age group and 23 percent of those in the 25–34 age group report reasons that are categorized as "other" in the survey. For men in the 16–24 age group, 78 percent report attending school as the reason. For men in the 25–34 age group, the reasons are more varied: 26 percent report disability or illness; 12 percent report other labor market–related reasons, namely that they lack employment opportunities, or that they are waiting to hear back from an employment inquiry, or to start an accepted employment offer; 9 percent report that the reason is because it is off-season; and 29 percent report other, unspecified reasons.[3]

Given the low unemployment rate, we do not examine the correlates of unemployment. Instead, in annex 3A, table 3A.1, we present statistics on the composition of those who are unemployed.

FIGURE 3.1

Self-reported reasons for being not available to work, not employed youth, 2010–11

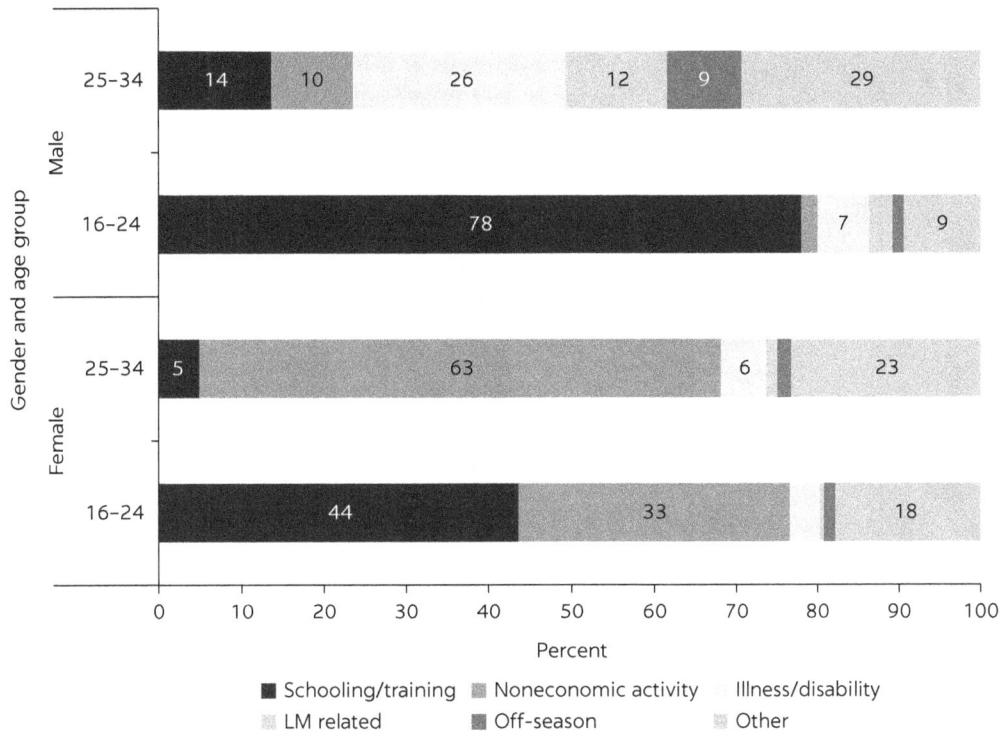

Source: Estimated using 2010–11 Nepal Living Standards Survey data.
Note: LM (labor market) related = three responses: (1) waiting to hear back from an employment inquiry; (2) thought no employment is available; and (3) waiting to start already-arranged employment. Estimates adjusted for sampling weights.

EMPLOYMENT

Employment status

Figure 3.2 shows labor force participation and employment rates. Given that the share of unemployed is low, we focus on employment rates. There are sharp differences in patterns by gender and by youth cohort. Women have lower employment rates than men. For example, for the 25–34 age group, rural women have an employment rate of 55 percent, compared to 77 percent for men. In the 16–24 age group, urban residents have lower employment rates than rural residents, driven by school attendance, as we will show. For example, rural women in that age group have an employment rate of 43 percent, compared to 29 percent for their urban counterparts.

School attendance and employment status

Figure 3.3 shows the distribution of individuals by combinations of school attendance and employment status. There are sharp differences in patterns by gender and by youth cohort. In the 16–24 age group, most are attending school, regardless of whether they are working, although the share of those attending school is smaller for women than men. In addition, the share of those attending school is larger in urban areas than rural areas.

In the 25–34 age group, most men are working only (73 percent of rural men and 75 percent of urban men). However, 13 percent of urban men and 22 percent

FIGURE 3.2

Labor force participation and employment rates among youth, 2010–11

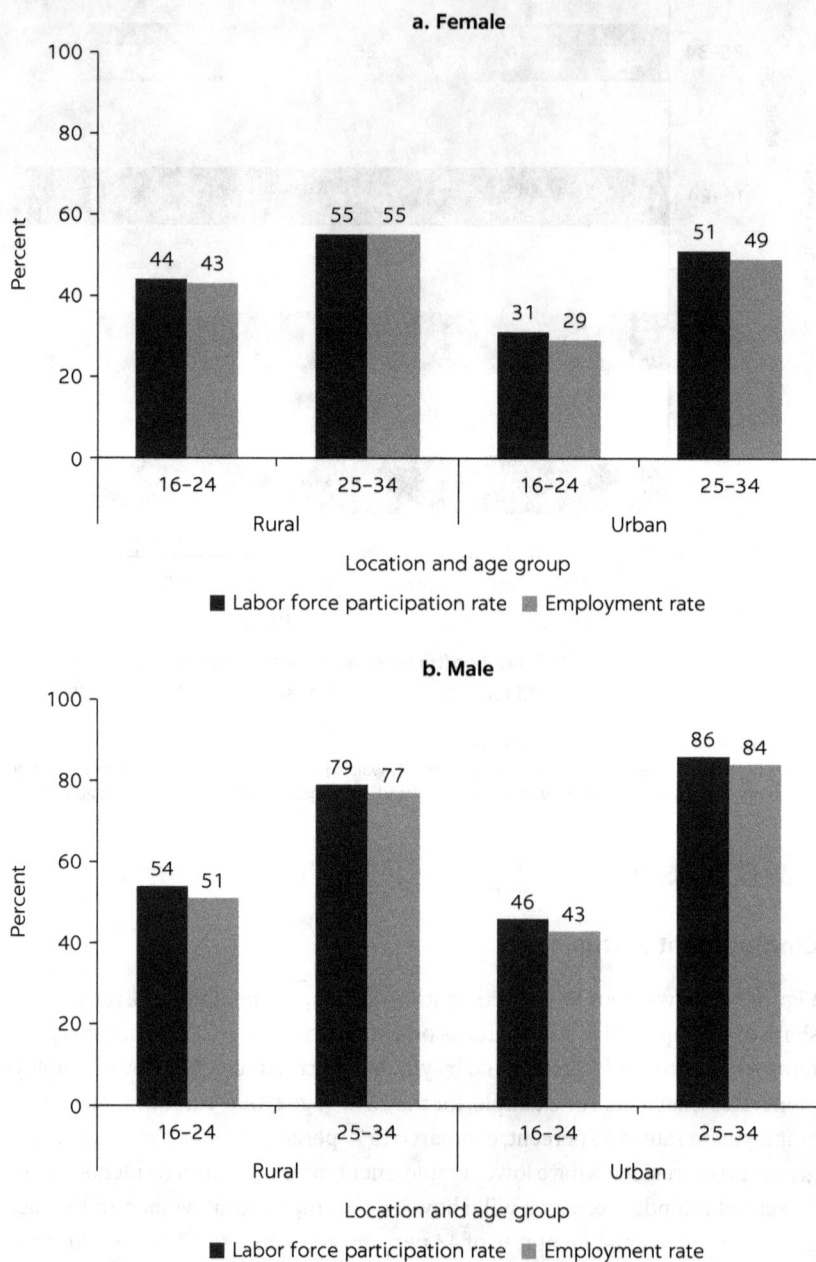

a. Female

b. Male

Source: Estimated using 2010–11 Nepal Living Standards Survey data.
Note: Estimates are adjusted for sampling weights.

of rural men are neither attending school nor working. The shares of women who are working only or neither attending school nor working are roughly comparable. For example, 53 percent of rural women are working only, whereas 45 percent are neither attending school nor working. Irrespective of school attendance or employment status, the majority of men and especially women are engaged in noneconomic activities. As tables 3.10 and 3.11 show later in the chapter, among those in the 25–34 age group, more than 90 percent of women and 60 percent of men are engaged in noneconomic activities.[4]

FIGURE 3.3

Distribution of schooling and employment activity status among youth, 2010–11

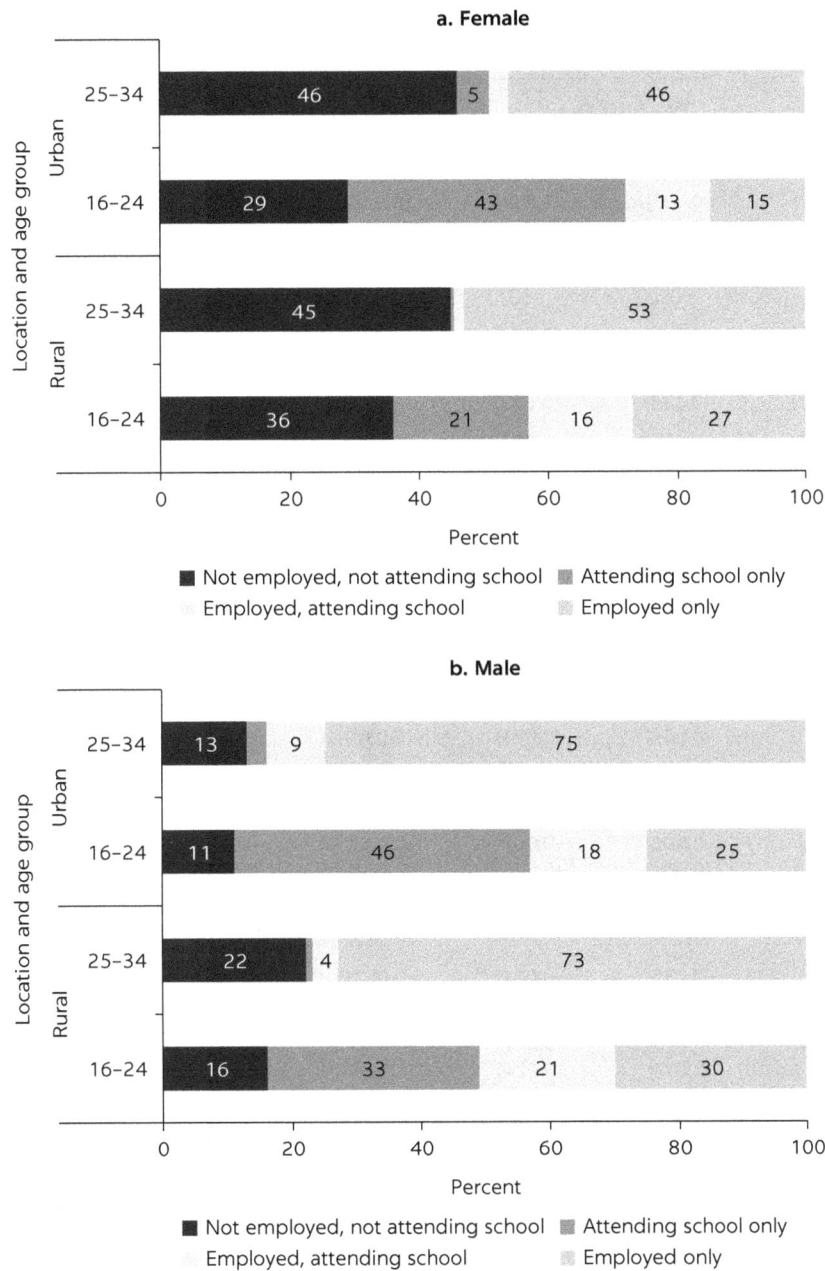

a. Female

b. Male

Source: Estimated using 2010–11 Nepal Living Standards Survey data.
Note: Estimates are adjusted for sampling weights.

Table 3.2 reports regression results for schooling and employment activity status. The reference category for the regression results is those neither attending school nor working. Current school attendance status and education attainment are expected to be strongly associated. Holding age constant, and assuming that the grade repetition rate does not differ by school attendance status, those attending school are expected have higher education attainment. Consistent with expectations, for both women and men, relative to neither attending

TABLE 3.2 **Multinomial logit regression results for activity status, youth, 2010–11**

Average marginal effects

FACTOR	FEMALE			MALE		
	IN SCHOOL ONLY	IN SCHOOL, EMPLOYED	EMPLOYED ONLY	IN SCHOOL ONLY	IN SCHOOL, EMPLOYED	EMPLOYED ONLY
	(1)	(2)	(3)	(4)	(5)	(6)
Reference category: Not in school, not employed						
Age	−0.041***	−0.037***	0.035***	−0.046**	−0.070***	0.081***
	(0.012)	(0.010)	(0.013)	(0.021)	(0.017)	(0.015)
Age squared	0.001**	0.001***	−0.000	0.000	0.001***	−0.001***
	(0.000)	(0.000)	(0.000)	(0.001)	(0.000)	(0.000)
Ever married	−0.081***	−0.063***	−0.020	−0.085***	−0.021	0.118***
	(0.010)	(0.009)	(0.024)	(0.022)	(0.021)	(0.020)
Head of household	0.001	−0.032	0.007	−0.032	0.028	0.068***
	(0.023)	(0.024)	(0.022)	(0.027)	(0.025)	(0.021)
Disability or chronic illness	−0.018	0.014	−0.022	−0.006	−0.032	−0.006
	(0.018)	(0.017)	(0.020)	(0.033)	(0.032)	(0.026)
Illness or injury in the last month	−0.001	0.013	−0.050***	0.012	−0.009	−0.039*
	(0.012)	(0.012)	(0.018)	(0.018)	(0.018)	(0.020)
Engaged in noneconomic activity	−0.064***	0.056***	0.235***	−0.004	0.014	0.021
	(0.014)	(0.015)	(0.035)	(0.013)	(0.013)	(0.015)
Completed grades 6–10	0.107***	0.082***	−0.116***	0.139***	0.097***	−0.168***
	(0.019)	(0.021)	(0.018)	(0.029)	(0.032)	(0.020)
Passed SLC	0.148***	0.146***	−0.153***	0.198***	0.185***	−0.305***
	(0.022)	(0.024)	(0.025)	(0.031)	(0.032)	(0.026)
Completed intermediate or higher	0.158***	0.173***	−0.204***	0.232***	0.247***	−0.372***
	(0.024)	(0.024)	(0.030)	(0.036)	(0.034)	(0.027)
Household size	−0.003	0.005**	−0.002	−0.004	0.003	0.011***
	(0.002)	(0.002)	(0.003)	(0.003)	(0.003)	(0.003)
Poor	0.012	−0.027*	0.004	0.014	−0.056***	−0.008
	(0.014)	(0.014)	(0.018)	(0.020)	(0.021)	(0.020)
Terai middle caste	−0.006	−0.035	−0.084***	−0.067**	0.043*	0.031
	(0.022)	(0.025)	(0.031)	(0.027)	(0.025)	(0.029)
Dalit	−0.038**	0.016	−0.041*	−0.027	0.007	−0.003
	(0.016)	(0.018)	(0.024)	(0.024)	(0.024)	(0.028)
Newar	−0.039***	0.010	0.079***	−0.065***	0.040	0.077**
	(0.014)	(0.017)	(0.028)	(0.023)	(0.025)	(0.031)
Janajati	−0.023**	0.004	0.021	−0.043***	0.001	−0.000
	(0.012)	(0.011)	(0.020)	(0.015)	(0.016)	(0.019)
Log time to nearest paved road	−0.007**	0.004	0.011**	−0.005	0.013***	−0.009*
	(0.003)	(0.003)	(0.005)	(0.004)	(0.004)	(0.005)
Natural disaster in last 5 years	−0.003	0.014	0.002	0.012	0.006	−0.040**
	(0.012)	(0.012)	(0.021)	(0.017)	(0.017)	(0.019)
Easier to find work than 5 years ago	0.009	0.009	−0.017	0.022	−0.004	−0.015
	(0.013)	(0.014)	(0.021)	(0.018)	(0.017)	(0.022)
Harder to find work than 5 years ago	0.015	−0.012	−0.057**	0.020	−0.036*	0.006
	(0.013)	(0.013)	(0.024)	(0.019)	(0.019)	(0.023)
Net increase in population in last 5 years	0.045***	−0.028*	−0.033	0.003	0.003	−0.050*
	(0.016)	(0.016)	(0.029)	(0.026)	(0.026)	(0.029)
Net decrease in population in last 5 years	0.016	−0.012	−0.031	0.005	−0.009	−0.072***
	(0.015)	(0.014)	(0.026)	(0.022)	(0.021)	(0.026)

continued

TABLE 3.2, *continued*

FACTOR	FEMALE			MALE		
	IN SCHOOL ONLY	IN SCHOOL, EMPLOYED	EMPLOYED ONLY	IN SCHOOL ONLY	IN SCHOOL, EMPLOYED	EMPLOYED ONLY
	(1)	(2)	(3)	(4)	(5)	(6)
Movement but net zero change in last 5 years	0.024 (0.018)	0.007 (0.019)	−0.044 (0.029)	−0.001 (0.026)	0.001 (0.026)	−0.039 (0.030)
Active user group present	−0.011 (0.016)	0.019 (0.019)	0.079*** (0.023)	−0.023 (0.022)	0.032 (0.021)	0.019 (0.025)
Urban Hills	−0.004 (0.018)	0.029 (0.018)	0.012 (0.037)	−0.038 (0.027)	0.030 (0.029)	−0.018 (0.037)
Rural Hills	−0.024 (0.018)	0.049*** (0.018)	0.024 (0.035)	−0.032 (0.027)	0.017 (0.029)	−0.053 (0.033)
Mountains	−0.050* (0.026)	0.106*** (0.025)	0.071 (0.052)	−0.033 (0.040)	0.087** (0.039)	−0.017 (0.056)
Urban Terai	0.043** (0.018)	−0.050** (0.020)	−0.074** (0.033)	0.012 (0.025)	−0.036 (0.026)	0.014 (0.033)
Rural Terai	−0.025 (0.019)	0.029 (0.020)	−0.069* (0.036)	−0.047* (0.027)	−0.018 (0.030)	−0.010 (0.034)
Observations		4,606			3,212	

Source: Estimated using 2010–11 Nepal Living Standards Survey data.
Note: SLC = School Leaving Certificate. Estimates are adjusted for sampling weights. Robust standard errors, clustered at the primary sampling unit level, are reported in parentheses.
*p<0.1, **p<0.05, ***p<0.01.

school nor working, those with at least some secondary education are more likely to be attending school, and less likely to be working only.

For both women and men, relative to neither attending school nor working, younger individuals are more likely to be attending school; older individuals are more likely to be working; those who are married are less likely to be attending school (and, for men only, those who are married are more likely to be working); those who have a recent injury or illness are less likely to be working; and those who are Newar instead of Brahmin or Chhetri are less likely to be attending school only, and more likely to be working. Relative to neither attending school nor working, women who are engaged in noneconomic activities are less likely to be attending school only, and more likely to be working (although engagement in noneconomic activities does not appear to be associated with school attendance or employment for men); those who reside in communities with active user groups are more likely to be working; and those who reside in urban Terai instead of the Kathmandu Valley are more likely to be attending school only, and less likely to be working, whereas those who reside in the Mountains instead of the Kathmandu Valley are less likely to be attending school only, and more likely to be working.

Sector and type of employment

Figure 3.4 shows the distribution of employed youth by sector and by type of main employment activity. There are sharp differences in patterns between urban and rural workers and by gender. In urban areas, the majority of female and male workers are employed in nonagricultural activities. Although the share of those wage-employed in agriculture is negligible, the share of those

FIGURE 3.4

Distribution of type and sector of main employment among youth, 2010–11

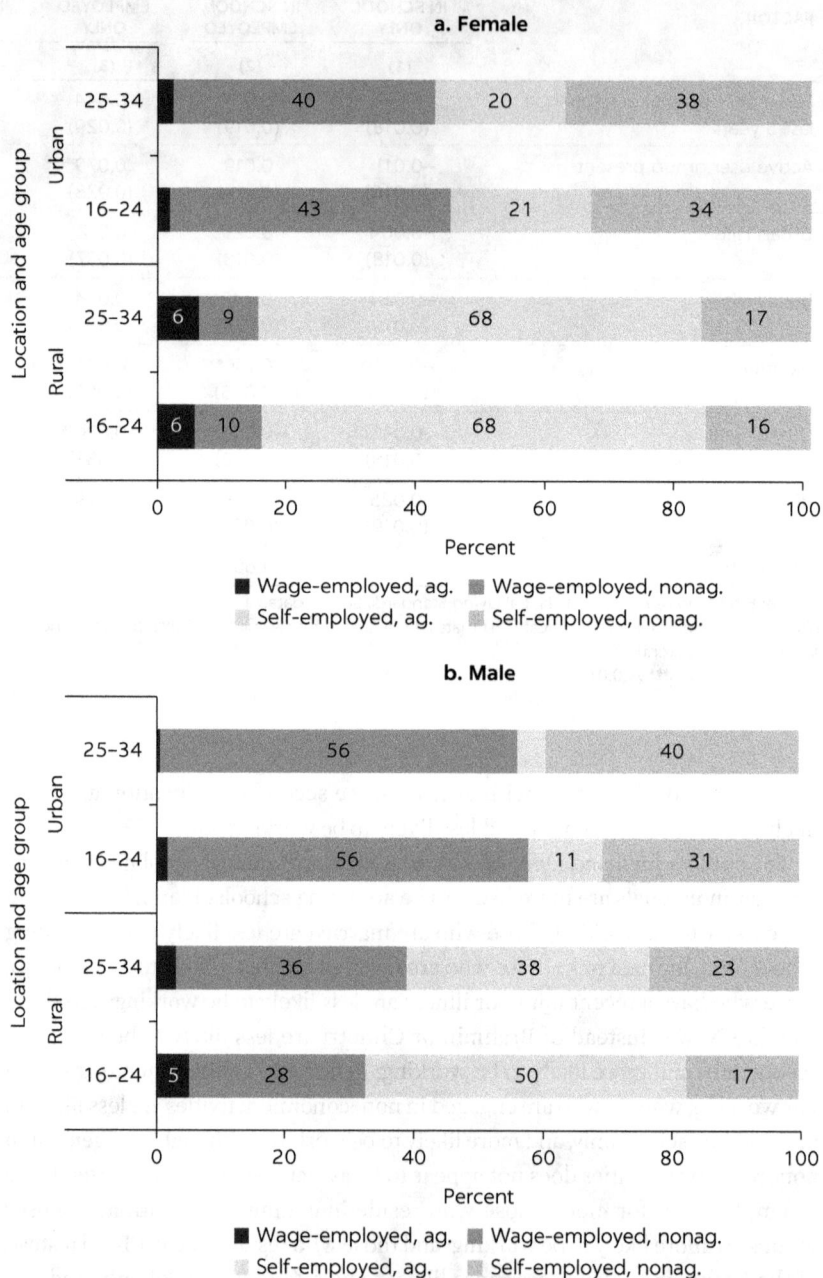

a. Female

b. Male

Source: Estimated using 2010–11 Nepal Living Standards Survey data.
Note: In the case of multiple employment activities, the employment activity with the most hours worked in the reference week is set as the main employment activity. Estimates are adjusted for sampling weights.

self-employed in agriculture is nontrivial, especially for female workers. For example, 20 percent of female workers in the 25–34 age group are self-employed in agriculture. Within nonagriculture, male workers are more likely than female workers to be wage-employed than self-employed.

In rural areas, the majority of female workers are self-employed in agriculture. Compared to female workers, male workers are more likely to be employed in nonagriculture. In addition, within nonagriculture, male workers are more likely to be wage-employed than self-employed, whereas the reverse holds for female workers.

The NLSS also asked workers a question about their occupation, which allows us to split nonagriculture into industry (which includes agroprocessing and construction) and services (which includes transportation). Annex figure 3A.1 shows the distribution of workers using the more refined measure of sector and type of employment. The main additional finding is that male workers are more likely to be engaged in industry than female workers.

Table 3.3 reports regression results for the correlates of sector (originally defined) and type of main employment. Those who are wage-employed in agriculture are omitted from the regressions because of small sample sizes. The reference category for the regression results is those who are self-employed in agriculture.

In terms of the likelihood of wage-employment in nonagriculture relative to self-employment in agriculture, for both women and men, those who are engaged in noneconomic activities, who come from a larger household, who reside in a community that is remote, who have experienced a natural disaster in the recent past, or who live in a region other than the Kathmandu Valley are less likely to be wage-employed in nonagriculture. On the other hand, those who are older, who have completed at least higher-secondary education, who are Dalit, or who reside in a community where it is harder to find work than in the recent past are

TABLE 3.3 **Multinomial logit regression results for sector and type of employment, employed youth, 2010–11**

Average marginal effects

	FEMALE		MALE	
FACTOR	WAGE-EMPLOYED IN NONAG.	SELF-EMPLOYED IN NONAG.	WAGE-EMPLOYED IN NONAG.	SELF-EMPLOYED IN NONAG.
	(1)	(2)	(3)	(4)
Reference category: Self-employed in agriculture				
Age	0.068***	−0.019	0.068***	−0.029
	(0.015)	(0.019)	(0.023)	(0.021)
Age squared	−0.001***	0.000	−0.001***	0.001
	(0.000)	(0.000)	(0.000)	(0.000)
Ever married	−0.067***	0.021	−0.009	0.011
	(0.020)	(0.028)	(0.034)	(0.027)
Head of household	0.011	−0.017	0.009	0.071**
	(0.022)	(0.027)	(0.031)	(0.029)
Disability or chronic illness	−0.023	0.037	0.001	0.012
	(0.022)	(0.030)	(0.048)	(0.039)
Illness or injury in the last month	−0.034*	0.018	0.024	−0.036
	(0.020)	(0.024)	(0.031)	(0.030)
Engaged in noneconomic activity	−0.110***	−0.001	−0.069***	0.003
	(0.033)	(0.047)	(0.026)	(0.023)
Currently attending school	0.020	−0.039	−0.074**	−0.001
	(0.027)	(0.030)	(0.036)	(0.031)
Completed grades 6–10	−0.023	0.052**	−0.046	0.076***
	(0.023)	(0.024)	(0.029)	(0.029)

continued

TABLE 3.3, *continued*

FACTOR	FEMALE		MALE	
	WAGE-EMPLOYED IN NONAG.	SELF-EMPLOYED IN NONAG.	WAGE-EMPLOYED IN NONAG.	SELF-EMPLOYED IN NONAG.
	(1)	(2)	(3)	(4)
Passed SLC	0.081***	0.080**	−0.046	0.110***
	(0.025)	(0.031)	(0.038)	(0.036)
Completed intermediate or higher	0.179***	0.065*	0.125***	0.079**
	(0.025)	(0.039)	(0.044)	(0.040)
Household size	−0.008**	−0.002	−0.013**	0.006
	(0.004)	(0.005)	(0.005)	(0.004)
Poor	0.016	−0.055*	0.098***	−0.074**
	(0.021)	(0.031)	(0.033)	(0.031)
Terai middle caste	−0.052	0.141***	−0.055	0.015
	(0.045)	(0.044)	(0.045)	(0.045)
Dalit	0.088***	−0.018	0.135***	−0.049
	(0.026)	(0.033)	(0.038)	(0.041)
Newar	0.001	0.031	−0.038	0.073*
	(0.024)	(0.035)	(0.042)	(0.038)
Janajati	0.026	0.074***	0.010	−0.014
	(0.019)	(0.023)	(0.033)	(0.032)
Log time to nearest paved road	−0.014***	−0.034***	−0.031***	−0.019***
	(0.005)	(0.006)	(0.008)	(0.007)
Natural disaster in last 5 years	−0.033*	−0.032	−0.058*	0.009
	(0.020)	(0.027)	(0.031)	(0.029)
Easier to find work than 5 years ago	0.045**	0.044	0.001	0.049
	(0.019)	(0.028)	(0.035)	(0.034)
Harder to find work than 5 years ago	0.067***	0.022	0.082**	0.042
	(0.020)	(0.032)	(0.034)	(0.035)
Net increase in population in last 5 years	0.015	0.053	0.030	0.094**
	(0.027)	(0.041)	(0.046)	(0.046)
Net decrease in population in last 5 years	−0.014	0.065*	−0.030	0.030
	(0.025)	(0.036)	(0.042)	(0.044)
Movement but net zero change in last 5 years	−0.026	0.056	−0.043	0.045
	(0.028)	(0.040)	(0.048)	(0.045)
Active user groups present	0.014	−0.063	0.003	0.032
	(0.025)	(0.040)	(0.039)	(0.039)
Urban Hills	−0.250***	−0.254***	−0.237***	−0.117*
	(0.047)	(0.072)	(0.067)	(0.062)
Rural Hills	−0.273***	−0.270***	−0.241***	−0.203***
	(0.043)	(0.069)	(0.063)	(0.058)
Mountains	−0.247***	−0.231***	−0.196**	−0.122
	(0.054)	(0.078)	(0.083)	(0.077)
Urban Terai	−0.197***	−0.164**	−0.150**	0.003
	(0.044)	(0.068)	(0.064)	(0.056)
Rural Terai	−0.272***	−0.253***	−0.310***	−0.090
	(0.042)	(0.068)	(0.063)	(0.055)
Observations	2,096		1,971	

Source: Estimated using 2010–11 Nepal Living Standards Survey data.
Note: SLC = School Leaving Certificate. Workers who are mainly wage-employed in agriculture are omitted because few observations exist. Estimates are adjusted for sampling weights. Robust standard errors, clustered at the primary sampling unit level, are reported in parentheses.
*p < 0.1, **p < 0.05, ***p < 0.01.

more likely to be wage-employed in nonagriculture. In addition, for women only, those who are married or who have had a recent illness or injury are also less likely to be wage-employed in agriculture. For men only, those who are attending school are less likely to be wage-employed in nonagriculture, whereas those who come from a poor household are more likely to be wage-employed in nonagriculture.

In terms of the likelihood of self-employment in nonagriculture relative to self-employment in agriculture, for both women and men, those who have completed at least some secondary education are more likely to be self-employed in nonagriculture, whereas those who come from a poor household or who reside in a more remote community are less likely to be self-employed in nonagriculture. Women who reside in any region outside the Kathmandu Valley and men who reside in the Hills instead of the Kathmandu Valley are less likely to be self-employed in nonagriculture. In addition, for women only, those who are Terai middle caste or Janajati instead of Brahmin or Chhetri, or who reside in a community with a net decrease in population in the recent past, are more likely to be self-employed in nonagriculture. For men only, those who are the head of a household, who are Newar, or who reside in a community with a net increase in population in the recent past are more likely to be self-employed in nonagriculture.

Hours worked

Table 3.4 reports median hours worked in the reference week in the worker's main employment activity (section a), and all employment activities (section b). Because of small sample sizes, median hours worked are not reported for urban workers who are mainly wage-employed in agriculture. Median hours worked tend to be higher for wage-employed workers than for self-employed workers. In general, median hours worked for women who are self-employed in nonagriculture and for men who are self-employed are lower for the 16–24 age group than for the 25–34 age group. Median hours worked for urban workers are either similar to, or higher than, those for rural workers. These patterns hold for both genders, and for hours worked in the main employment activity or in all employment activities.

Table 3.5 reports regression results for the correlates of log hours worked by the worker in all employment activities. Although not reported, the regression results for log hours worked in the main employment activity are qualitatively similar.[5]

The regressions for men appear to explain a larger share of the variation in hours worked than those for women (30 percent versus 14 percent). In terms of factors significantly associated with hours worked for both genders, those who are attending school work fewer hours (21 percent fewer hours for women, and 19 percent fewer hours for men). Compared to women who live in the Kathmandu Valley, women who reside in the rural Hills, the Terai, and the Mountains work fewer hours (ranging from 16 percent to 26 percent fewer hours across these regions), and men who reside in the rural Terai work 12 percent fewer hours. Consistent with the bivariate patterns noted previously, relative to those who are self-employed in agriculture, those in other types of employment work more hours (between 25 percent to 58 percent more hours for women, and between 36 percent to 68 percent more hours for men, depending on the type of employment). Factors such as engagement in noneconomic activities, household poverty status, caste and ethnicity, and the

TABLE 3.4 **Median hours worked per week, employed youth, 2010–11**

MAIN EMPLOYMENT TYPE	16-24 YEARS		25-34 YEARS	
	RURAL	URBAN	RURAL	URBAN
	(1)	(2)	(3)	(4)
a. Main employment activity				
Female				
Self-employed, agriculture	22	24	22	21
Wage-employed, agriculture	35	—	36	—
Self-employed, nonagriculture	21	26	28	36
Wage-employed, nonagriculture	40	42	36	42
Male				
Self-employed, agriculture	18	32	27	26
Wage-employed, agriculture	28	—	32	—
Self-employed, nonagriculture	28	40	48	56
Wage-employed, nonagriculture	48	49	48	48
b. All employment activities				
Female				
Self-employed, agriculture	24	27	23	22
Wage-employed, agriculture	49	—	42	—
Self-employed, nonagriculture	21	28	33	41
Wage-employed, nonagriculture	42	42	40	45
Male				
Self-employed, agriculture	20	35	28	26
Wage-employed, agriculture	42	—	42	—
Self-employed, nonagriculture	34	42	56	60
Wage-employed, nonagriculture	48	50	50	51

Source: Estimated using 2010–11 Nepal Living Standards Survey data.
Note: — = omitted because few observations exist. In the case of multiple employment activities, the employment activity with the most hours worked in the reference week is set as the main activity. Estimates are adjusted for sampling weights.

TABLE 3.5 **OLS regression results for log hours worked, all employment activities, employed youth, 2010–11**

FACTOR	FEMALE	MALE
	(1)	(2)
Age	−0.005 (0.034)	0.138*** (0.030)
Age squared	0.000 (0.001)	−0.002*** (0.001)
Ever married	−0.111** (0.054)	0.030 (0.046)
Head of household	−0.104* (0.055)	0.031 (0.043)
Disability or chronic illness	−0.035 (0.054)	−0.166** (0.065)

continued

TABLE 3.5, *continued*

FACTOR	FEMALE (1)	MALE (2)
Illness or injury in last month	−0.003 (0.046)	−0.014 (0.048)
Engaged in noneconomic activity	−0.129 (0.092)	−0.023 (0.033)
Currently attending school	−0.214*** (0.060)	−0.192*** (0.049)
Completed grades 6–10	−0.012 (0.052)	0.032 (0.039)
Passed SLC	−0.117* (0.066)	−0.011 (0.053)
Completed intermediate or higher	0.031 (0.063)	−0.016 (0.054)
Wage-employed in agriculture	0.580*** (0.073)	0.363*** (0.099)
Wage-employed in nonagriculture	0.598*** (0.058)	0.675*** (0.047)
Self-employed in nonagriculture	0.242*** (0.056)	0.501*** (0.057)
Household size	0.006 (0.008)	0.010* (0.006)
Poor	−0.033 (0.044)	−0.040 (0.041)
Terai middle caste	0.066 (0.087)	0.065 (0.058)
Dalit	−0.033 (0.060)	0.035 (0.052)
Newar	0.095 (0.064)	−0.025 (0.059)
Janajati	0.008 (0.051)	−0.023 (0.045)
Log time to nearest paved road	0.025* (0.014)	−0.010 (0.012)
Natural disaster in last 5 years	−0.006 (0.049)	−0.114** (0.045)
Easier to find work than 5 years ago	0.055 (0.062)	0.001 (0.051)
Harder to find work than 5 years ago	0.068 (0.060)	0.054 (0.051)
Net increase in population in last 5 years	−0.078 (0.074)	−0.114* (0.061)
Net decrease in population in last 5 years	−0.060 (0.068)	−0.081 (0.064)
Movement but net zero change in last 5 years	−0.071 (0.072)	−0.001 (0.061)
Active user groups present	0.107* (0.059)	0.011 (0.048)
Urban Hills	−0.054 (0.091)	−0.025 (0.100)

continued

TABLE 3.5, *continued*

FACTOR	FEMALE	MALE
	(1)	(2)
Rural Hills	−0.168*	−0.125
	(0.090)	(0.080)
Mountains	−0.257**	0.084
	(0.125)	(0.103)
Urban Terai	−0.200**	−0.101
	(0.094)	(0.064)
Rural Terai	−0.237***	−0.122*
	(0.088)	(0.071)
Intercept	3.260***	1.443***
	(0.454)	(0.381)
Observations	2,138	1,988
R^2 statistic	0.135	0.309

Source: Estimated using 2010–11 Nepal Living Standards Survey data.
Note: SLC = School Leaving Certificate. Hours-worked data are trimmed at the 1st and 99th percentiles. Estimates are adjusted for sampling weights. Robust standard errors, clustered at the primary sampling unit level, are reported in parentheses.
*$p < 0.1$, **$p < 0.05$, ***$p < 0.01$.

level of difficulty of finding work compared to the recent past in the community do not appear to be associated with hours worked.

Some other factors are significantly associated with hours worked for one gender but not the other. For women only, those who are married work 11 percent fewer hours; those who are heads of households work 10 percent fewer hours; and those who have only passed the SLC work 12 percent fewer hours than those with primary education or less. In addition, those who reside in communities with active user groups work 11 percent more hours. For men, hours worked increase with age (14 percent for an additional year). In addition, those who suffer from a disability or chronic illness work 16 percent fewer hours, and both those who reside in a community with a net increase in population in the recent past and those who reside in a community that experienced a natural disaster in the recent past work 11 percent fewer hours.

Time-related underemployment

Table 3.6 reports time-related underemployment rates. We define underemployment in the standard way, on the basis of how many hours the worker worked, whether the worker is available for more work, and whether the worker actively searched for more work, all in the reference week. We also relax the standard definition by excluding the active search condition, to allow for the possibility that the worker may be discouraged from searching. The denominator for all rates is those employed.

The underemployment rate, based on either the standard or relaxed definition, is low. Depending on the gender and the youth cohort, the standard underemployment rate ranges from 2 percent to 7 percent for working 35 hours or less, and from 2 percent to 4 percent for working 15 hours or less. When we relax the definition, the underemployment rate increases by 2 to 6 percentage points, depending on the hours-worked range (≤35 hours or ≤15 hours), gender, and youth cohort.

TABLE 3.6 **Time-related underemployment among youth, 2010–11**

	FEMALE		MALE	
	16–24 YEARS	**25–34 YEARS**	**16–24 YEARS**	**25–34 YEARS**
	(1)	**(2)**	**(3)**	**(4)**
a. Rates				
Underemployment rate, ≤35 hours (%)	4	2	7	5
Underemployment rate, ≤35 hours (relaxed def.) (%)	9	8	13	10
Underemployment rate, ≤15 hours (%)	2	2	4	2
Underemployment rate, ≤15 hours (relaxed def.) (%)	5	5	7	5
b. Decomposition of underemployment conditions				
(1) Employed, >36 hours (%)	38	43	51	71
(2) Employed, 16–35 hours (%)	38	35	28	20
(3) Of (2), available for more work (%)	11	8	24	26
(4) Of (3), actively searched for more work (%)	40	25	54	52
(5) Employed, ≤15 hours (%)	27	25	23	11
(6) Of (5), available for more work (%)	20	19	29	44
(7) Of (6), actively searched for more work (%)	35	35	54	44

Source: Estimated using 2010–11 Nepal Living Standards Survey data.
Note: Def. = definition. Estimates are adjusted for sampling weights.

Analogous to the investigation for unemployment in the previous section, we examine which of the conditions in the definition of underemployment (hours worked, availability for more work, or actively searched for more work) matters more in determining the levels of underemployment. Section b of table 3.6 reports the share of employed workers in each condition. A sizable share of employed workers worked less than full time. Depending on the gender and the youth cohort, the share of workers who worked 16–35 hours ranges from 20 percent to 38 percent, and the share who worked 15 hours or less ranges from 11 percent to 27 percent.

The share of workers reporting that they are available for more work ranges from 11 percent to 44 percent, depending on the hours-worked range, gender, and youth cohort. Conditional on availability for more work, the share of workers who report that they have actively searched for more work ranges from 25 percent to 54 percent, depending on the hours-worked range, gender, and youth cohort. As we find for unemployment, unavailability for more work is driving the observed levels of underemployment.

For those who worked less than 40 hours and report that they are unavailable for more work in the reference week, the survey asks the reason for their unavailability. Figure 3.5 shows the distribution of self-reported reasons for those who worked 35 hours or less. Similar to what we find when we examine the reasons for unavailability among those who are not working, the main reason for unavailability among those in the 16–24 age group is because they are attending school (43 percent of women and 64 percent of men). For women, engagement in noneconomic activities is another main reason (reported by 33 percent of those in the 16–24 age group, and 67 percent of those in the 25–34 age group).

For men in the 25–34 age group, the reasons are more varied: Twenty-two percent report that the reason is because it is off-season; 25 percent report that they have adequate work; and 13 percent report other, unspecified reasons.

FIGURE 3.5

Self-reported reasons for being not available to work more hours, employed youth, less than 36 hours worked in the reference week, 2010–11

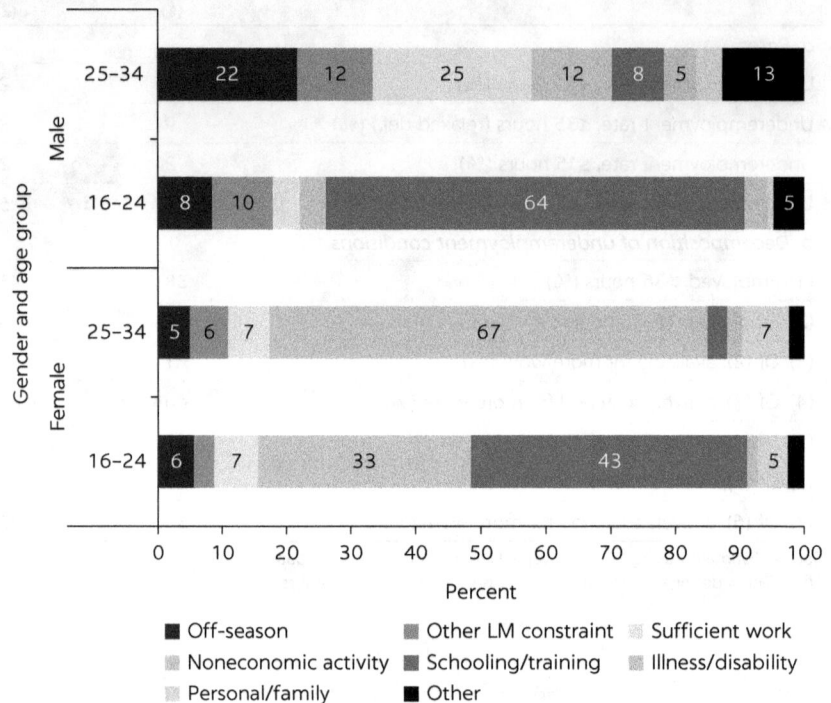

Source: Estimated using 2010–11 Nepal Living Standards Survey data.
Note: Other labor market (LM) constraint comprises four responses: (1) lack of financing or raw materials; (2) machinery, electrical, or other breakdown; (3) industrial dispute; and (4) lack of business or could not find more work. Estimates are adjusted for sampling weights.

Twelve percent report an employment-related constraint, such as lack of business funds or supplies, lack of sales, machinery breakdown, or strikes.

Given the low underemployment rate, we do not examine the correlates of underemployment. Instead, in annex 3A, table 3A.1, we present statistics on the composition of those who are underemployed.

Wage earnings

Table 3.7 reports median hourly earnings for the worker's main wage-employment activity (section a) and for all wage-employment activities (section b). Median hourly earnings are not reported for urban workers who are mainly wage-employed in agriculture because of small sample sizes. Median labor earnings are higher for nonagricultural workers than for agricultural workers; they are either similar or higher for urban workers than for rural workers; and they are higher for the 25–34 age group than for the 16–24 age group. The patterns are consistent with how we expect the levels of education attainment, labor market experience, and cost of living—all potential determinants of earnings—will vary between subgroups. The patterns hold for both the main wage-employment activity and all wage-employment activities.

Table 3.8 reports regression results for log hourly earnings for all wage-employment activities held by the worker. Although some workers who are

TABLE 3.7 **Median hourly wage earnings, wage-employed youth, 2010–11**

MAIN EMPLOYMENT TYPE	16–24 YEARS		25–34 YEARS	
	RURAL	URBAN	RURAL	URBAN
	(1)	(2)	(3)	(4)
a. Main wage-employment activity				
Female				
Wage-employed, agriculture	15	—	17	—
Wage-employed, nonagriculture	19	25	23	26
Male				
Wage-employed, agriculture	19	—	25	—
Wage-employed, nonagriculture	25	23	30	40
b. All wage-employment activities				
Female				
Wage-employed, agriculture	19	—	19	—
Wage-employed, nonagriculture	23	25	25	29
Male				
Wage-employed, agriculture	19	—	30	—
Wage-employed, nonagriculture	29	24	38	42

Source: Estimated using 2010–11 Nepal Living Standards Survey data.
Note: — = omitted because few observations exist. Hourly earnings are in 2010–11 Nepalese rupees. In the case of multiple wage employment activities, the wage employment activity with the most hours worked in the reference week is set as the main activity. In the case of multiple employment activities, the employment activity with the most hours worked in the reference week is set as the main activity. Estimates are adjusted for sampling weights.

TABLE 3.8 **OLS regression results for log hourly wage earnings for youth, all wage-employment activities, 2010–11**

FACTOR	FEMALE	MALE
	(1)	(2)
Age	0.027	−0.016
	(0.068)	(0.056)
Age squared	−0.000	0.001
	(0.001)	(0.001)
Ever married	0.123*	0.136**
	(0.074)	(0.061)
Head of household	0.206**	0.027
	(0.101)	(0.069)
Disability or chronic illness	−0.031	0.227**
	(0.106)	(0.098)
Illness or injury in last month	0.122	−0.012
	(0.080)	(0.063)
Engaged in noneconomic activity	−0.217*	0.084
	(0.116)	(0.052)
Currently attending school	0.120	−0.028
	(0.098)	(0.081)

continued

TABLE 3.8, *continued*

FACTOR	FEMALE	MALE
	(1)	**(2)**
Completed grades 6–10	0.208**	−0.011
	(0.091)	(0.060)
Passed SLC	0.075	0.070
	(0.111)	(0.098)
Completed intermediate or higher	0.520***	0.484***
	(0.112)	(0.089)
Wage-employed in nonagriculture	0.011	0.183*
	(0.090)	(0.099)
Household size	0.013	−0.031***
	(0.013)	(0.012)
Poor	−0.079	−0.060
	(0.086)	(0.069)
Terai middle caste	0.278	0.122
	(0.195)	(0.101)
Dalit	−0.004	0.132
	(0.106)	(0.084)
Newar	0.011	−0.087
	(0.095)	(0.080)
Janajati	0.059	0.108
	(0.077)	(0.068)
Log time to nearest paved road	0.036	0.029*
	(0.022)	(0.015)
Natural disaster in last 5 years	0.041	0.023
	(0.087)	(0.061)
Easier to find work than 5 years ago	0.052	−0.012
	(0.088)	(0.065)
Harder to find work than 5 years ago	−0.063	−0.030
	(0.092)	(0.061)
Net increase in population in last 5 years	0.271**	0.002
	(0.106)	(0.076)
Net decrease in population in last 5 years	0.089	−0.001
	(0.112)	(0.085)
Movement but net zero change in last 5 years	0.019	−0.090
	(0.101)	(0.081)
Active user groups present	−0.040	0.077
	(0.084)	(0.064)
Urban Hills	−0.062	−0.110
	(0.137)	(0.129)
Rural Hills	−0.355***	−0.194*
	(0.135)	(0.105)
Mountains	−0.258	0.061
	(0.198)	(0.120)
Urban Terai	−0.530***	−0.241**
	(0.126)	(0.094)
Rural Terai	−0.365***	−0.199**
	(0.130)	(0.097)

continued

TABLE 3.8, *continued*

FACTOR	FEMALE (1)	MALE (2)
Intercept	2.615***	3.126***
	(0.842)	(0.702)
Observations	532	881
R^2 statistic	0.209	0.212

Source: Estimated using 2010–11 Nepal Living Standards Survey data.
Note: OLS = ordinary least squares; SLC = School Leaving Certificate. Hourly earnings data are trimmed at the 1st and 99th percentiles. Estimates are adjusted for sampling weights. Robust standard errors, clustered at the primary sampling unit level, are reported in parentheses.
*$p<0.1$, **$p<0.05$, ***$p<0.01$.

mainly self-employed also engage in wage-employment activities, the regressions are restricted to workers who are mainly wage-employed. Although not reported, the regression results for log hourly earnings in the main wage-employment activity are qualitatively similar.[6]

The share of variation in earnings explained by both the female and male regressions is about 20 percent. In terms of factors that are significantly associated with earnings for both genders, we find that higher levels of education are associated with higher earnings. For women, the effect emerges when they have completed some secondary education, whereas for men, the effect emerges when they have at least higher-secondary education. Relative to primary education or less, women with some secondary education earn 21 percent more, and both women and men with at least higher-secondary education earn about 50 percent more. Workers in regions outside of the Kathmandu Valley earn less. In terms of significant effects, those from the rural Hills and rural and urban Terai earn less (between 36 percent and 53 percent less in earnings for women, and between 19 percent and 24 percent less in earnings for men, depending on the region).

Some factors are significantly associated with earnings for only one of the genders. For men, those who have ever married earn 14 percent more, and those who are wage-employed in nonagriculture earn 18 percent more. Earnings are positively associated with the time from the worker's home to the nearest paved road, indicating that the supply of male wage labor may be tighter in more remote communities. Surprisingly, those who have a disability or chronic illness earn 23 percent more, and earnings decrease with household size (3 percent less in earnings for each additional household member). Additional urban- and rural-specific regressions indicate that the disability effect appears for rural residents, and the household size effect appears for urban residents. For women, those who are heads of households earn 21 percent more, and those who reside in a community with a net increase in population earn 27 percent more, the latter suggesting that they benefit from a growing labor market.

Factors that do not appear to be associated with earnings include age, recent illness or injury, current school attendance, caste or ethnicity, household poverty status, experience with a natural disaster in the recent past in the community, the level of difficulty finding employment compared to five years ago in the community, and the presence of active user groups in the community. These patterns hold for both women and men.

TIME TRENDS IN LABOR PATTERNS

How have labor patterns evolved over time for youth? Figure 3.6 shows the changes that occurred between 2003–04 and 2010–11 in terms of the distribution of women by activity status (panel a), labor force status (panel b), and type of main employment (panel c). Figure 3.7 shows analogous information for men.

FIGURE 3.6

Distribution of female youth by activity status, labor force status, and employment type, by youth cohort, location, and survey year

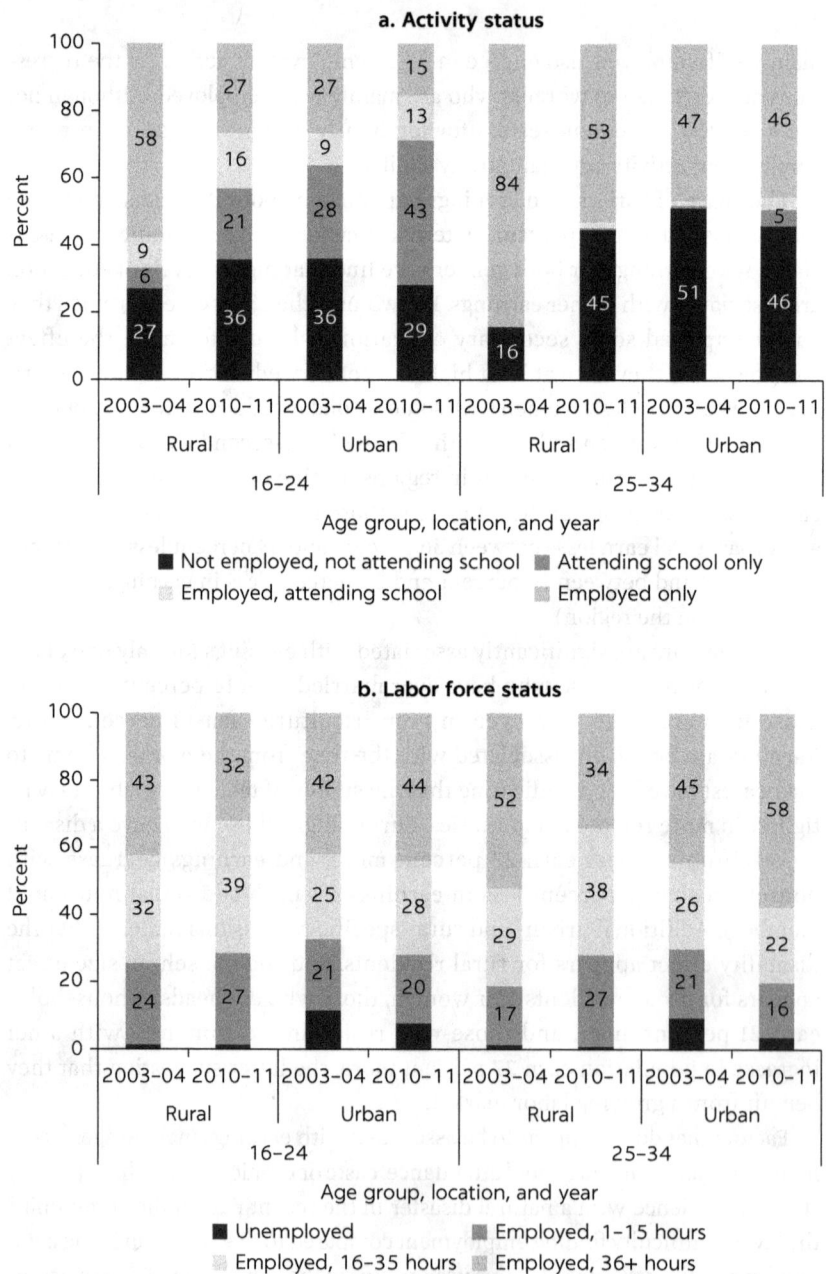

a. Activity status

b. Labor force status

continued

FIGURE 3.6, *continued*

c. Main employment type

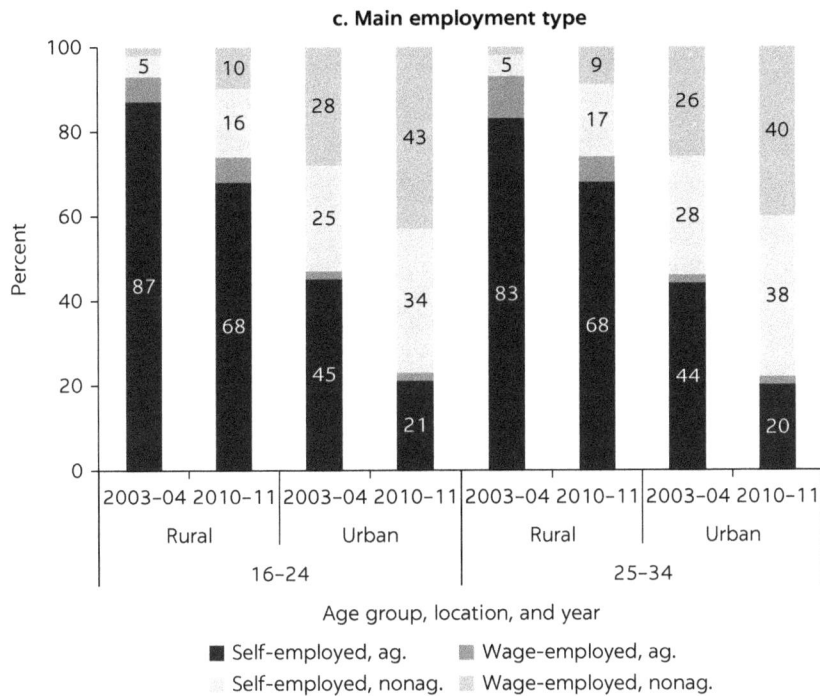

Age group, location, and year

■ Self-employed, ag.   ▨ Wage-employed, ag.
▫ Self-employed, nonag.   ▨ Wage-employed, nonag.

Source: Estimated using 2003–04 and 2010–11 Nepal Living Standards Survey data.
Note: In the case of multiple employment activities, the employment activity with the most hours worked in the reference week is set as the main activity. Estimates are adjusted for sampling weights.

FIGURE 3.7

Distribution of male youth by activity status, labor force status, and employment type, by youth cohort, location, and survey year

a. Activity status

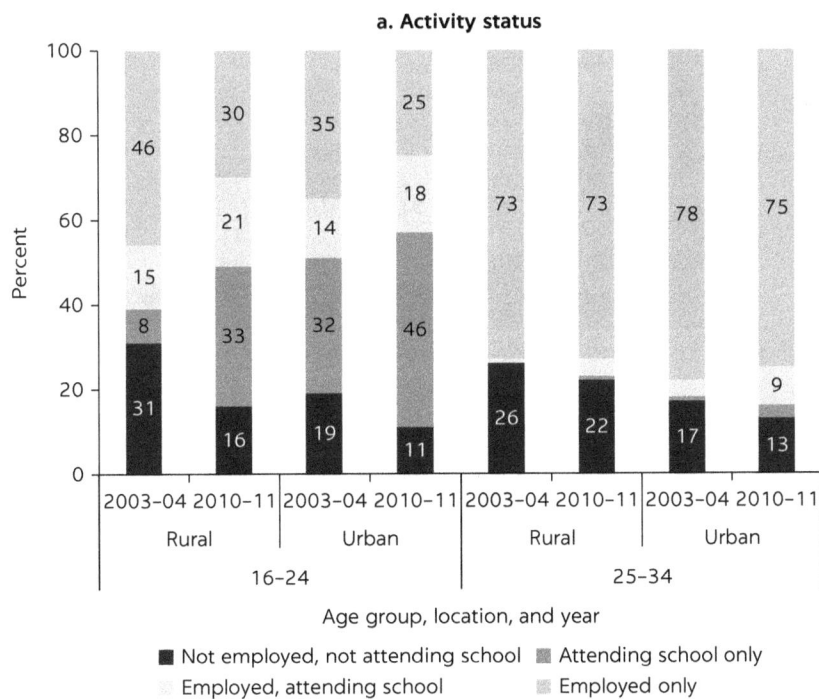

Age group, location, and year

■ Not employed, not attending school   ▨ Attending school only
▫ Employed, attending school   ▨ Employed only

continued

FIGURE 3.7, *continued*

b. Labor force status

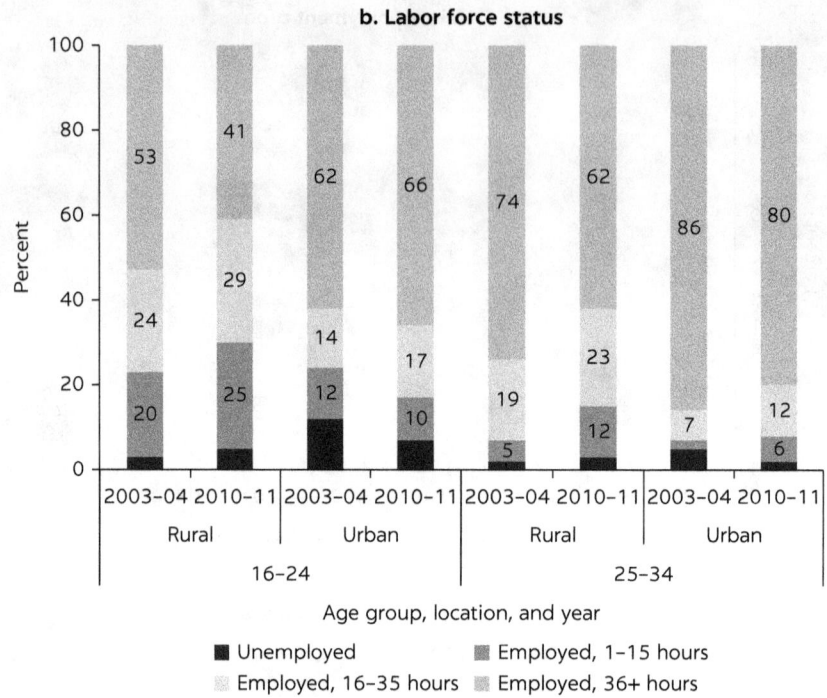

Unemployed — Employed, 1–15 hours
Employed, 16–35 hours — Employed, 36+ hours

c. Main employment type

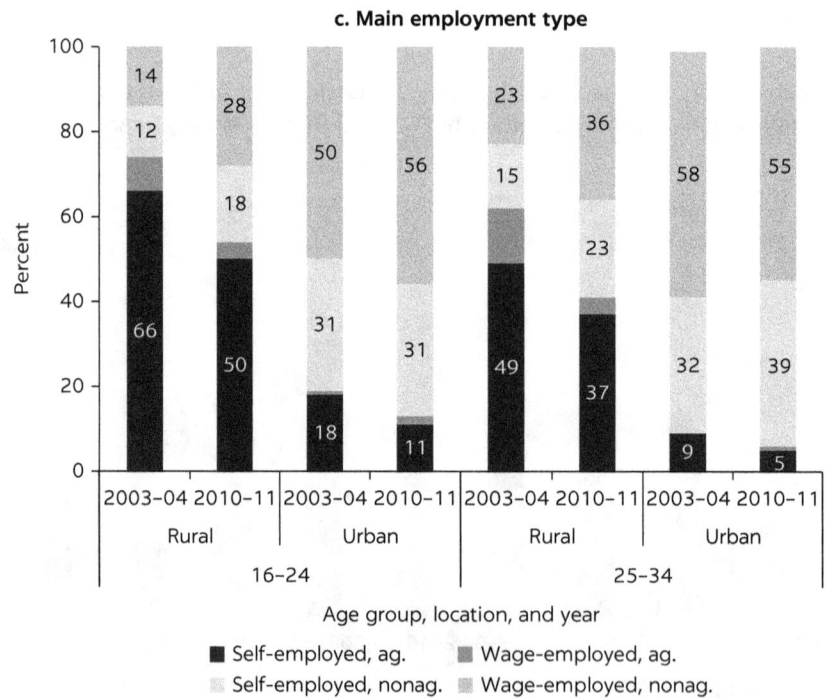

Self-employed, ag. — Wage-employed, ag.
Self-employed, nonag. — Wage-employed, nonag.

Source: Estimated using 2003–04 and 2010–11 Nepal Living Standards Survey data.
Note: In the case of multiple employment activities, the employment activity with the most hours worked in the reference week is set as the main activity. Estimates are adjusted for sampling weights.

In terms of activity status, for the 16–24 age group, the share who are attending school has risen markedly, whereas the share who are employed has declined. This pattern of change is qualitatively similar for both genders. The share of rural female youth who are neither employed nor attending school has risen. The increase is especially large for the 25–34 age group in percentage-point terms (from 16 percent in 2003–04 to 45 percent in 2010–11). This pattern of change is not observed for rural male youth.

In terms of labor force status, the share of rural youth working 36 or more hours in the reference week (that is, full-time work) has declined. This pattern of change holds for both youth cohorts, and for both genders. Labor force status patterns for urban youth are more stable over time.

In terms of employment type, the share who are self-employed in agriculture has decreased, whereas the share who are wage- or self-employed in nonagriculture has increased. This pattern of change holds for both urban and rural areas, for both youth cohorts, and for both genders. However, the pattern of change is more pronounced for women than men in percentage-point terms.

Table 3.9 reports how median real hourly earnings for the worker's main wage employment activity have evolved between 2003–04 and 2010–11. We do not report how median earnings have evolved for urban workers who are mainly wage-employed in agriculture, given the small sample sizes for the subgroup. For female youth, those in the 16–24 age group who are mainly wage-employed in nonagriculture in urban areas observe a gain in median earnings of 24 percent. In contrast, their counterparts in rural areas observe a change in median earnings of –36 percent. Changes in median earnings for other subgroups are negligible, ranging from –4 percent to 5 percent.

For male youth, those who are mainly wage-employed in agriculture in rural areas observe the largest gains in median earnings (21 percent for the 16–24 age group, and 50 percent for the 25–34 age group). Changes in median earnings for those who are mainly wage-employed in nonagriculture are negligible, ranging between –10 percent and 4 percent.

TABLE 3.9 **Change in median real hourly wage earnings, main wage employment activity, youth**

MAIN EMPLOYMENT TYPE	16-24 YEARS				25-34 YEARS			
	RURAL		URBAN		RURAL		URBAN	
	2010-11	% Δ FROM 2003-04	2010-11	% Δ FROM 2003-04	2010-11	% Δ FROM 2003-04	2010-11	% Δ FROM 2003-04
	(1)	(2)	(3)	(4)	(5)	(6)	(7)	(8)
a. Female								
Wage-employed, ag.	15	5	—	—	17	5	—	—
Wage-employed, nonag.	19	-36	25	24	23	5	26	-4
b. Male								
Wage-employed, ag.	19	21	—	—	25	50	—	—
Wage-employed, nonag.	25	4	23	-8	30	1	40	-10

Source: Estimated using 2003–04 and 2010–11 Nepal Living Standards Survey data.
Note: — = omitted because few observations exist. Hourly earnings are in 2010–11 Nepalese rupees. In the case of multiple wage employment activities, the wage employment activity with the most hours worked in the reference week is set as the main activity. In the case of multiple employment activities, the employment activity with the most hours worked in the reference week is set as main activity. Estimates are adjusted for sampling weights.

FIGURE 3.8

Evolution of salary and wage indexes

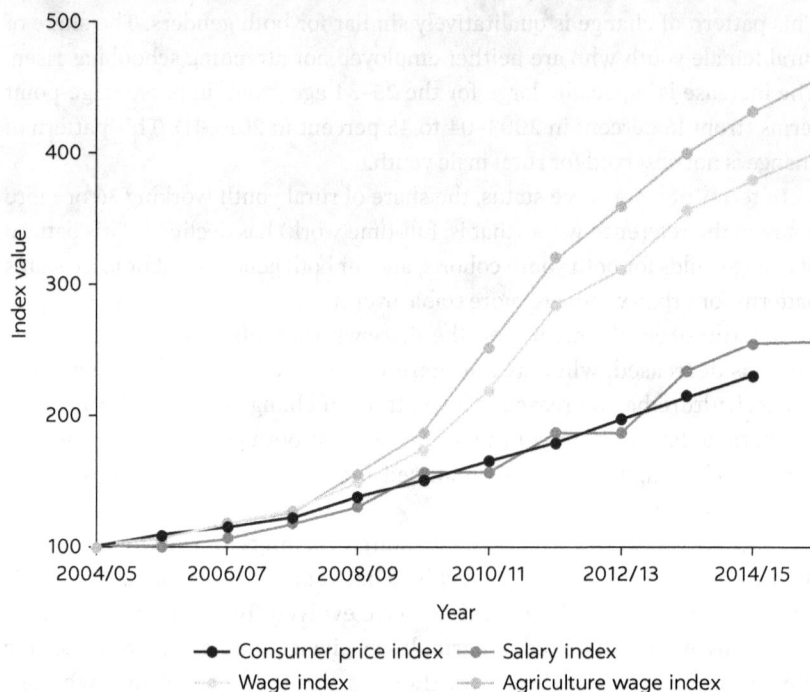

Source: Statistics obtained from the government of Nepal's Economic Surveys for the various fiscal years.
Note: The base year for all indexes is 2004/05.

Large gains in agricultural wages are also reflected in salary and wage data gathered by the Nepal government through its annual Economic Surveys. Figure 3.8 shows the evolution of nominal salary, wage, and agricultural wage indexes, as well as the urban consumer price index, between 2004–05 and 2015–16. The salary index reflects salaries for public and private sector workers, and the wage index reflects wages for construction, agricultural, and industrial workers. Comparing the nominal trend in wages and salaries to the trend in consumer prices, we find that agricultural wages see the largest real gains over the period, whereas salaries see little real gain.

YOUTH VERSUS NONYOUTH LABOR OUTCOMES

How do mean labor outcomes compare between youth and nonyouth? Table 3.10 reports mean female labor and other outcomes for the two youth cohorts, and for nonyouth. Table 3.11 reports analogous information for male labor and other outcomes. Given that a large share of those in the 16–24 age group are attending school, we compare outcomes between those in the 25–34 age group and nonyouth. School attendance rates for the 25–34 age group are low—in the single digits for most subgroups.

For those in the 25–34 age group, education levels are higher, measured in terms of the share who currently attend school, ever attended school, or passed the SLC; the rural share who are engaged in economic activities (that is, the rural employment-to-population ratio) is smaller; the unemployment rate is higher;

TABLE 3.10 **Comparison of labor and other indicators between female youth and nonyouth, 2010-11**

INDICATOR	RURAL			URBAN		
	16-24 YEARS	25-34 YEARS	35-54 YEARS	16-24 YEARS	25-34 YEARS	35-54 YEARS
	(1)	(2)	(3)	(4)	(5)	(6)
Share currently attending school (%)	38	2	0	57	8	0
Share who attended school in the past (%)	77	45	15	92	76	48
Share who passed SLC (%)	22	9	2	48	35	18
Share engaged in economic activities (%)	43	55	63	29	49	52
Share engaged in noneconomic activities (%)	91	95	95	87	96	95
Median hours in noneconomic activities in ref. week	21	28	21	17	28	21
Unemployment rate (%)	1	1	0	8	4	1
Unemployment rate (relaxed definition) (%)	5	2	1	16	9	6
Median hours worked in ref. week, main employment activity	24	25	24	35	40	40
Median hours worked in ref. week, all employment activities	27	28	26	35	42	42
Underemployment rate, ≤35 hours in ref. week (%)	3	2	2	4	3	1
Underemployment rate, ≤15 hours in ref. week (%)	2	2	1	3	2	1
Share wage-employed in agriculture (%)	6	6	7	2	2	3
Share self-employed in agriculture (%)	68	68	71	21	20	27
Share wage-employed in nonagriculture (%)	10	9	5	43	40	28
Share self-employed in nonagriculture (%)	16	17	16	34	38	43
Share in agriculture (%	75	76	81	27	23	33
Share in industry (including construction and agroprocessing) (%)	9	9	7	17	18	15
Share in services (including transportation) (%)	16	14	13	57	58	52
Median hourly wage earnings, main wage-employment activity	18	19	19	25	25	27
Median hourly wage earnings, all wage-employment activities	19	23	19	25	27	27

Source: Estimated using 2010-11 Nepal Living Standards Survey data.
Note: SLC = School Leaving Certificate; ref. = reference. Sample restricted to household members. Relaxed definition for unemployment excludes the active search condition. Sector and type of employment information are for the main employment activity. Median hourly wage earnings are in 2010-11 Nepalese rupees. Estimates are adjusted for sampling weights.

TABLE 3.11 **Comparison of labor and other indicators between male youth and nonyouth, 2010-11**

INDICATOR	RURAL			URBAN		
	16-24 YEARS	25-34 YEARS	35-54 YEARS	16-24 YEARS	25-34 YEARS	35-54 YEARS
	(1)	(2)	(3)	(4)	(5)	(6)
Share currently attending school (%)	56	4	1	65	12	2
Share attended school in the past (%)	93	82	60	98	92	83
Share passed SLC (%)	28	23	12	52	54	40
Share engaged in economic activities (%)	53	80	83	44	86	84

continued

TABLE 3.11, *continued*

INDICATOR	RURAL			URBAN		
	16–24 YEARS	25–34 YEARS	35–54 YEARS	16–24 YEARS	25–34 YEARS	35–54 YEARS
	(1)	(2)	(3)	(4)	(5)	(6)
Share engaged in noneconomic activities (%)	52	66	75	50	67	68
Median hours in noneconomic activities in ref. week	5	8	7	5	7	6
Unemployment rate (%)	4	3	1	7	3	2
Unemployment rate (relaxed definition) (%)	8	5	2	14	6	4
Median hours worked in ref. week, main employment activity	28	40	36	48	49	48
Median hours worked in ref. week, all employment activities	30	43	42	48	56	48
Underemployment rate, ≤35 hours in ref. week (%)	8	5	4	3	3	2
Underemployment rate, ≤15 hours in ref. week (%)	4	2	2	1	2	1
Share wage-employed in agriculture (%)	5	3	6	2	1	1
Share self-employed in agriculture (%)	50	38	44	11	4	11
Share wage-employed in nonagriculture (%)	28	36	27	56	56	48
Share self-employed in nonagriculture (%)	17	23	23	31	40	40
Share in agriculture (%)	56	44	54	15	6	14
Share in industry (including construction and agroprocessing) (%)	17	25	21	28	25	19
Share in services (including transportation) (%)	26	31	26	57	69	67
Median hourly wage earnings, main wage-employment activity	25	30	31	23	40	50
Median hourly wage earnings, all wage-employment activities	26	38	38	24	42	50

Source: Estimated using 2010–11 Nepal Living Standards Survey data.
Note: SLC = School Leaving Certificate; ref. = reference. Sample restricted to household members. Relaxed definition for unemployment excludes the active search condition. Sector and type of employment information are for the main employment activity. Median hourly wage earnings are in 2010–11 Nepalese rupees. Estimates are adjusted for sampling weights.

and the share of those who are wage-employed in nonagriculture is larger, all relative to nonyouth. These patterns hold for both genders. In addition, for urban men, median hourly earnings are lower for those in the 25–34 age group than for nonyouth.

CONCLUSION

The findings presented in this chapter point to directions for policy and research. Youth unemployment and time-related underemployment rates, whether based on standard or relaxed definitions, tend to be low. The main determining factor appears to be the unavailability of individuals for (more) work. The main self-reported reasons for unavailability are school attendance and, in the case of women, engagement in noneconomic activities. However, the reported reasons may be proximate, concealing a more extensive underlying labor demand problem. Two patterns signal such a possibility: the nontrivial share of women and men who are neither attending school nor working, and the nontrivial share of female and male workers who are working much less than full time.

Time trends indicate two major shifts in labor patterns for youth in general. First is the increasing share of youth who are attending school, which indicates more years of formal schooling and, thus, later entry into the labor market. Second is the declining share of workers who are self-employed in agriculture, and the increasing share of workers in self- and wage-employment in nonagriculture, a transition that is stronger for youth than for nonyouth.

In addition, we find three major shifts in labor patterns for rural youth: (1) a declining employment rate for women, (2) declining mean hours worked by female and male workers, and (3) increasing real hourly earnings for rural male wage workers in agriculture, with relatively little or no real gain in earnings for other types of wage workers. Plausible explanations for the patterns are (1) a high out-migration rate of rural male youth for employment elsewhere, (2) a high inflow rate of remittances from labor migrants to rural households, and (3) the cessation of the armed conflict in 2006, which has allowed rural residents to reengage in previously disrupted economic and development activities that are more in line with traditional divisions and intensities of labor. The effects of male youth labor out-migration and remittances on the labor outcomes of youth household members are explored in chapter 5.

The earnings trends are corroborated by annual wage data, which show that, although agricultural workers have experienced the largest real gains in wages, salaried workers have experienced essentially no real gains in salaries. Given that salaried workers tend to be more educated than wage workers, the labor-earnings returns to education appear to be declining over time. The combination of potentially declining labor-earnings returns to education and increasing education attainment in the labor force suggests that the increase in the demand for educated workers is deficient relative to the increase in the supply of these workers. The problem may be more acute in urban areas given the higher share of more-educated workers in these areas.

Compared to nonyouth, youth (specifically those in the 25–34 age group, who had mostly completed their education) have a higher level of education attainment, a lower rural employment rate, and a higher unemployment rate, and account for a larger share of wage-employment in nonagriculture. These patterns are consistent with what general labor market theory predicts—specifically, that youth can face frictions when they transition from formal education to the labor market, and that nonyouth can obtain higher earnings with longer labor market experience and job tenure (even if partly offset by the higher level of education attainment among youth). Thus, the patterns do not necessarily signal that youth face labor market disadvantages that may persist over their working lives. The open question is to what extent youth—who are much more educated on average than nonyouth—are likely to find the right employment match, at least in terms of maximizing their private returns, in comparison to nonyouth when they themselves were youth.

ANNEX 3A

TABLE 3A.1 **Composition of unemployed and underemployed youth, 2010–11**

CHARACTERISTIC	FEMALE			MALE		
	UNEMPLOYED	UNDEREMPLOYED, ≤35 HOURS	UNDEREMPLOYED, ≤15 HOURS	UNEMPLOYED	UNDEREMPLOYED, ≤35 HOURS	UNDEREMPLOYED, ≤15 HOURS
	(1)	(2)	(3)	(1)	(2)	(3)
Age	24	24	25	23	24	24
Ever married (%)	58	74	79	54	63	59
Head of household (%)	27	17	16	12	21	20
Disability or chronic illness (%)	12	16	15	4	7	10
Recent illness or injury (%)	21	14	15	11	8	5
Engaged in noneconomic activities (%)	96	94	96	39	56	53
Attending school (%)	30	21	17	28	14	13
Grade 5 or lower (%)	27	46	40	30	42	42
Grades 6–10 (%)	33	32	33	28	36	37
Passed SLC only (%)	19	17	20	19	13	14
Higher secondary or above (%)	22	6	7	23	9	7
Household size (no. of members)	5	5	6	6	7	7
Poor (%)	12	27	26	24	38	38
Brahmin or Chhetri (%)	47	38	41	35	25	24
Terai middle caste (%)	9	1	0	10	16	17
Dalit (%)	3	17	14	10	13	10
Newar (%)	10	4	4	7	4	3
Janajati (%)	28	35	32	26	33	35
Muslim (%)	3	4	6	9	9	12
Other (%)	0	1	2	4	0	0
Kathmandu Valley (%)	32	4	5	14	5	3
Urban Hills (%)	6	4	3	4	2	0
Rural Hills (%)	20	37	32	22	26	23
Mountains (%)	3	5	0	2	5	6
Urban Terai (%)	14	11	14	10	8	9
Rural Terai (%)	25	38	46	49	55	59

Source: Estimated using 2010–11 Nepal Living Standards Survey data.
Note: SLC = School Leaving Certificate. Estimates are adjusted for sampling weights.

FIGURE 3A.1

Distribution of sector and type of employment among youth, 2010–11

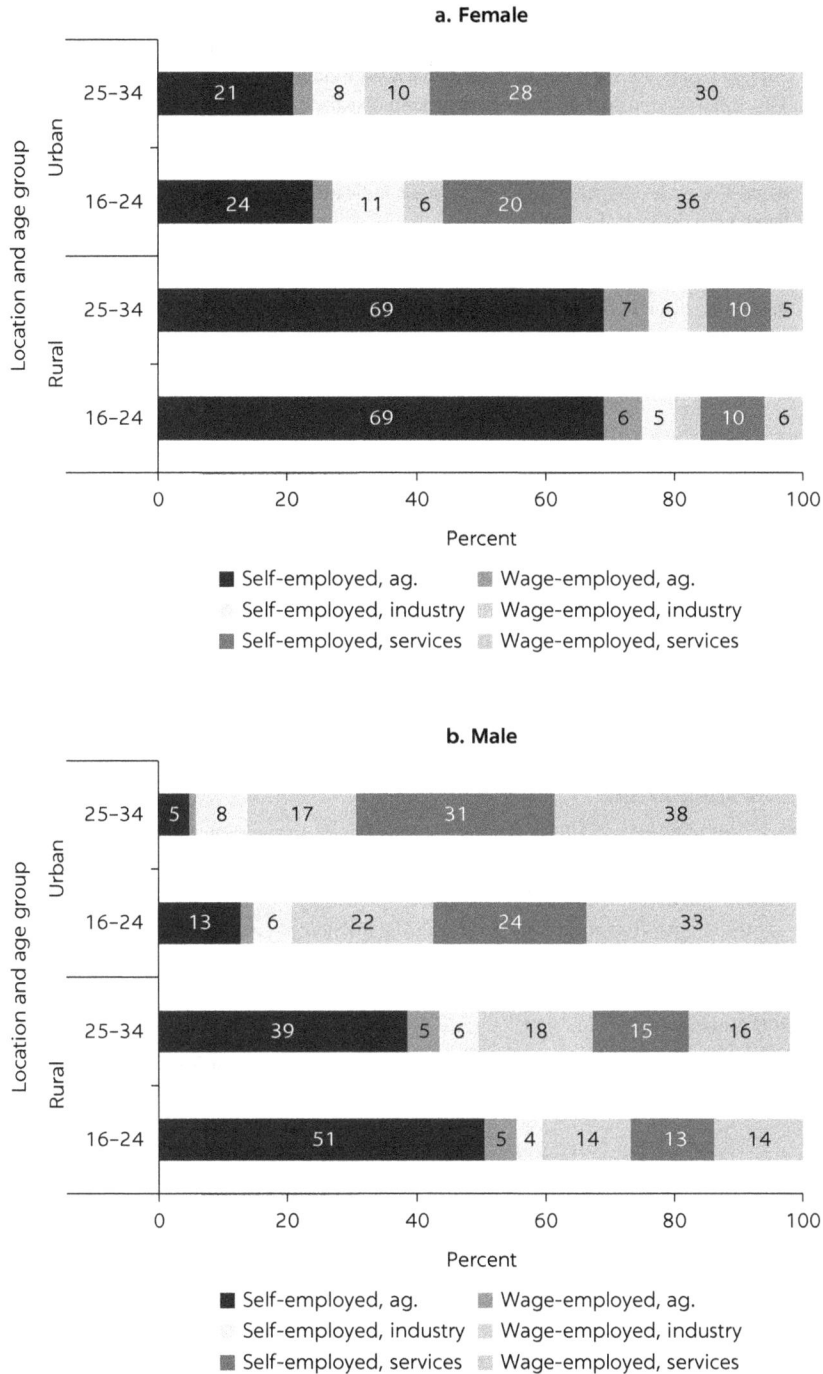

a. Female

Location and age group

Urban
- 25–34: 21 | 8 | 10 | 28 | 30
- 16–24: 24 | 11 | 6 | 20 | 36

Rural
- 25–34: 69 | 7 | 6 | 10 | 5
- 16–24: 69 | 6 | 5 | 10 | 6

Percent

■ Self-employed, ag. ▨ Wage-employed, ag.
□ Self-employed, industry ▨ Wage-employed, industry
■ Self-employed, services ▨ Wage-employed, services

b. Male

Location and age group

Urban
- 25–34: 5 | 8 | 17 | 31 | 38
- 16–24: 13 | 6 | 22 | 24 | 33

Rural
- 25–34: 39 | 5 | 6 | 18 | 15 | 16
- 16–24: 51 | 5 | 4 | 14 | 13 | 14

Percent

■ Self-employed, ag. ▨ Wage-employed, ag.
□ Self-employed, industry ▨ Wage-employed, industry
■ Self-employed, services ▨ Wage-employed, services

Source: Estimated using 2010–11 Nepal Living Standards Survey data.
Note: Sectors are derived from worker occupation data based on Nepal Standard Codes for Occupation (NSCO). Industry includes construction and agroprocessing. Services include transportation. Estimates are adjusted for sampling weights.

NOTES

1. The latest available survey is the 2015–16 NAHS. The report for this survey (Government of Nepal and UNDP 2016a) has been released publicly, but the unit data have not. The 2015–16 NAHS does not, however, contain a labor module.
2. The SLC is offered on the basis of passing a standardized exam offered to grade 10 students annually by the SLC Exam Board of the Nepal government. The student's SLC scores and pass status matter for further education within Nepal.
3. Some of the reasons reported by individuals indicate that unavailability for work is conflated with the lack of search.
4. Mean hours of noneconomic activities in the reference week are much lower for men than women (7–8 hours versus 28 hours).
5. Results are available upon request.
6. Results are available upon request.

REFERENCES

DFID (UK Department for International Development) and World Bank. 2006. *Unequal Citizens: Gender, Caste, and Ethnic Exclusion in Nepal.* Kathmandu: World Bank.

Government of Nepal. 2004. *Nepal Living Standards Survey 2003/04: Statistical Report, Volume 1.* Kathmandu: Central Bureau of Statistics, National Planning Commission Secretariat, Government of Nepal.

——. 2009. *Report on the Nepal Labour Force Survey 2008.* Kathmandu: Central Bureau of Statistics, National Planning Commission Secretariat, Government of Nepal.

——. 2011. *Nepal Living Standards Survey 2010/11: Statistical Report, Volume 1.* Kathmandu: Central Bureau of Statistics, National Planning Commission Secretariat, Government of Nepal.

Government of Nepal and UNDP (United Nations Development Programme). 2016a. *Annual Household Survey 2015/16: Major Findings.* Kathmandu: Central Bureau of Statistics, National Planning Commission Secretariat, Government of Nepal.

——. 2016b. *Annual Household Survey 2014/15: Major Findings.* Kathmandu: Central Bureau of Statistics, National Planning Commission Secretariat, Government of Nepal.

ILO (International Labour Organization). 2017a. *World Employment and Social Outlook: Trends 2017.* Geneva: ILO.

——. 2017b. *Global Employment Trends for Youth 2017: Pathways to a Better Working Future.* Geneva: ILO.

4 Labor Market Perceptions and Sentiments among Youth Workers

DHUSHYANTH RAJU AND SCOTT ABRAHAMS

INTRODUCTION

What views do youth workers have about their current labor market conditions and outcomes and their future labor market prospects? Standard labor economics research is based on revealed preferences, that is, the analysis of data on observed behaviors and outcomes of workers and employers. A labor force survey mainly captures such data. Policy making based on evidence from objective data has a sound footing, to the extent that the worker's revealed preferences are consistent with his or her true preferences. However, observed labor choices may not reflect the true interests of the worker, and they reveal little about either the thought process or the actual process followed by the worker. They also do not reveal what opportunities and constraints the worker may have experienced in making his or her labor choices.

To shed light on the underlying labor processes and interests of workers, this chapter describes the self-reported perceptions, motivations, intentions, and aspirations of Nepalese youth with respect to the domestic labor market—that is, their own explanations for their labor behavior. The data come from the 2013 School-to-Work Transition Survey (SWTS), a nationally representative sample survey of individuals ages 15–29 years. In our analysis, we define youth as those ages 16–29 years and exclude individuals who are age 15 years, given that Nepalese law classifies them as children.

We examine workers' views regarding employment search strategies, main difficulties in finding employment, the relevance of their qualifications for employment, employment satisfaction, and desire to change employment, among other things. Except for Serriere and CEDA (2014), which analyze these same data, prior research on self-reported explanations for the labor behavior of workers in Nepal is absent. On the basis of the 2008 Nepal Labour Force Survey, the government of Nepal (2009) reports the distribution of responses of unemployed workers on employment search length and search strategies, variables we also examine in this chapter. We deepen the existing evidence by performing all analyses separately for urban and rural areas, and by examining the sociodemographic and employment correlates of selected workers' sentiments. For example, we ask what factors determine whether a worker (1) reports that insufficient employment opportunities or inadequate qualifications were the main difficulty in finding employment, (2) is dissatisfied with current employment, or (3) desires to change current employment. Our findings hold for workers present in their households at the time of the survey, which is a highly selected group, given the substantial outflow of male workers from Nepal to other countries. According to the 2010–11 Nepal Living Standards Survey (NLSS), 29 percent of Nepalese men ages 16–29 years were absent from their households because they had migrated to other countries for employment.

With respect to employed workers, most found employment by either joining their family's income-generating activity or asking friends or family for assistance. Only a minority of workers formally applied for employment, and a negligible share used public employment service centers as part of their employment search. Employment search length tends to be short; the majority of workers found employment in less than three months. In rural areas, more-educated workers and workers who obtained wage employment with written contracts are more likely to have had longer employment searches. The majority of workers feel that their qualifications are relevant, but a sizable minority feel that they need additional education or training.

Most employed workers report that the main difficulty they experience in finding employment is either insufficient employment opportunities or inadequate qualifications. In rural areas, wage workers are more likely to report that insufficient employment opportunities were the main difficulty, whereas unpaid family workers are more likely to report that inadequate qualifications were the main difficulty. Although workers tend to work full time, a large share of workers, particularly agricultural workers, desire additional hours of work.

Most workers are dissatisfied with their employment, at a rate that is much higher than for workers in other SWTS-surveyed countries. Wage workers with written contracts are less likely to be dissatisfied with their employment than other types of workers. The vast majority of workers, including wage workers, feel that their employment is secure. Regardless, a large share of workers desire to change employment, mainly to find employment that has better working conditions, offers more work hours, or better matches their qualifications.

With respect to unemployed workers, as expected, they had longer employment searches, and they are more likely than employed workers to have refused employment offers and to have formally applied for employment. The main reason unemployed workers give for turning down an offer is low wages; but urban unemployed workers also tend to care about other aspects, such as the match between their qualifications and the employment offer, and the convenience of the employment location. Rural unemployed workers are particularly open to moving to the Kathmandu Valley or another country for employment.

Similar to employed workers, most unemployed workers report that the main difficulty they face in finding employment is either insufficient employment opportunities or inadequate qualifications. Nepalese unemployed workers are more likely than their counterparts in other SWTS-surveyed countries to report that insufficient employment opportunities are the main difficulty. Within Nepal, more-educated unemployed workers are more likely to report that insufficient employment opportunities are the main difficulty.

For both employed and unemployed workers, their region of residence matters at times for their perceptions and sentiments. Inadequate qualifications appear to be more of an issue in the Kathmandu Valley, whereas insufficient employment opportunities appear to be more of an issue in the Hills, for both urban and rural residents.

The collective evidence suggests that employment creation appears to be a critical issue, specifically the creation of decent, formal-wage employment.

The remainder of the chapter is organized as follows. The next section discusses the data, sample, and structure of the analysis. The following section presents the results. The final section discusses the implications of our findings.

DATA, SAMPLE, AND STRUCTURE OF THE ANALYSIS

We analyze data from the 2013 round of the SWTS for Nepal (Serriere and CEDA 2014). The SWTS is representative at the national level, for the six regions of the country and for urban and rural areas within each region. Only individuals ages 15–29 years were interviewed. Our analysis excludes individuals age 15 years because they are considered children and not adults under Nepalese law (Government of Nepal 2000).

The survey data suffer from two important problems. The first problem likely matters less for statistical inference than the second. First, data were not collected for eligible members in each sample household who were not present at the time of the interview. The missing or nonresponse rate is a substantial 29 percent. To the extent that most of the missing eligible individuals are those who have migrated to other countries, our results can be interpreted as applying to youth residing in their households.

Second, there appears to be a problem with the gender data. The male–female gender ratio in our data is 1.2. However, the male–female ratio for individuals ages 15–29 years is 0.9, according to 2011 population census data (Government of Nepal 2012), and 0.7 for the same age group, according to data from the 2010–11 NLSS. Given this, we do not perform any subgroup analysis by gender; nor do we include gender as a factor in any regressions. On the basis of the analysis of other household survey data conducted in other chapters in this book, we find that labor patterns often diverge in direction between genders or that the patterns are similar in direction but more pronounced for one gender. Thus, the results from the aggregated analysis of patterns in these data are expected to suffer from attenuation bias.

The survey had one main module for employed workers and another for unemployed workers. Following this, our analysis is disaggregated by whether the worker is employed or unemployed. Employed is defined as engaged in an economic activity in the reference week. Unemployed is defined as not employed, available for work in the reference week, and actively looked for work in the last month.[1] The analysis sample contains 1,300 employed workers (39 percent of all individuals) and 341 unemployed workers (10 percent of all individuals).

All analyses are performed separately for urban and rural workers. In the analysis sample, 30 percent of workers are urban residents. As other chapters in this book show, labor patterns and trends differ substantially for rural versus urban areas, such as with respect to education qualifications, type and sector of employment, and labor out-migration. Indeed, for many labor indicators, the differences between rural and urban areas are much larger than differences between other key subgroups (such as gender or household poverty status). Thus, we expect that self-reported explanations and sentiments regarding labor behavior will differ between rural and urban workers as well.

Table 4.1 reports mean sociodemographic and employment characteristics for workers separately by status (employed, unemployed) and location of

TABLE 4.1 **Mean characteristics, by worker status, workers ages 16–29 years, 2013**

CHARACTERISTIC	RURAL		URBAN	
	EMPLOYED	UNEMPLOYED	EMPLOYED	UNEMPLOYED
	(1)	(2)	(3)	(4)
Age	22.83	21.29	23.75	22.04
Married	0.57	0.26	0.41	0.27
Number of children	0.69	0.33	0.38	0.22
Currently attending school	0.24	0.57	0.40	0.69
Highest education				
Primary or less	0.45	0.21	0.16	0.13
Secondary	0.35	0.35	0.35	0.29
Tertiary	0.20	0.44	0.49	0.59
Relative economic status				
More well off than average	0.13	0.14	0.39	0.35
Average well off	0.56	0.59	0.53	0.51
Less well off than average	0.31	0.27	0.08	0.14
Father's education				
None	0.42	0.29	0.18	0.12
Primary	0.39	0.27	0.30	0.35
Secondary	0.14	0.35	0.32	0.34
Tertiary	0.05	0.10	0.19	0.20
Life goal				
Occupational	0.13	0.36	0.32	0.30
Societal	0.11	0.13	0.10	0.13
Financial	0.28	0.18	0.22	0.17
Familial	0.48	0.33	0.37	0.39
Hours worked	39.07	n.a.	38.82	n.a.
Employment type				
Wage employee, written contract	0.12	n.a.	0.25	n.a.
Wage employee, verbal contract	0.28	n.a.	0.28	n.a.
Employer, own-account worker	0.17	n.a.	0.20	n.a.
Unpaid family worker	0.44	n.a.	0.27	n.a.
Sector				
Agriculture	0.51	n.a.	0.11	n.a.
Industry	0.14	n.a.	0.14	n.a.
Services	0.34	n.a.	0.75	n.a.
Region				
Rural Hills	0.48	0.54	n.a.	n.a.
Mountains	0.12	0.08	n.a.	n.a.
Rural Terai	0.40	0.38	n.a.	n.a.
Kathmandu Valley	n.a.	n.a.	0.48	0.49
Urban Hills	n.a.	n.a.	0.25	0.23
Urban Terai	n.a.	n.a.	0.27	0.27
Observations	970	204	369	143

Source: Estimated using 2013 School-to-Work Transition Survey data.

Note: n.a. = not applicable. Italicized indicators represent reference categories in the regressions we estimate. All estimates are adjusted for sampling weights.

residence (rural, urban). Sociodemographic characteristics comprise age, marital status, number of children, current school participation status, education level, relative household economic status, father's education level, life goal, and region of residence. Employment characteristics comprise hours worked in the reference week, employment type, and employment sector.

In terms of some key patterns, compared to employed workers, unemployed workers are younger on average, less likely to be married, have fewer children on average, and are more likely to be attending school. Urban workers tend to be more educated than rural workers, and unemployed workers tend to be more educated than employed workers. Relative to urban workers, rural workers are more likely to report that they are economically worse off than average and less likely to report that they are economically better off than average. Patterns for reported relative economic status are similar between employed and unemployed workers.

Employed workers worked full time on average (that is, 36 or more hours in the reference week). Unpaid family employment is more common for rural employed workers than for urban ones (44 percent versus 27 percent), and wage employment with written contracts is more common for urban employed workers than for their rural counterparts (25 percent versus 12 percent). Rural employed workers are more likely to be engaged in agriculture than urban employed workers (51 percent versus 11 percent) and are less likely to be engaged in services (34 percent versus 75 percent).

In all the regressions we estimate, we examine the relationship between the outcome of interest and sociodemographic characteristics. In the regressions for employed workers, we also examine the relationship between the outcome of interest and employment characteristics. The reference categories for categorical sociodemographic and employment regression factors are italicized in table 4.1. Finally, depending on the specific outcome, we include other potentially relevant factors in the regressions. All factors are identical in the rural- and urban-specific regressions except for region of residence. The regions in the rural-specific regressions are the Hills (reference category), the Terai, and the Mountains, whereas the regions in the urban-specific regressions are the Kathmandu Valley (reference category), the Hills, and the Terai. Note that the regressions for unemployed workers suffer from small sample sizes (between 100 to 200 observations); therefore, the results should be read with more caution.

All outcomes are binary by construction. Consequently, we estimate binomial logit regressions, and transform the estimated coefficients into average marginal effects, which we report. Inference is based on robust standard errors clustered at the primary sampling unit level. All estimates—patterns and correlates—are adjusted for survey sampling weights.

EMPLOYED YOUTH WORKERS

Employment search: Employed youth workers (hereafter in the subsection, referred to as workers) found employment mainly through informal strategies. Forty-three percent of workers simply joined their family's income-generating activity, while another 20 percent found employment by asking family and friends for assistance. Twenty-nine percent of workers found employment by following formal strategies, such as registering at public employment service centers (specifically, where relevant, labor offices, vocational and skill development training centers, or employment information offices), placing or responding to an employment advertisement, applying or interviewing for employment, directly inquiring with employers, or obtaining permits to start a business. Compared to urban workers, rural workers are more likely to report joining the family income-generating activity (46 percent versus 29 percent) and less likely to have asked family and friends for search assistance (18 percent versus 31 percent).

As part of their employment search, only 23 percent of workers formally applied for employment in the year before they found employment, with a higher rate for urban workers than rural workers (37 percent versus 20 percent). Seven percent of workers refused an employment offer, with a higher rate for urban workers than rural workers (18 percent versus 5 percent). Workers rarely used public employment service centers as part of their employment search: Only 7 percent of workers used these centers, with similar rates for rural and urban workers.

Main difficulties finding employment. The two most commonly reported main difficulties in finding employment are insufficient employment opportunities (26 percent) and inadequate qualifications (19 percent). Ten percent of workers report that they did not experience any difficulty in finding employment. The response patterns are roughly similar between rural and urban workers.

Table 4.2 reports regression results for the correlates of whether the worker reports that insufficient employment opportunities were the main difficulty in finding employment, as well as regression results for the correlates of whether the worker reports that inadequate qualifications were the main difficulty. In rural areas, unpaid family workers are less likely to report insufficient employment opportunities than wage workers with written contracts. For both urban and rural workers, region of residence matters: those from the Hills are more likely to report insufficient employment opportunities.

TABLE 4.2 **Correlates of type of difficulty finding work, employed workers ages 16–29 years, 2013**

MLE logit regression results, average marginal effects

FACTOR	INSUFFICIENT EMPLOYMENT OPPORTUNITIES		INADEQUATE QUALIFICATIONS	
	RURAL	URBAN	RURAL	URBAN
	(1)	(2)	(3)	(4)
Age	0.007	0.002	−0.019***	−0.000
	(0.006)	(0.011)	(0.006)	(0.007)
Married	−0.112***	−0.060	0.137***	−0.068
	(0.043)	(0.076)	(0.039)	(0.050)
Number of children	0.024	0.041	0.008	0.033
	(0.020)	(0.065)	(0.019)	(0.040)
Secondary education	−0.009	−0.028	0.021	−0.164*
	(0.045)	(0.088)	(0.037)	(0.096)
Tertiary education	0.002	−0.004	0.101*	−0.247**
	(0.060)	(0.088)	(0.060)	(0.109)
Currently attending school	−0.008	0.016	0.039	0.075
	(0.069)	(0.061)	(0.045)	(0.071)
Average well off	−0.004	0.041	0.004	0.010
	(0.043)	(0.055)	(0.055)	(0.048)
Less well off than average	−0.073	−0.131*	0.023	0.211*
	(0.062)	(0.074)	(0.063)	(0.124)

continued

TABLE 4.2, *continued*

| FACTOR | INSUFFICIENT EMPLOYMENT OPPORTUNITIES | | INADEQUATE QUALIFICATIONS | |
	RURAL	URBAN	RURAL	URBAN
	(1)	(2)	(3)	(4)
Father: primary education	0.128**	0.105	−0.120***	0.060
	(0.060)	(0.089)	(0.041)	(0.089)
Father: secondary education	−0.064	−0.077	−0.026	−0.035
	(0.058)	(0.065)	(0.042)	(0.054)
Father: tertiary education	0.048	−0.048	−0.026	0.070
	(0.054)	(0.073)	(0.038)	(0.051)
Life goal: societal contribution	−0.073**	−0.119	0.039	0.061
	(0.031)	(0.091)	(0.034)	(0.052)
Life goal: financial	−0.051	−0.117	0.041	0.111
	(0.051)	(0.089)	(0.042)	(0.082)
Life goal: familial	−0.035	−0.138	−0.019	−0.004
	(0.086)	(0.100)	(0.088)	(0.064)
Hours worked	0.001	−0.002	0.001	0.001
	(0.001)	(0.002)	(0.001)	(0.001)
Wage employee, verbal contract	−0.004	0.057	−0.028	−0.018
	(0.079)	(0.055)	(0.050)	(0.049)
Employer/own-account worker	−0.034	0.048	0.023	0.025
	(0.086)	(0.063)	(0.057)	(0.066)
Unpaid family worker	−0.163**	−0.046	0.122**	0.002
	(0.073)	(0.055)	(0.055)	(0.075)
Industry	−0.051	−0.111	0.182**	0.069
	(0.056)	(0.106)	(0.071)	(0.101)
Services	−0.067	−0.029	−0.004	−0.026
	(0.045)	(0.092)	(0.036)	(0.080)
Mountains	−0.192***	n.a.	−0.062	n.a.
	(0.066)		(0.074)	
Terai	−0.137***	n.a.	−0.018	n.a.
	(0.047)		(0.037)	
Hills	n.a.	0.205***	n.a.	−0.058
		(0.069)		(0.056)
Terai	n.a.	0.082	n.a.	−0.088
		(0.070)		(0.059)
Observations	739	297	739	297

Source: Estimated using 2013 School-to-Work Transition Survey data.
Note: n.a. = not applicable. Robust standard errors, clustered at the primary sampling unit level, are reported in parentheses. All estimates are adjusted for sampling weights.
*$p<0.1$, **$p<0.05$, ***$p<0.01$.

In rural areas, unpaid family workers are more likely to report inadequate qualifications than wage workers with written contracts, and industrial workers are more likely to report inadequate qualifications than agricultural workers. For urban workers, those with higher levels of education are less likely to report inadequate qualifications (as one would expect), but few other factors appear to be associated with inadequate qualifications.

Employment search length. As may be expected given the informal nature of finding employment, the employment search length tends to be short. Seventy-five percent of workers found employment in less than three months, with similar rates for rural and urban workers.

Table 4.3 presents regression results for the correlates of whether the worker searched for employment for at least three months (a longer search). In rural areas, those with tertiary education are more likely to have had a longer search than those with primary education or less. In urban areas, those who report that inadequate qualifications were the main difficulty they experienced finding employment are more likely to have had a longer search, whereas insufficient employment opportunities do not appear to be correlated with the likelihood of

TABLE 4.3 Correlates of employment search duration of at least three months, employed workers ages 16–29 years, 2013

MLE logit regression results, average marginal effects

FACTOR	RURAL (1)	URBAN (2)
Age	0.001 (0.006)	0.011 (0.010)
Married	0.031 (0.048)	−0.005 (0.065)
Number of children	0.010 (0.024)	0.060 (0.048)
Secondary education	0.030 (0.060)	−0.127 (0.105)
Tertiary education	0.150** (0.074)	−0.105 (0.135)
Currently attending school	0.007 (0.061)	0.092 (0.070)
Average well off	0.023 (0.050)	0.086 (0.058)
Less well off than average	0.075 (0.057)	0.022 (0.120)
Life goal: societal contribution	−0.101 (0.075)	−0.062 (0.082)
Life goal: financial	−0.085 (0.066)	−0.057 (0.076)
Life goal: familial	−0.025 (0.063)	0.014 (0.067)
Father: primary education	0.060 (0.045)	0.030 (0.077)
Father: secondary education	0.085 (0.058)	0.056 (0.088)
Father: tertiary education	−0.044 (0.093)	0.086 (0.104)
Hours worked	0.001 (0.001)	0.003** (0.001)
Insufficient employment opportunities	0.015 (0.039)	0.043 (0.061)
Inadequate qualifications	0.077 (0.058)	0.115** (0.058)
Wage employee, verbal contract	0.054 (0.077)	−0.039 (0.081)

continued

TABLE 4.3, *continued*

FACTOR	RURAL	URBAN
	(1)	(2)
Employer/own-account worker	−0.097	−0.028
	(0.088)	(0.083)
Unpaid family worker	−0.171**	−0.242***
	(0.086)	(0.086)
Industry	−0.056	0.107
	(0.059)	(0.134)
Services	0.041	0.081
	(0.055)	(0.109)
Mountains	−0.204***	n.a.
	(0.070)	
Terai	−0.107*	n.a.
	(0.056)	
Hills	n.a.	0.197**
		(0.089)
Terai	n.a.	0.188**
		(0.075)
Observations	739	297

Source: Estimated using 2013 School-to-Work Transition Survey data.
Note: n.a. = not applicable. Robust standard errors, clustered at the primary sampling unit level, are reported in parentheses. All estimates are adjusted for sampling weights.
*p<0.1, **p<0.05, ***p<0.01.

longer employment search for either rural or urban workers. In both urban and rural areas, unpaid family workers are less likely to have had a longer employment search than wage workers with written contracts. Finally, region of residence matters: among rural workers, those from the Hills are more likely to have had a longer search, and among urban workers, those from the Hills and the Terai are more likely to have had a longer search.

Education and training. Fifty-five percent of workers report that they feel that their academic and professional qualifications are relevant for their current employment, whereas 26 percent report that they need more education or training. Rural workers are less likely than urban workers to feel that their qualifications are relevant (53 percent versus 67 percent), and are more likely to report that they need more education or training (28 percent versus 13 percent).

Table 4.4 presents regression results for the correlates of whether the worker reports that he or she needs training or that his or her skills are not relevant. As expected, those with higher levels of education are less likely to report the need for training or that their skills are not relevant. Those who are currently attending school and those who feel that they are not economically better off than average are more likely to report the need for training or that their skills are not relevant. Those who worked more hours are less likely to report the need for training or that their skills are not relevant. Finally, among urban workers, those from the Hills or the Terai are more likely than those from the Kathmandu Valley to report the need for training or that their skills are not relevant.

Hours. Both urban and rural workers worked on average 39 hours in the reference week. Forty-two percent of workers report that they would like to work more hours, with a higher share for rural workers than urban workers (44 percent versus 38 percent). Workers desire an additional 20 hours of work weekly on average, with urban workers desiring fewer additional hours weekly than rural workers on average (16 hours versus 20 hours).

Conditional on desiring more hours of work, 57 percent of workers report that they desire these hours in their current job followed by 33 percent who report that they desire these hours by getting an additional job. Only a small minority of workers (8 percent) report that they desire additional hours by leaving their current job. The distribution of responses is similar between rural and urban workers.

Table 4.4 also presents regression results for the correlates of whether the worker reports that he would like to work more hours. In urban areas, those with relatively less education, those who feel that they are economically less well off than average, and those from the Hills are more likely to desire more hours, whereas those who worked more hours, and industrial and service workers, are less likely to desire more hours. In rural areas, industrial workers are more likely to desire more hours than agricultural workers. In both urban and rural areas, wage workers are more likely to desire more hours than other types of workers.

Employment satisfaction. Fifty-eight percent of workers report that they are at least somewhat dissatisfied with their current employment, with a much higher rate of dissatisfaction among rural workers than urban workers (61 percent versus 40 percent).

TABLE 4.4 **Correlates of "needs training" and "desires more hours," employed workers ages 16–29 years, 2013**

MLE binomial logit regression results, average marginal effects

FACTOR	NEEDS TRAINING / SKILLS NOT RELEVANT		DESIRES MORE WORK HOURS	
	RURAL	URBAN	RURAL	URBAN
	(1)	(2)	(3)	(4)
Age	0.006	0.001	−0.011	0.000
	(0.006)	(0.008)	(0.007)	(0.010)
Married	−0.044	0.027	−0.021	−0.110
	(0.036)	(0.042)	(0.043)	(0.069)
Number of children	0.012	0.016	0.022	−0.023
	(0.024)	(0.031)	(0.028)	(0.050)
Secondary education	−0.178***	−0.205*	−0.012	−0.126*
	(0.050)	(0.114)	(0.048)	(0.076)
Tertiary education	−0.155**	−0.431***	−0.040	−0.126
	(0.064)	(0.119)	(0.061)	(0.091)
Currently attending school	0.143**	0.173**	−0.090	−0.020
	(0.060)	(0.073)	(0.061)	(0.069)
Average well off	0.193***	0.088**	−0.098*	−0.014
	(0.044)	(0.044)	(0.053)	(0.053)
Less well off than average	0.302***	0.263**	−0.109*	0.285***
	(0.051)	(0.125)	(0.064)	(0.109)
Father: primary education	−0.110	−0.215***	−0.034	−0.002
	(0.075)	(0.052)	(0.072)	(0.092)
Father: secondary education	−0.119*	−0.078	−0.009	−0.005
	(0.063)	(0.055)	(0.064)	(0.099)
Father: tertiary education	−0.102**	−0.067	0.057	0.109
	(0.047)	(0.048)	(0.068)	(0.069)
Life goal: societal contribution	−0.125***	−0.082	0.071*	0.116**
	(0.039)	(0.064)	(0.042)	(0.058)

continued

TABLE 4.4, *continued*

FACTOR	NEEDS TRAINING / SKILLS NOT RELEVANT		DESIRES MORE WORK HOURS	
	RURAL	URBAN	RURAL	URBAN
	(1)	(2)	(3)	(4)
Life goal: financial	−0.136**	−0.085	−0.024	0.136*
	(0.055)	(0.070)	(0.069)	(0.072)
Life goal: familial	−0.240***	0.050	−0.023	0.133*
	(0.081)	(0.080)	(0.102)	(0.074)
Hours worked in reference week	−0.002**	−0.004***	−0.001	−0.003*
	(0.001)	(0.001)	(0.002)	(0.002)
Wage employee, verbal contract	0.087	0.001	−0.001	−0.022
	(0.070)	(0.065)	(0.088)	(0.102)
Employer/own-account worker	0.061	−0.050	−0.307***	−0.242***
	(0.071)	(0.056)	(0.078)	(0.063)
Unpaid family worker	0.028	−0.011	−0.185**	−0.400***
	(0.077)	(0.075)	(0.091)	(0.062)
Industry	−0.031	0.008	0.196***	−0.228**
	(0.053)	(0.081)	(0.072)	(0.108)
Services	−0.070*	0.034	−0.009	−0.221***
	(0.041)	(0.063)	(0.062)	(0.083)
Mountains	0.068	n.a.	0.088	n.a.
	(0.047)		(0.054)	
Terai	0.004	n.a.	−0.080	n.a.
	(0.047)		(0.057)	
Hills	n.a.	−0.147**	n.a.	0.354***
		(0.070)		(0.080)
Terai	n.a.	−0.127*	n.a.	0.050
		(0.068)		(0.071)
Observations	819	319	789	314

Source: Estimated using 2013 School-to-Work Transition Survey data.
Note: n.a. = not applicable. Robust standard errors, clustered at the primary sampling unit level, are reported in parentheses. All estimates are adjusted for sampling weights.
*$p<0.1$, **$p<0.05$, ***$p<0.01$.

Table 4.5 reports regression results for the correlates of whether the worker is dissatisfied with his or her current employment. In both rural and urban areas, compared to wage workers with written contracts, all other types of workers are much more likely to be dissatisfied with their current employment, possibly indicating the undesirability of other forms of employment relative to formal wage employment.

Employment change. Employment security does not register as an issue. About 90 percent of urban and rural workers report that they are either very likely or likely to retain their employment over the next year if they desire. (The rates are similar when we examine wage workers only.) Nonetheless, 45 percent of employed workers report that they desire to change their employment, with similar rates for rural and urban workers. Common explanations reported by those who desire to change employment are that they want to seek a better match with their qualifications (31 percent), that their current employment is temporary (21 percent), that they want to work more hours (20 percent), or that they want better working conditions (15 percent). Seeking a better match with qualifications is a more common response among urban workers than rural workers (38 percent versus 30 percent), whereas seeking better working conditions is a more common response for rural workers than urban workers (16 percent versus 10 percent). Notwithstanding, workers tend not to have made any effort to change employment; only 35 percent and 26 percent of workers who desire to change employment sought new employment or additional employment in the last month, respectively, with slightly higher reported effort rates among rural workers than urban workers.

Table 4.5 also presents regression results for the correlates of whether the worker reports the desire to change employment. In urban areas, older or married workers are less likely to report that they desire to change employment, whereas those currently attending school are more likely to report that they desire to do so. In rural areas, industrial workers are less likely than agricultural workers to report that they desire to change employment. Unsurprisingly, in both rural and urban areas, those who are dissatisfied with their current employment are much more likely to report that they desire to change employment. Also in both rural and urban areas, employers and own-account workers are much less likely to report that they desire to change employment than wage workers with written contracts.

Comparison with other countries

To provide an international point of reference, based on information given by Elder (2014), we compare selected results for Nepal to those of other countries where the SWTS was conducted, namely Bangladesh (in 2013), Cambodia (in 2012), Samoa (in 2012), and Vietnam (in 2012–13). Note that the international comparisons are based on results for the full sample of individuals ages 15–29 years. As a result, the statistics for Nepal could differ from those from our analysis, which excluded those age 15 years.

TABLE 4.5 **Correlates of employment dissatisfaction and desire to change employment, employed workers ages 16–29 years, 2013**

MLE binomial logit regression results, average marginal effects

FACTOR	DISSATISFIED WITH EMPLOYMENT		DESIRE TO CHANGE EMPLOYMENT	
	RURAL	URBAN	RURAL	URBAN
	(1)	(2)	(3)	(4)
Age	−0.004	−0.012	−0.004	0.019**
	(0.005)	(0.010)	(0.006)	(0.009)
Married	−0.022	0.034	−0.012	−0.115**
	(0.043)	(0.051)	(0.041)	(0.057)
Number of children	−0.012	0.050	0.019	−0.049
	(0.018)	(0.041)	(0.027)	(0.054)
Secondary education	−0.015	−0.069	0.089*	−0.013
	(0.043)	(0.090)	(0.050)	(0.077)
Tertiary education	0.001	−0.126	0.044	−0.080
	(0.065)	(0.111)	(0.062)	(0.082)
Currently attending school	0.117**	0.091	0.036	0.188***
	(0.058)	(0.066)	(0.056)	(0.065)
Average well off	0.046	0.119***	−0.051	0.009
	(0.050)	(0.040)	(0.048)	(0.049)

continued

TABLE 4.5, *continued*

FACTOR	DISSATISFIED WITH EMPLOYMENT		DESIRE TO CHANGE EMPLOYMENT	
	RURAL	URBAN	RURAL	URBAN
	(1)	(2)	(3)	(4)
Less well off than average	0.134**	0.140	−0.035	0.149
	(0.054)	(0.090)	(0.058)	(0.123)
Father: primary education	0.074	0.052	0.060	−0.001
	(0.072)	(0.077)	(0.058)	(0.070)
Father: secondary education	0.093*	−0.111*	0.160***	0.011
	(0.055)	(0.058)	(0.059)	(0.077)
Father: tertiary education	0.070	−0.037	0.069	−0.000
	(0.055)	(0.058)	(0.051)	(0.056)
Life goal: societal contribution	−0.053	−0.021	−0.005	0.194***
	(0.039)	(0.061)	(0.039)	(0.075)
Life goal: financial	0.041	0.146**	0.025	0.175**
	(0.049)	(0.074)	(0.051)	(0.086)
Life goal: familial	−0.051	0.112	−0.057	0.098
	(0.070)	(0.080)	(0.076)	(0.093)
Dissatisfied with current employment	n.a.	n.a.	0.365***	0.212***
			(0.035)	(0.057)
Overqualified	−0.004***	−0.003**	−0.001	−0.003*
	(0.001)	(0.001)	(0.001)	(0.001)
Need training / skills not relevant	−0.015	0.130	−0.043	0.002
	(0.042)	(0.107)	(0.046)	(0.077)
Hours worked in reference week	−0.018	0.074	−0.061	0.088
	(0.033)	(0.077)	(0.043)	(0.087)
Wage employee, verbal contract	0.246***	0.209***	0.087	0.141*
	(0.062)	(0.063)	(0.069)	(0.084)
Employer/own-account worker	0.320***	0.091	−0.237***	−0.145**
	(0.063)	(0.082)	(0.071)	(0.070)
Unpaid family worker	0.602***	0.611***	−0.118	−0.071
	(0.059)	(0.069)	(0.075)	(0.088)
Industry	−0.028	−0.135	−0.109**	0.054
	(0.046)	(0.099)	(0.055)	(0.101)
Services	−0.035	−0.021	−0.070	−0.076
	(0.043)	(0.080)	(0.046)	(0.089)
Mountains	0.028	n.a.	0.014	n.a.
	(0.062)		(0.049)	
Terai	−0.032	n.a.	0.028	n.a.
	(0.038)		(0.043)	
Hills	n.a.	−0.046	n.a.	0.025
		(0.056)		(0.069)
Terai	n.a.	0.027	n.a.	0.025
		(0.065)		(0.080)
Observations	819	319	819	319

Source: Estimated using 2013 School-to-Work Transition Survey data.
Note: n.a. = not applicable. Robust standard errors, clustered at the primary sampling unit level, are reported in parentheses. All estimates are adjusted for sampling weights.
*$p<0.1$, **$p<0.05$, ***$p<0.01$.

Three comparisons stand out (see figure 4.1). First, employment satisfaction rates range between 74 percent and 90 percent in the other countries, but the rate is markedly lower for Nepal, at 41 percent. Second, consistent with Nepal's much lower employment-satisfaction rate, 45 percent of Nepalese workers indicate that they desire to change employment, compared to a range of 13 percent to 42 percent in the other countries. Third, conditional

FIGURE 4.1

Comparison of sentiments and opinions of employed workers ages 15–29 years, Nepal versus other countries

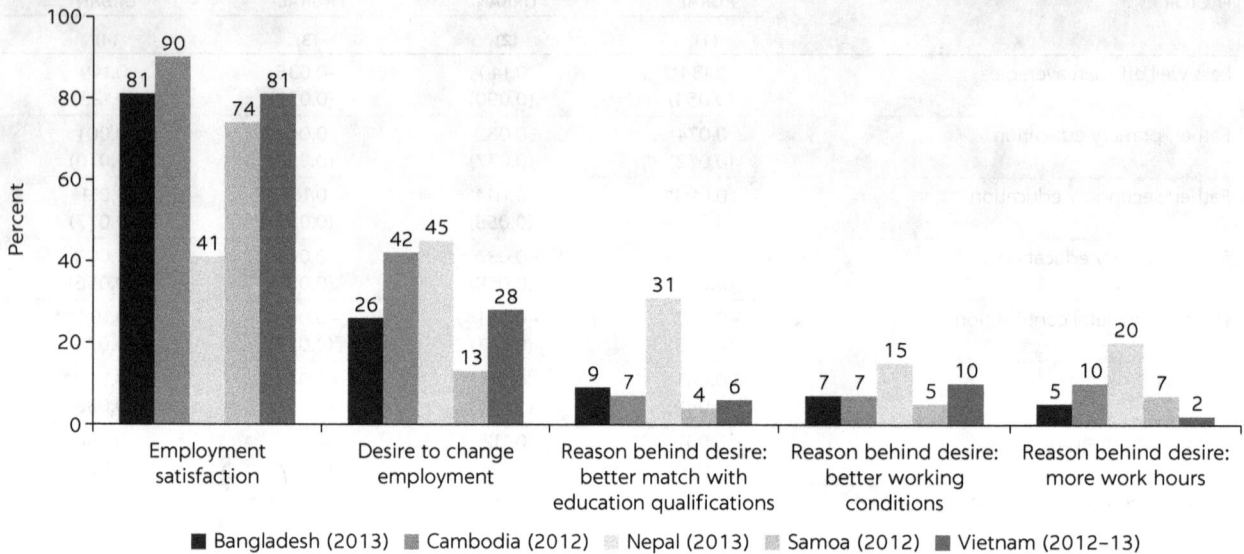

Source: Based on statistics drawn from Elder 2014.

on desiring to change employment, Nepalese workers are much more likely than workers in the other countries to report that the reason is to find a better match with their education qualifications, to obtain more work hours, or to seek better working conditions.

UNEMPLOYED YOUTH WORKERS

Employment search. The SWTS asks unemployed workers about the strategies they have used to search for employment. Unlike employed workers, for whom the question is on the specific strategy that led to employment (and thus they could only offer a single response), unemployed workers have the option to offer multiple responses. The most commonly used strategies by unemployed workers have been to ask friends and family for assistance (67 percent); to place, or respond to, an employment advertisement (45 percent); to inquire directly with employers (21 percent); and to register at a public employment service center (14 percent). Rural unemployed workers are more likely than urban unemployed workers to have registered with a public employment service center (18 percent versus 5 percent), more likely to have asked friends and family for assistance (67 percent versus 58 percent), and less likely to have placed, or responded, to employment advertisements (43 percent versus 52 percent). In terms of inquiring directly with employers, rural and urban unemployed workers have similar rates.

On the basis of comparable questions, it appears that unemployed workers are more likely to have formally applied for employment than employed workers, presumably given the former's need to explore other options to find employment. Fifty-nine percent of unemployed workers report that they have formally applied for employment in the last year, with a higher rate for urban unemployed workers than for their rural counterparts (66 percent versus 56 percent). (In comparison, only 23 percent of employed workers had formally applied for employment in the year before they became employed.)

As discussed in the previous section, a large share of employed workers—when asked about how they found their employment—report that they joined the family income-generating activity. The SWTS does not ask if the unemployed worker's family has an income-generating activity. Thus, we do not know if the unemployed worker has a family income-generating activity that he did not join, or if he does not have a family income-generating activity.

Desired employment. Fifty-five percent of unemployed workers desire to work in the public sector, followed by 24 percent who prefer the private wage sector. Rural unemployed workers have a higher interest in public employment than urban unemployed workers (55 percent versus 48 percent). Conversely, urban unemployed workers have a higher interest in private wage employment than rural unemployed workers (32 percent versus 21 percent).

Employment refusal. Twenty-five percent of unemployed workers report that they have refused an employment offer, with a higher rate for rural than urban workers (26 percent versus 21 percent). Sixty-three percent of unemployed workers who have refused an employment offer have done so because of low wages, with a much higher rate for rural workers than urban workers (70 percent versus 40 percent). Compared to their rural counterparts, urban unemployed workers more frequently cited other reasons for refusing an employment offer, such as a lack of interest in the offer, an inconvenient employment location, or a mismatch between qualifications and the offer.

Employment search length. Fifty percent of unemployed workers have been both without work and actively looking for employment for less than three months; 23 percent for three months to less than one year; and 27 percent for one year or more. Employment search length is somewhat more likely to be longer for urban than rural unemployed workers: 56 percent of urban unemployed workers have been looking for employment for at least three months, compared to 48 percent of rural unemployed workers. Being choosy about employment does not appear to influence employment search length; a simple bivariate correlation test indicates that unemployed workers who have been looking for employment for at least three months are in fact *less* likely to have refused an employment offer.

Moving for employment. The SWTS asks unemployed workers whether they would move for employment; the workers could provide multiple responses on where they would go. Thirty-three percent report that they would not move for employment, with a higher rate for urban than rural unemployed workers (52 percent versus 27 percent). Forty-two percent of those outside the Kathmandu Valley report that they would consider moving to the Valley for employment, with a higher rate for rural than other urban unemployed workers (44 percent versus 26 percent). Forty percent report that they would consider moving to another country for employment, again with a higher rate for rural than urban unemployed workers (46 percent versus 25 percent).

Labor value of education. Although their qualifications may be insufficient, most unemployed workers feel that their education is useful for employment; 78 percent report that they feel their education is either useful or somewhat useful, with similar rates for rural and urban unemployed workers.

Main difficulties finding employment. The two most commonly reported main difficulties in finding employment are insufficient employment opportunities

(33 percent) and inadequate qualifications (32 percent). The response patterns are similar between rural and urban unemployed workers.

Table 4.6 presents regression results for the correlates of whether an unemployed worker reports that insufficient employment opportunities are the main difficulty, as well as the regression correlates of whether the unemployed worker reports that inadequate qualifications are the main difficulty. More-educated unemployed workers are less likely to report that inadequate qualifications are

TABLE 4.6 **Correlates of main difficulty in finding employment, unemployed workers ages 16–29 years, 2013**

MLE binomial logit regression results, average marginal effects

	INSUFFICIENT EMPLOYMENT OPPORTUNITIES		INADEQUATE QUALIFICATIONS	
FACTOR	RURAL	URBAN	RURAL	URBAN
	(1)	(2)	(3)	(4)
Age	−0.008	−0.003	0.024*	−0.010
	(0.016)	(0.017)	(0.015)	(0.015)
Married	−0.038	0.152	−0.120*	−0.032
	(0.139)	(0.099)	(0.071)	(0.105)
Number of children	−0.019	−0.088	−0.033	−0.136
	(0.156)	(0.078)	(0.062)	(0.088)
Secondary education	0.200**	0.046	−0.183	−0.398***
	(0.096)	(0.067)	(0.142)	(0.104)
Tertiary education	0.401***	0.344***	−0.422**	−0.695***
	(0.144)	(0.106)	(0.193)	(0.123)
Currently attending school	−0.114	−0.111	−0.191**	0.034
	(0.104)	(0.096)	(0.094)	(0.088)
Average well off	0.074	−0.006	−0.121	0.064
	(0.081)	(0.088)	(0.108)	(0.068)
Less well off than average	0.118	0.113	−0.135	0.005
	(0.117)	(0.131)	(0.102)	(0.120)
Father: primary education	−0.091	0.020	0.180	−0.032
	(0.135)	(0.089)	(0.127)	(0.129)
Father: secondary education	−0.219**	0.014	−0.122	−0.028
	(0.109)	(0.121)	(0.100)	(0.094)
Father: tertiary education	−0.156*	0.112	0.051	0.012
	(0.080)	(0.121)	(0.082)	(0.091)
Life goal: societal contribution	−0.139	0.059	0.076	−0.018
	(0.111)	(0.090)	(0.087)	(0.098)
Life goal: financial	0.083	−0.046	−0.087	0.049
	(0.112)	(0.107)	(0.104)	(0.133)
Life goal: familial	−0.026	−0.016	−0.072	−0.115
	(0.128)	(0.114)	(0.155)	(0.134)
Mountains	n.a.	n.a.	0.463***	n.a.
			(0.130)	
Terai	−0.262**	n.a.	0.186***	n.a.
	(0.116)		(0.068)	
Hills	n.a.	0.174*	n.a.	−0.155**
		(0.099)		(0.068)
Terai	n.a.	0.119	n.a.	−0.166**
		(0.112)		(0.080)
Observations	177	136	189	136

Source: Estimated using 2013 School-to-Work Transition Survey data.
Note: n.a. = not applicable. Robust standard errors, clustered at the primary sampling unit level, are reported in parentheses. All estimates are adjusted for sampling weights.
*$p < 0.1$, **$p < 0.05$, ***$p < 0.01$.

the main difficulty, and more likely to report that insufficient employment opportunities are the main difficulty.

Region of residence matters. Among rural workers, those from the Terai are less likely than those in the Hills to report that insufficient employment opportunities are the main difficulty, whereas those from the Mountains and the Terai are more likely than those in the Hills to report that inadequate qualifications are the main difficulty. Among urban workers, those from the Hills are more likely than those from the Kathmandu Valley to report that insufficient employment opportunities are the main difficulty, and those from the Hills and the Terai are less likely than those from the Kathmandu Valley to report that inadequate qualifications are the main difficulty.

Comparison with other countries

Using statistics drawn from Elder (2014) for unemployed workers ages 15–29 years, we compare selected results for Nepal to other SWTS-surveyed countries (see figure 4.2). As noted earlier, our results for Nepal exclude those individuals who are age 15 years. Three comparisons stand out. First, 31 percent of Nepalese unemployed workers report searching for work for a year or more, lower than in Bangladesh (45 percent), but much higher than in Cambodia (17 percent) or Vietnam (7 percent). Second, 52 percent of Nepalese unemployed workers report that they prefer public employment, much higher than in the other countries, where the rates range from 7 percent to 32 percent. Third, 25 percent of Nepalese unemployed workers report that insufficient employment opportunities are the main difficulty they face in finding employment, compared to lower rates of 8 percent to 15 percent in the other countries. In addition, 43 percent of Nepalese unemployed workers report that inadequate education qualifications are the main difficulty, lower than in Bangladesh (63 percent) but much higher than in Cambodia (23 percent) or Vietnam (6 percent).

FIGURE 4.2

Comparison of sentiments and opinions of unemployed workers ages 15–29 years, Nepal versus other countries

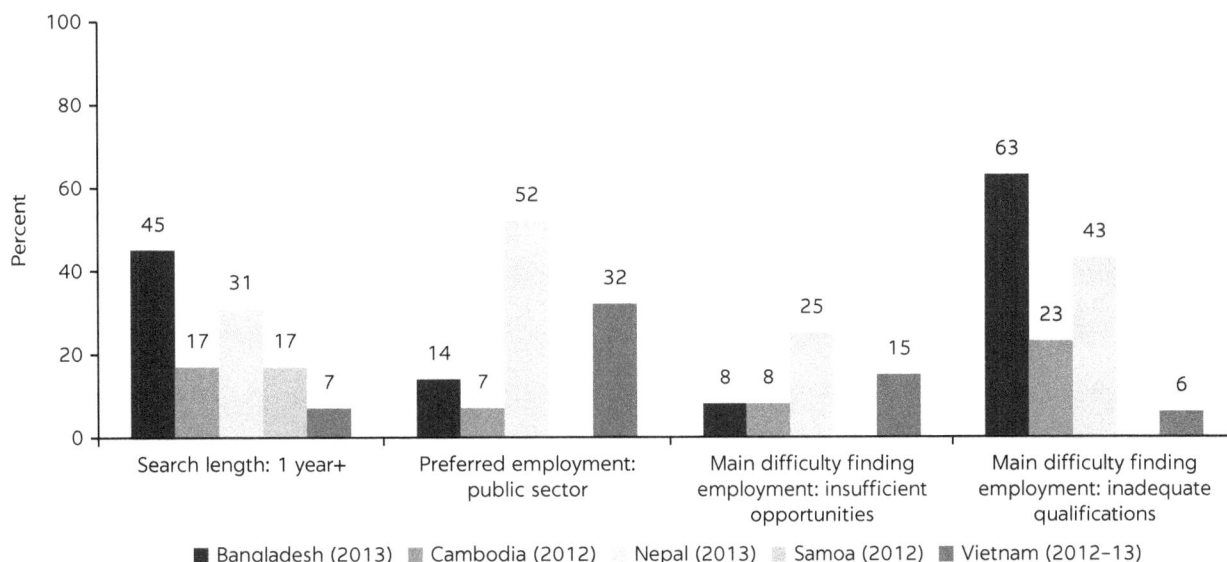

Source: Based on statistics drawn from Elder 2014.

CONCLUSION

The results from our analysis in this chapter suggest that employment creation is a critical issue for Nepal, particularly the creation of decent, formal wage employment, which is desired by youth workers. Inadequate qualifications also appear to be an issue, such as for those in the Kathmandu Valley. However, it is possible that insufficient employment opportunities create the impression among workers that inadequate qualifications are the binding constraint, if employers select workers for scarce but highly demanded formal wage employment on the basis of worker qualifications (that is, using education as the main screening mechanism). We posit that unemployed workers may have difficulty finding employment because they are more disadvantaged compared to employed workers in terms of the quality of family and friend networks that they can tap into to look for employment, or of their family's position in terms of having an income-generating activity they could join.

Although apparently less desirable, self-employment—that is, by becoming an own-account or an unpaid family worker—may serve as a safety valve for the labor market, complicating efforts by analysts to gauge the market's health. The other safety valve is employment in India, the Middle East, or other countries, an option chosen by many Nepalese youth.

NOTE

1. The definition of unemployed is more relaxed than the standard definition, which sets the active search condition in relation to the reference week.

REFERENCES

Elder, Sara. 2014. *Labour Market Transitions of Young Women and Men in Asia and the Pacific*. Work4Youth Publication 19. Geneva: International Labour Office.

Government of Nepal. 2000. *Child Labor (Prohibition and Regulation) Act, 2056 (2000)*. Kathmandu: Government of Nepal.

———. 2009. *Report on the Nepal Labour Force Survey 2008*. Kathmandu: Central Bureau of Statistics, National Planning Commission Secretariat, Government of Nepal.

———. 2012. *National Population and Housing Census 2011 (National Report)*. Kathmandu: Central Bureau of Statistics, Government of Nepal.

Serriere, Nicolas, and CEDA (Centre for Economic Development and Administration). 2014. *Labour Market Transitions of Young Women and Men in Nepal*. Work4Youth Publication 12. Geneva: International Labour Office.

5 Youth Labor Migration

LAURENT BOSSAVIE AND ANASTASIYA DENISOVA

INTRODUCTION

The extent of labor migration by Nepalese youth is so large that it deserves special attention within the broader discussion of Nepal's youth employment. One-third of households in Nepal report receiving remittances from members who have migrated—a very large share compared to other South Asian countries.

Nepal's labor migration destinations largely fall into three main categories: (1) within the country (which we refer to as "internal"), (2) to India, and (3) to other countries (which we refer to as "other external destinations"). Labor migration within Nepal and to India is unregulated. Labor migration to other countries generally takes place under bilateral agreements with the Nepal government, with workers migrating as temporary contract labor. Temporary labor migration to countries other than India is referred to as "foreign employment." Private recruitment agencies based in Nepal recruit workers for foreign employment.[1] The Department of Foreign Employment (DOFE) under the Nepal Ministry of Labor and Employment maintains documentation on foreign employment workers and provides each worker traveling legally with an employment (or exit) permit prior to departure.

This chapter examines internal and external labor migration of Nepalese youth, on the basis of an analysis of nationally representative household survey and government administrative data, namely the 2010–11 Nepal Living Standards Survey (NLSS) and 2010–16 DOFE employment permit data, as well as a review of documentation and research. Youth are defined as individuals ages 16–34 years. In particular, the chapter aims to answer the following questions about Nepalese youth:

- What is the extent of labor migration?
- What are the patterns of where labor migrants come from, where they go, and what employment they obtain at their destination?

- What factors are associated with labor migration and with particular destination choices?
- What are the strengths and weaknesses of the institutional arrangements behind the foreign employment process?
- What effects did macro factors in Nepal, including the severe earthquake in 2015, and in destination countries have on foreign employment outflows?
- What are the effects of labor migration on the labor outcomes of youth household members who remain behind (stayers)?
- What share of youth labor migrants have returned, and how do the labor outcomes of returned youth labor migrants (returnees) differ from youth nonmigrants?

We find that youth labor migration is extensive in Nepal, and that it is male dominated. The three regions in Nepal with the highest rates of male youth labor out-migration are the rural Terai, rural Hills, and Mountains. Most female youth labor migrants move internally, whereas most male youth migrants go to other countries. Irrespective of gender, most youth migrants are wage-employed, particularly when they go to other countries, and engage in services. Labor migrants who move within Nepal or go to India tend to obtain information about employment at their destination through informal channels, such as friends or relatives, whereas labor migrants who go to other countries tend to obtain such information from recruitment agencies.

On the correlates of youth labor migration, female youth who are more educated or who come from richer households are more likely to migrate for labor, suggesting positive selection in their labor migration decision. In contrast, male youth who are less educated are more likely to migrate for labor, and household economic status does not appear to be associated with the likelihood of labor migration, suggesting negative or neutral selection in their labor migration decision. Male youth are more likely to migrate for labor from more agricultural communities, especially if they are landless or smallholder farmers, indicating that the state and structure of the home economy serve as push factors. Evidence also suggests negative selection in labor migration to India, which is presumably facilitated by the low costs of migrating to that country, and positive selection in the decision to migrate internally, indicating that the domestic urban labor market is more attractive to male youth with more human capital and other resources.

Most foreign employment workers go to four countries: Malaysia, Qatar, Saudi Arabia, and the United Arab Emirates. Although reasonable on paper, institutional arrangements that guide the foreign employment process appear to suffer from implementation shortcomings. In addition, recruitment agencies are seen to have substantial market power, which may raise the monetary costs of, and reduce the expected gains from, workers obtaining foreign employment. Foreign employment outflow appears to be influenced mainly by macroeconomic and other forces in destination countries, rather than by forces in Nepal. The 2015 earthquake in Nepal appears to have had a negative effect on the outflow of foreign employment workers who went through recruitment agencies (mostly new foreign employment workers), but not on foreign employment workers who did not use recruitment agencies (mostly workers who have renewed contracts with their foreign employers).

Male youth labor migration appears to have negative effects on the likelihood of employment and hours worked for both female and male youth stayers, although the effects are not consistently significant. Male youth labor migration has significant positive effects on school enrollment and years of education for children in the household, and the effects appear to be mediated through remittances.

A large share of male youth labor migrants return home. The share is highest for those who migrated to India, which is consistent with the view that migrants to this country engage in circular or seasonal labor migration, facilitated by the low costs of migrating to India. Comparing labor outcomes at home between youth returnees and youth who have not migrated, returnees from countries other than India appear to do worse.

The remainder of the chapter is structured as follows. The next section describes the main data sources. The subsequent section discusses the structure of the analysis, using one of the main data sources, the 2010–11 NLSS. Then we discuss the patterns and correlates, respectively, of youth labor migration. "Foreign Employment" discusses the institutional arrangements in Nepal for foreign employment, the process that workers follow to seek and secure such work, foreign employment trends, and macro determinants of these trends. The next section discusses the effects of male youth labor migration on the labor outcomes of male and female youth stayers, and on the education outcomes of children in the household. Then we focus on returned youth labor migrants, and compare labor outcomes for this group to those for youth who did not migrate. The final section concludes by examining the implications of the findings for data, research, and policy.

DATA

The main sources of data for this study are the 2010–11 NLSS and DOFE employment permit data.

Nepal Living Standards Survey

The third round in a series, the 2010–11 NLSS is representative at the national level, as well as for 12 regions within the country. The original sample was 7,200 households from 600 primary sampling units (PSUs). Out of this total sample, 1,200 households from 100 PSUs were drawn from the second NLSS round (the 2003–04 NLSS) to constitute a panel sample, and 6,000 households from 500 PSUs were drawn to constitute a new cross-sectional sample (see Government of Nepal 2011 for survey design details). We use the new cross-sectional sample, for which 5,988 households from 599 primary sampling units were successfully interviewed.

The survey comprises both a household questionnaire and a community questionnaire. In the household questionnaire, the survey gathers information from the household respondent on household members who were absent at the time of the survey but are expected to return. The information includes the reason for absence, which allows us to identify labor migrants. It also includes age at departure, marital status, education, destination district within Nepal or other country, employment at destination, and remittances. The household questionnaire also asks household members who were present at the time of the survey whether they migrated for labor for at least two consecutive months over the past five years, as well as the reason for their migration. This information allows us to identify labor migrants who have returned.

The survey has at least two important limitations. First, information on labor outcomes of migrants at their destination is limited. In particular, the survey does not gather information on migrant wages at their destination. Second, the survey does not gather information on whether the returned labor migrant intends to migrate again. Thus, we are not able to distinguish between circular migration and permanent return, a potential meaningful distinction for the returned migrant's labor market attachment and outcomes at home.

DOFE employment permit data

DOFE data comprise employment permit data from January 2010 to May 2016 for foreign employment workers who went through recruitment agencies (which we refer to as "agency-based foreign employment workers") and employment permit data from September 2011 to May 2016 for foreign employment workers who did not use recruitment agencies (which we refer to as "individual foreign employment workers"). In the data, individual foreign employment workers are categorized into three groups: (1) new, (2) repeat (those who renewed their employment permits), and (3) legalized (those who initially left Nepal without an employment permit but were allowed to later apply to DOFE for legalization of their status). For all foreign employment workers, we have data on the worker's age, gender, district of origin, destination country, date of permit issue, recruitment agency, foreign employer, occupation, and wage.

Our DOFE data have at least three important limitations. First, the date of birth is missing for more than 40 percent of workers who received foreign employment permits prior to 2013. Second, we have wage data only for agency-based foreign employment workers. These wage data should also be interpreted with caution. Recruitment agencies may have overreported wages to comply with the minimum wage at destination mandated by DOFE. At the same time, conversely, the worker's actual earnings may be higher than the wages reported to DOFE due to tips, bonuses, and overtime pay. Third, the data allow us to identify whether a foreign employment worker is new or a repeat only for individual foreign employment workers.

STRUCTURE OF THE ANALYSIS USING NLSS DATA

We use 2010–11 NLSS data for an analysis of the patterns of youth labor migration, the correlates of youth labor migration, and the effects on youth labor out-migration on the labor outcomes of youth stayers. We also use these data for an analysis of the home labor outcomes of returned youth labor migrants. Although we perform the full set of analyses for male youth, the analyses for female youth were partial, contingent on sufficient sample sizes.

Most of our results are based on multiple regression analyses. Factors for individual-level regressions for youth comprise age (in quadratic form), marital status, education level, caste or ethnicity group, household economic status (in consumption expenditure quintiles), a standardized community amenities index (constructed on the basis of principal-components analysis), amount of time to the nearest road, household size (including absent members), household farmland ownership status, share of households engaged in farming in the community, and identifiers for regions (urban Hills, rural Hills, the Mountains [rural], urban Terai, rural Terai, and the Kathmandu Valley [urban]). By community, we mean the PSU.

The outcome variables for our various regressions are binomial, multinomial, or continuous. For the binomial and multinomial structures, we estimate appropriate logit regressions, and transform the estimated coefficients into average marginal effects, which we report. Inferences for all regressions are based on robust standard errors clustered at the level of the PSU. Other relevant methodological steps are discussed just before we present the results.

Although we report regression results for all Nepal, we also estimate regressions for the three regions in the country (taken together) that have the largest male youth labor migration outflows—namely the rural Hills, rural Terai, and Mountains—under the assumption that patterns and correlates may be stronger for these regions. We find that the results for all Nepal and for these three regions are qualitatively similar.

In addition, recognizing that the panel sample presumably differs from the cross-sectional sample because of the nature of attrition, as a robustness test, we estimate regressions of the correlates of labor migration, the effects at home from labor migration, and the home labor outcomes for returned labor migrants, using 2003–04 values for the factors. We find that the results are qualitatively similar when we use 2010–11 regression factors in the cross-sectional sample or the 2003–04 regression factors in the panel sample. The results for the panel sample are available upon request.

PATTERNS IN YOUTH LABOR MIGRATION

We present statistics for youth who were labor migrants at the time the 2010–11 NLSS was administered to households. Labor migration is extensive, and it is dominated by youth and men. Eighteen percent of Nepalese youth have migrated for labor. Disaggregated by gender, we find that 30 percent of male youth have migrated for labor, compared to 5 percent of female youth. Seventy-two percent of labor migrants are youth, and 87 percent of youth labor migrants are male.

Data to compare Nepal's youth labor migration rate to those in other South Asian countries are unavailable. However, data are available to estimate the share of households that receive remittances, and we use these numbers as a rough proxy for the extent of labor migration. As figure 5.1 shows, Nepal stands out: 33 percent of Nepalese households received remittances in 2010–11, compared to 21 percent for Bangladesh in 2009–10, 19 percent for Pakistan in 2013–14, and 14 percent for Sri Lanka in 2009–10. The picture remains similar when we look at rural or urban households across these countries.

Figure 5.2 shows youth labor out-migration rates by region. Youth labor out-migration rates are higher for rural than urban regions. For male youth, the rate is highest for the rural Hills (36 percent), rural Terai (35 percent), and Mountains (35 percent), and lowest for the Kathmandu Valley (10 percent). Although the rate of male youth labor out-migration for the Kathmandu Valley is relatively low, it translates into a large absolute number because the region accounts for a significant share of the country's male youth population. Female youth labor out-migration rates are generally low, and vary little among regions (from a high of 7 percent for the Mountains to a low of 3 percent for rural Terai and the Kathmandu Valley).

Figure 5.3 shows the distribution of youth labor migrants by destination type. The most common destinations for female youth labor migrants are the rural and urban areas of Nepal (32 percent and 39 percent, respectively), followed by

FIGURE 5.1

Share of households that report receiving remittances, Nepal versus other South Asian countries

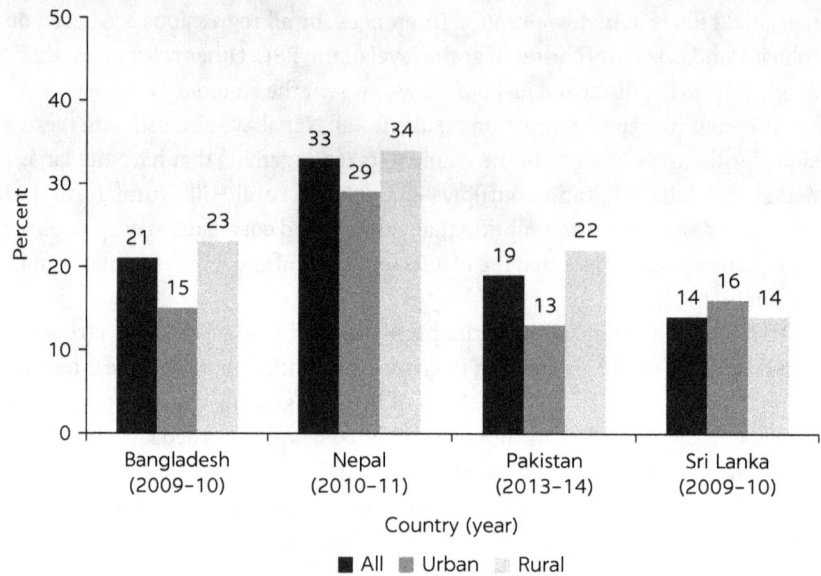

Source: Estimated using data from the 2009–10 Bangladesh Household Income and Expenditure Survey, the 2010–11 Nepal Living Standards Survey, the 2013–14 Pakistan Household Income and Expenditure Survey, and the 2009–10 Sri Lanka Household Income and Expenditure Survey.
Note: Estimates are adjusted for sampling weights.

FIGURE 5.2

Share of youth who have migrated for labor, by home region, 2010–11

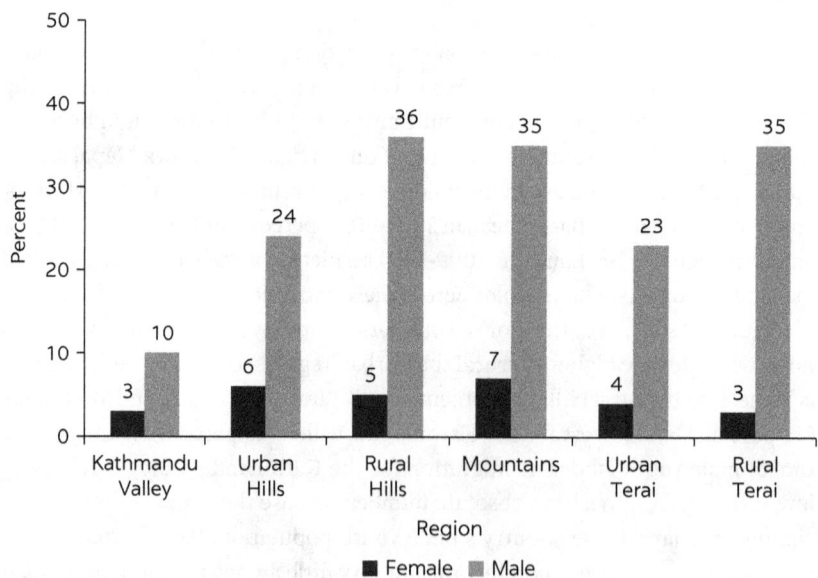

Source: Estimated using data from the 2010–11 Nepal Living Standards Survey (NLSS).
Note: A youth labor migrant is defined as an individual ages 16–34 years who was absent from the household for labor reasons at the time the 2010–11 NLSS was administered to the household and who has the intention to return, as reported by the household. Estimates are adjusted for sampling weights.

FIGURE 5.3

Distribution of male and female youth labor migration, by destination type, 2010–11

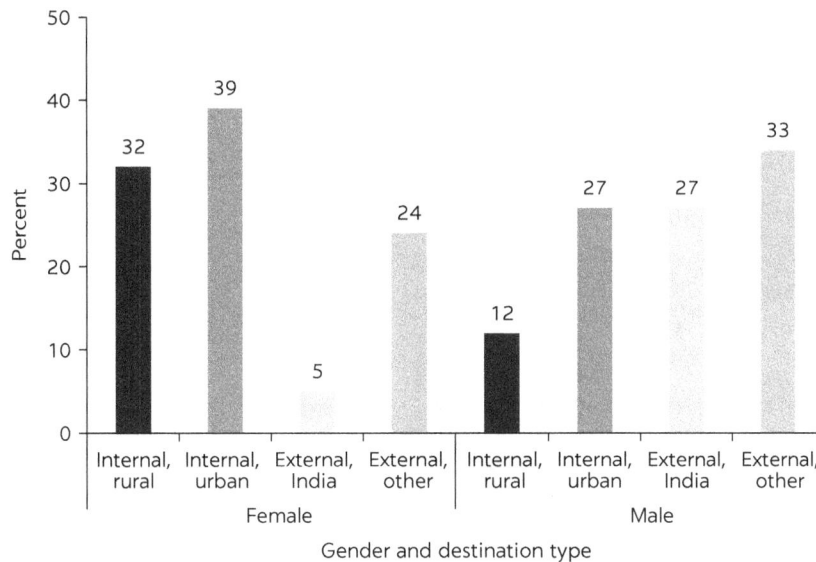

Source: Estimated using data from the 2010–11 Nepal Living Standards Survey (NLSS).
Note: A youth labor migrant is defined as an individual ages 16–34 years who was absent from the household for labor reasons at the time the 2010–11 NLSS was administered to the household and who has the intention to return, as reported by the household. Estimates are adjusted for sampling weights.

external destinations other than India (24 percent). Only 5 percent of female youth labor migrants go to India. The most common destinations for male youth labor migrants are India (27 percent), other external destinations (33 percent), and urban Nepal (27 percent).

Panel a of figure 5.4 shows the distribution of youth labor migrants by type of employment (wage or self-employment) at destination. Although the "do not know" share at times obscures the picture (especially for female youth labor migrants to India), the evidence suggests that the vast majority of youth labor migrants to external destinations are wage employed, irrespective of gender. The majority of male youth labor migrants to internal destinations are also wage employed, but a large share is self-employed. For female youth labor migrants to internal destinations, the share is similar for those who are wage-employed and those who are self-employed.

Panel b of figure 5.4 shows the distribution of youth labor migrants by sector of employment (agriculture, industry, construction, and services) at destination. Again, although the "do not know" share makes the picture less clear, employment in services dominates for both female and male youth labor migrants, across destinations. In addition, a sizable share of male youth labor migrants are employed in construction across destinations, whereas a sizable share of female youth labor migrants to internal destinations are employed in agriculture.

Finally, figure 5.5 shows the distribution of information on employment at destination for youth labor migrants by destination type. The main sources of this information for female and male youth labor migrants to internal destinations and India are family, friends, and neighbors. Although substantial shares of

FIGURE 5.4

Sector and type of employment at destination for youth labor migrants, by gender and destination type, 2011–11

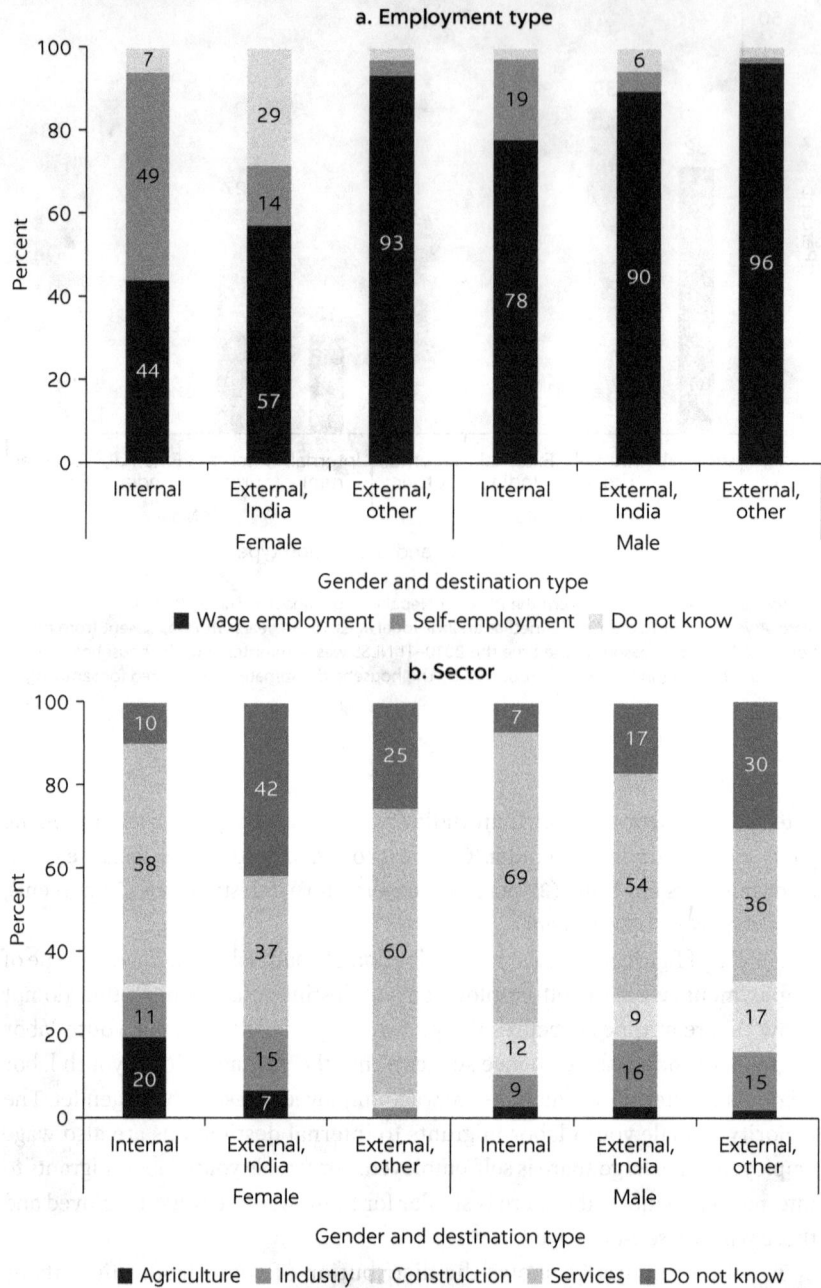

a. Employment type

b. Sector

Source: Estimated using data from the 2010–11 Nepal Living Standards Survey (NLSS).
Note: A youth labor migrant is defined as an individual ages 16–34 years who was absent from the household for labor reasons at the time the 2010–11 NLSS was administered to the household and who has the intention to return, as reported by the household. Estimates are adjusted for sampling weights.

female and male youth labor migrants to external destinations other than India also obtain information on employment at their destinations through family, friends, and neighbors, a greater percentage obtain this information through recruitment agencies. Interestingly, if the statistics are taken at face value, non-trivial shares of youth labor migrants to internal destinations and India also have received information on employment at destination from recruitment agencies.

FIGURE 5.5

Source of information on employment at destination for youth labor migrants, by gender and destination type, 2010–11

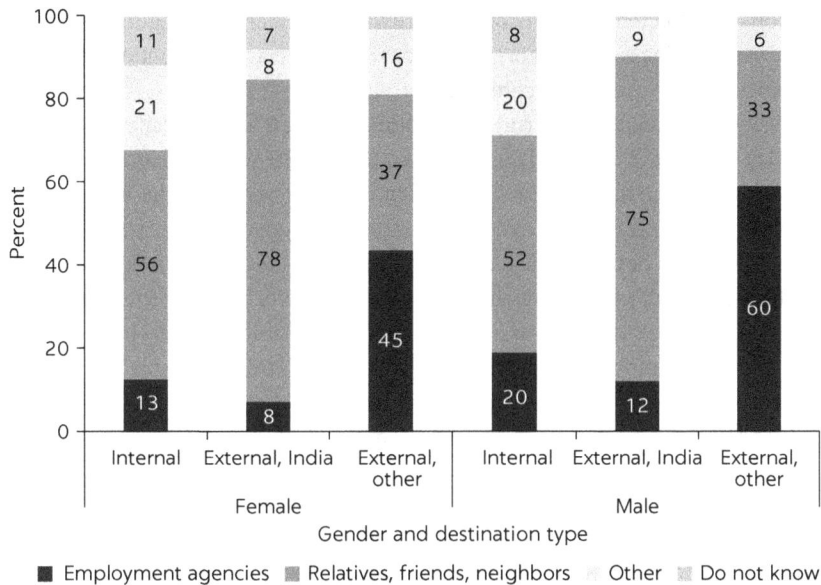

Source: Estimated using data from the 2010–11 Nepal Living Standards Survey (NLSS).
Note: A youth labor migrant is defined as an individual ages 16–34 years who was absent from the household for labor reasons at the time the 2010–11 NLSS was administered to the household and who has the intention to return, as reported by the household. Estimates are adjusted for sampling weights.

CORRELATES OF YOUTH LABOR MIGRATION

What factors are associated with youth labor migration, and with specific destinations? Although previous research has explored the correlates of labor migration, the factors associated with labor migration by Nepalese youth are not well understood. Evidence is particularly limited in terms of the factors associated with the choice of destination for labor migration by Nepalese youth.

A labor migrant is defined to be an individual who was absent for labor reasons from the household at the time the 2010–11 NLSS was administered to the household, departed from the household in the five years before the 2010–11 NLSS was administered, and has the intention to return, all as reported by the household.

Existing evidence for Nepal on the correlates of migration

Rigorous evidence based on representative data is limited for Nepal on the determinants of migration and choice of migration destination. Using village-level panel data over the period 2001–10, Shrestha (2017a) examines several potential pull and push factors in the decision to migrate among Nepalese. He finds that an income gain associated with rainfall increases the likelihood of migration to India—which is characterized as a destination with low costs of, and low economic gains from, migration—but that it has no effect on the likelihood of migration to other external destinations—which are characterized as high cost and high gain. He also finds that an increase in the intensity of the Maoist insurgency conflict (which occurred between 1996 and 2006), measured by deaths per 1,000 in the population, increases the likelihood of migration to external destinations. Additionally, he shows that an increase in migrant demand from external destinations, as reflected in their economic growth rates, increases migration to those destinations. These findings are consistent with the classical economic model of migration in the presence of credit constraints.

Using survey data from a rural agricultural setting (Chitwan Valley), Bhandari (2004) finds that households with less access to cultivated land are more likely to migrate, indicating the role of a push factor. On the basis of qualitative research in a village in Kathmandu District, Gaurab (2014) suggests that earnings differentials between home and destination influence the decision to migrate.

Existing evidence also suggests that social networks affect the decision to migrate. Using survey data for a small sample of agricultural households in eastern Chitwan District, Regmi, Paudel, and Williams (2014) find that the number of extended family members a migrant has at his or her destination—which serves as a measure of the migrant's social network—is positively associated with the decision to migrate.

Ethnicity also appears to influence the decision to migrate, including the choice of destination. Using nationally representative household survey data, Sharma et al. (2014) find that Terai Janajati and Hill Dalit workers are most likely to migrate internally and that Newar, Tarai Janajati, and Tarai Dalit workers are least likely to migrate externally. The authors also find that Muslim workers are most likely to migrate to Middle Eastern countries, whereas Hill Dalit workers are most likely to migrate to India.

Similarly, using the same data as the previous study, the World Bank (2011) finds that Dalit have more labor migrants in India than other ethnic groups. Ethnic groups from the Hills region in Nepal are overrepresented among Nepalese labor migrants to Middle East countries. There could be multiple pathways behind the association between ethnicity and migration. For example, ethnicity could influence the decision to migrate because it is associated with household wealth, and household wealth helps cover the costs of migration in the presence of credit constraints. Ethnicity-based networks at a migrant's destination could also have a bearing on the gains and costs from labor migration. These pathways, among others, are untested in the existing literature.

Finally, using data from the Chitwan Valley, Massey, Axinn, and Ghimire (2010) find that favorable environmental conditions, measured by the extent of area covered in flora and the time needed to gather firewood, decrease the likelihood of migration. Using the same data, Shrestha and Bhandari (2007) find that environmental insecurity at home, as measured by less access to forest resources, is positively associated with the decision to migrate.

Correlates of youth labor migration

Figure 5.6 reports the bivariate relationship between the likelihood of labor migration and education attainment (measured in years of schooling) among youth. The likelihood of labor migration is high among male youth with low levels of schooling, at about 50 percent; but the share declines in an almost linear fashion for individuals who have completed more than six years of schooling. This suggests negative, skill-based selection in the labor migration decisions among male youth. For female youth, the likelihood of labor migration is low throughout the distribution of years of schooling, with a small increase after 12 years of schooling.

FIGURE 5.6

Likelihood of youth labor migration, by education attainment and gender, 2010–11

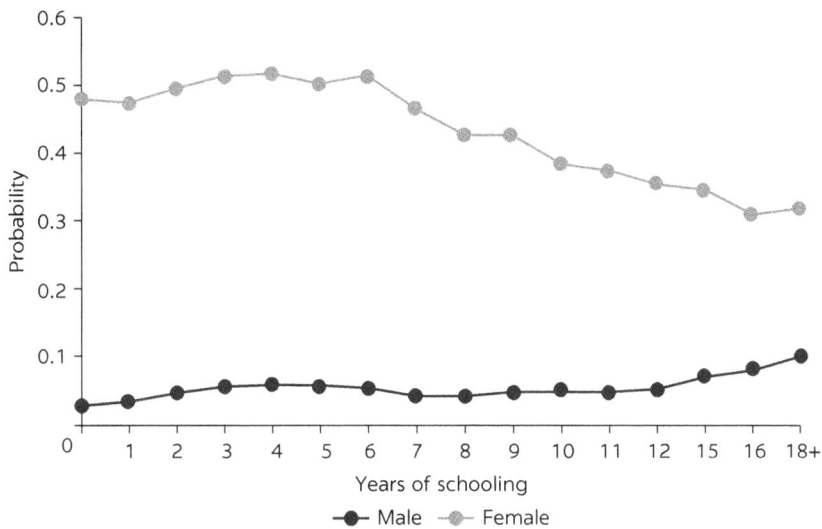

Source: Estimated using data from the 2010–11 Nepal Living Standards Survey (NLSS).
Note: A youth labor migrant is defined as an individual ages 16–34 years who was absent from the household at the time the 2010–11 NLSS was administered to the household, left the household in the five years before the 2010–11 NLSS was administered, and has the intention to return, all as reported by the household. All estimates are adjusted for sampling weights.

Table 5.1 reports the regression results of the correlates of labor migration to any destination, separately for male and female youth. For male youth, those with higher levels of education (School Leaving Certificate or higher) are less likely to migrate, controlling for other factors, which is consistent with the bivariate relationship shown in figure 5.6. Compared to youth from the Brahmin community, those from the Dalit and Muslim communities are more likely to migrate, whereas those from the Terai middle-caste community are less likely to migrate. The likelihood of migration increases with the share of households engaged in agriculture in the community, controlling for, among other things, the level of development in the community as captured by a community infrastructure index. In other words, workers tend to migrate from more agricultural communities, suggesting a potential push factor. On the other hand, workers from households that own at least 1 hectare of agricultural land are less likely to migrate, suggesting that relatively large land ownership discourages labor migration.[2]

For female youth, those who are married are less likely to migrate, whereas those who have higher levels of education attainment, who come from richer households, or who reside in a community with a higher level of development are more likely to migrate. The agriculture-related characteristics of the household or the community do not appear to be associated with the labor migration decisions of female youth. The nature of the association between migration and education attainment, household economic status, and the level of community development indicates that female youth labor migration is positively selected by skills and other dimensions.

For both male and female youth, those from regions outside of the Kathmandu Valley are more likely to migrate. Neither household size (accounting for absent members) nor whether the community experienced a natural disaster in the last five years appears to be associated with the likelihood of labor migration.

TABLE 5.1 **Correlates of youth labor migration, by gender, 2010–11**

Binomial logit estimations, average marginal effects

FACTOR	MALE	FEMALE
	(1)	(2)
Age	0.190*** (0.013)	0.058*** (0.009)
Age squared	−0.003*** (0.000)	−0.001*** (0.000)
Married	−0.027 (0.020)	−0.039*** (0.011)
Education (reference category: less than SLC)		
SLC or 11th grade	−0.046** (0.018)	0.035*** (0.011)
Grade 12 and above	−0.129*** (0.030)	0.052*** (0.016)
Consumption quintile (reference category: 1st quintile)		
2nd	0.005 (0.027)	0.036** (0.015)
3rd	0.012 (0.028)	0.037** (0.016)
4th	0.041 (0.029)	0.032* (0.018)
5th (richest)	0.048 (0.032)	0.071*** (0.018)
Ethnicity/caste (reference category: Brahmin)		
Terai middle class	−0.098*** (0.033)	−0.023* (0.012)
Dalit	0.075*** (0.028)	0.025 (0.015)
Newar	−0.035 (0.037)	0.021 (0.023)
Janajati	−0.010 (0.021)	0.036*** (0.010)
Muslim	0.074* (0.044)	−0.037*** (0.014)
Other	−0.148*** (0.051)	−0.036* (0.020)
Community amenities index	0.003 (0.018)	0.012** (0.006)
Time to nearest paved road (in hours)	−0.003* (0.002)	−0.000 (0.001)
Natural disaster in the past five years	−0.006 (0.023)	0.010 (0.010)
Household size (including absentees)	0.003 (0.003)	0.002 (0.002)
Household owns at least 1 hectare of agricultural land	−0.073*** (0.026)	0.014 (0.011)
Share of household heads in PSU employed in agriculture	0.267*** (0.038)	0.018 (0.016)

continued

TABLE 5.1, *continued*

FACTOR	MALE (1)	FEMALE (2)
Region (Reference category: Kathmandu Valley)		
Urban Hills	0.152*** (0.034)	0.050*** (0.017)
Rural Hills	0.275*** (0.033)	0.048*** (0.010)
Mountains	0.328*** (0.052)	0.084*** (0.026)
Urban Terai	0.189*** (0.037)	0.034*** (0.012)
Rural Terai	0.302*** (0.031)	0.052*** (0.012)
Observations	4,937	4,827

Source: Estimated using data from the 2010–11 Nepal Living Standards Survey (NLSS).
Note: PSU = primary sampling unit. A youth labor migrant is defined as an individual ages 16–34 years who was absent from the household at the time the 2010–11 NLSS was administered to the household, left the household in the five years before the 2010–11 NLSS was administered, and has the intention to return, all as reported by the household. SLC = School Leaving Certificate. Robust standard errors, clustered at the PSU level, are reported in parentheses. Estimates are all adjusted for sampling weights. *p < 0.1, **p < 0.05, ***p < 0.01.

Correlates of youth labor migration by destination type

Individual, household, and community factors may also influence the labor migrant's destination choice. In the basic economic model, the migrant evaluates his or her expected utility in each possible destination choice and decides to migrate to the destination where the expected utility is highest (Sjaastad 1962).

Figure 5.7 shows the association between the likelihood of labor migration to a given destination type and years of schooling for male youth (panel a) and female youth (panel b). The associations for male youth differ markedly by destination type. For labor migration to India, the likelihood of migration is relatively high at low levels of schooling, but decreases sharply after six years of schooling. This indicates negative selection in the decision to migrate for labor to India. For labor migration to other external destinations, the likelihood of migration increases with years of schooling for up to 10 years, but decreases after that. For internal destinations, the likelihood of migration increases with years of schooling, indicating positive selection in the decision to migrate for labor to these destinations.

For female youth, the difference across destination types in the association between the likelihood of labor migration and years of schooling is less striking. For internal destinations, the likelihood of labor migration increases slightly up to five years of schooling and is then relatively flat. It is higher than the likelihood of labor migration to India or to other external destinations for all years of schooling. For India and other external destinations, the likelihood of labor migration is virtually zero for up to 12 years of schooling, and then increases, especially for labor migration to other external destinations.

Table 5.2 presents regression results of the correlates of destination type for male youth labor migrants. The reference category is male youth who did not migrate for labor. We do not estimate the regression relationship for female youth because of small sample sizes.

The association between years of schooling and destination type shown in figure 5.7 is robust, controlling for other factors. Those with more years of

FIGURE 5.7

Likelihood of youth labor migration, by education attainment and destination type, 2010–11

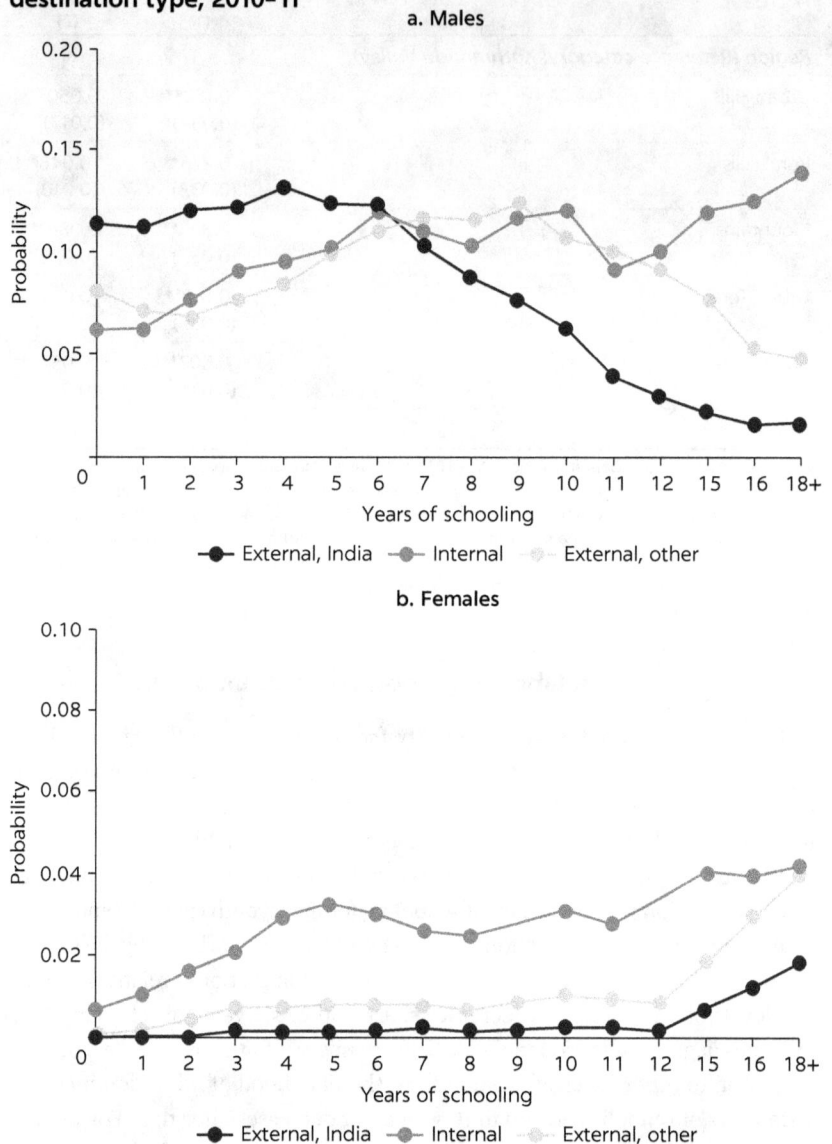

a. Males

b. Females

Source: Estimated using data from the 2010–11 Nepal Living Standards Survey (NLSS).
Note: A youth labor migrant is defined as an individual ages 16–34 years who was absent from the household at the time the 2010–11 NLSS was administered to the household, left the household in the five years before the 2010–11 NLSS was administered, and has the intention to return, all as reported by the household. Estimates are adjusted for sampling weights.

schooling are more likely to migrate internally, and less likely to migrate to India and other countries. In terms of household economic status, those from richer households are more likely to migrate internally or to external destinations other than India, and less likely to migrate to India. The education-related results suggest that the earnings gain is higher from internal migration than external migration for those with a high level of education attainment. On the basis of education attainment and household economic status, it appears that migration to India is negatively selected, whereas internal labor migration is positively selected. Labor migration to other external destinations is negatively selected with respect to education attainment, and positively selected with respect to household economic status.

TABLE 5.2 **Correlates of choice of destination type, male youth labor migration only, 2010–11**

Multinomial logit estimation, average marginal effects

FACTOR	REFERENCE CATEGORY: DID NOT MIGRATE		
	DESTINATION TYPE		
	INTERNAL	EXTERNAL, INDIA	EXTERNAL, OTHER
	(1)	(2)	(3)
Age	0.048*** (0.013)	0.021** (0.010)	0.139*** (0.013)
Age squared	−0.001*** (0.000)	−0.000** (0.000)	−0.002*** (0.000)
Married	0.013 (0.017)	0.010 (0.016)	−0.049*** (0.015)
Education (reference category: less than SLC)			
SLC or 11th grade	0.053*** (0.016)	−0.107*** (0.019)	−0.002 (0.014)
Grade 12 and above	0.089*** (0.030)	−0.123*** (0.040)	−0.119*** (0.036)
Consumption quintile (reference category: 1st quintile)			
2nd	0.033 (0.025)	−0.034* (0.018)	0.027 (0.029)
3rd	0.038 (0.025)	−0.058*** (0.020)	0.059** (0.025)
4th	0.055** (0.027)	−0.097*** (0.024)	0.104*** (0.026)
5th (richest)	0.050* (0.029)	−0.101*** (0.029)	0.111*** (0.029)
Ethnicity/caste (reference category: Brahmin)			
Terai middle class	−0.048* (0.026)	−0.088*** (0.024)	0.030 (0.028)
Dalit	−0.003 (0.025)	0.028 (0.025)	0.031 (0.024)
Newar	0.084* (0.046)	−0.156*** (0.023)	0.002 (0.026)
Janajati	−0.004 (0.018)	−0.080*** (0.020)	0.073*** (0.017)
Muslim	−0.072** (0.033)	0.018 (0.045)	0.114*** (0.039)
Other	−0.030 (0.038)	−0.116*** (0.030)	−0.002 (0.053)
Community amenities index	−0.006 (0.011)	0.020** (0.008)	−0.019 (0.016)
Time to nearest paved road (in hours)	−0.001 (0.001)	−0.002* (0.001)	−0.000 (0.001)
Natural disaster in the past five years	−0.015 (0.020)	−0.006 (0.019)	0.011 (0.019)
Household size (including the absentee)	0.001 (0.003)	−0.001 (0.003)	0.003 (0.002)

continued

TABLE 5.2, *continued*

FACTOR	REFERENCE CATEGORY: DID NOT MIGRATE		
	DESTINATION		
	INTERNAL	EXTERNAL, INDIA	EXTERNAL, OTHER
	(1)	(2)	(3)
Household owns at least 1 hectare of agricultural land	−0.037* (0.021)	−0.087*** (0.020)	0.040** (0.018)
Share of household heads in PSU employed in ag.	0.066** (0.028)	0.106*** (0.033)	0.101*** (0.034)
Region (Reference category: Kathmandu Valley)			
Urban Hills	0.097*** (0.023)	0.051** (0.024)	0.004 (0.031)
Rural Hills	0.162*** (0.020)	0.115*** (0.023)	0.005 (0.028)
Mountains	0.243*** (0.045)	0.101*** (0.036)	−0.005 (0.034)
Urban Terai	0.079*** (0.016)	0.103*** (0.030)	0.014 (0.034)
Rural Terai	0.129*** (0.018)	0.149*** (0.022)	0.028 (0.028)
Observations	4,937		

Source: Estimates using data from the 2010–11 Nepal Living Standards Survey (NLSS).
Note: SLC = School Leaving Certificate. PSU = primary sampling unit. A youth labor migrant is defined as an individual ages 16–34 years who was absent from the household at the time the 2010–11 NLSS was administered to the household, departed from the household in the five years before the 2010–11 NLSS was administered, and has the intention to return, all as reported by the household. Robust standard errors, clustered at the PSU level, are reported in parentheses. All estimates are adjusted for sampling weights.
*$p<0.1$, **$p<0.05$, ***$p<0.01$.

The likelihood of migration increases with the share of households engaged in agriculture in the community, irrespective of destination type. However, controlling for the prevalence of agricultural activity in the community and for household economic status, those from households with relatively large agricultural land ownership are less likely to migrate internally or to India, and more likely to migrate to other external destinations.

With respect to other factors, the likelihood of migration increases with the individual's age, irrespective of destination type. Those who are married are less likely to migrate to other external destinations, and marital status does not appear to be associated with the likelihood of migrating internally or to India. Relative to those from the Brahmin community, those from the Newar community are more likely to migrate internally; those from the Janajati and Muslim communities are more likely to migrate to other external destinations; and those from the Terai middle caste, Newar, Janajati, and other communities are less likely to migrate to India. Compared to those from the Kathmandu Valley, those from the other regions in Nepal are more likely to migrate to internal destinations or to India. In contrast, the likelihood of migration to other external destinations appears to be similar across all of Nepal's regions.

FOREIGN EMPLOYMENT

This section provides an overview of the institutional arrangements for foreign employment, that is, temporary, contract-based labor migration to countries other than India. It also examines the efficiency of the process the worker follows to seek and secure foreign employment, using available documentation and data from the 2015 World Bank Global Knowledge Partnership on Migration and Development (KNOMAD) migration cost database and from the 2009 Nepal Migration Survey (NMS). Note that although this section discusses institutional arrangements prior to the recent reorganization of Nepal's government into a federal structure, we expect its conclusions to remain relevant.

The regulatory system

In the late 1990s and early 2000s, the Nepal government's policy on labor outmigration was focused on the creation of institutional mechanisms to facilitate temporary labor migration to countries other than India. Subsequently, partly because of the success of this policy and partly because of changing economic conditions, the labor migration flow to other countries increased markedly. The policy focus then shifted from one of labor migration promotion to one of regulation of the labor migration process to these new external destinations, with particular emphasis on protecting the rights and welfare of Nepalese workers. Evidence of this shift can be seen with the formulation of Nepal's Foreign Employment Policy in 2012; the preparation of legislation, directives, and manuals associated with the policy; and the creation of the National Strategic Action Plan 2015–22 focused on improving the welfare of foreign employment workers.

The 2012 Foreign Employment Policy has resulted in the creation of the following directives and manuals aimed at improving the foreign employment process and protecting the rights of foreign employment workers: the 2013 Standard on the Enlisting Process of the Health Examination, the 2013 Directive on the Procedure on Individual Labor Permits, the 2014 Manual on Registration and Renewal of Orientation Training Institutions, the 2014 Manual on Extending Objective Assistance to Skill Trained Human Resources, and the 2015 Directive on Sending Domestic Helpers for Foreign Employment. These directives and manuals complement the 2007 Foreign Employment Act (FEA), which prescribes penalties for misconduct by recruitment agencies, including for fraud, misrepresentation of work conditions, overcharging of foreign employment workers, and falsification and confiscation of documents.

The Nepal government also has institutions that seek to promote safe and decent foreign employment. The 2007 FEA mandated the creation of institutions designed to ensure the welfare of Nepalese foreign employment workers before departure and at destination. These include (1) the Foreign Employment Welfare Fund (FEWF), managed by the Foreign Employment Promotion Board (FEPB); (2) DOFE; and (3) the Foreign Employment Tribunal (FET).

Foreign Employment Promotion Board. FEPB is responsible for promoting foreign employment and providing for the social protection and welfare of foreign employment workers, including through management of FEWF. Using FEWF resources, the FEPB (1) conducts skill training and predeparture orientation; (2) engages in the rescue and rehabilitation of workers who run into problems in their destination country, and in the reintegration of foreign employment workers returning to Nepal; and (3) provides financial support and compensation to families for the occupational death or disability of foreign employment workers.

FEWF is financed through several sources, including (1) foreign employment worker fees (each worker is supposed to make a one-time payment of NPR 1,000) and interest earned from deposited fees; (2) license and deposit fees collected from recruitment agencies (recruitment agencies are mandated to pay a deposit of US$30,000 and a fee of US$200 upon registration of the agency, and a deposit of US$2,000 per registered individual agent); and (3) any other contributions received from foreign employment–related institutions or grants from local or foreign entities (Paoletti et al. 2014).

Labor attachés. FEA mandates that a Nepal embassy based in a host country with more than 5,000 Nepalese foreign employment workers must have a labor attaché to oversee the welfare of these workers. As of July 2015, Nepal had labor attachés in eight countries: Bahrain, Kuwait, Malaysia, Oman, Qatar, the Republic of Korea, Saudi Arabia, and the United Arab Emirates (ILO 2016). The main responsibilities of the labor attaché include assisting in resolving disputes between workers and employers, assisting with the rescue of workers as needed and the repatriation of a worker's body in case of death, informing the Nepal government about labor conditions in the destination country, and checking if the terms of the bilateral agreement between Nepal and the destination country are respected.

Department of Foreign Employment. DOFE is responsible for the regulation of recruitment agencies and the registration of foreign employment workers, with the aim of preventing fraud, such as the overcharging of workers or the provision of false information about foreign employment terms and conditions. DOFE is also responsible for grievance redressal.

Foreign Employment Tribunal. FET is a semijudicial body responsible for the resolution of complaints filed by individual prospective or incumbent foreign employment workers (that is, those not using recruitment agencies) and of other complaint cases that lie outside DOFE's jurisdiction.

Vocation and Skills Development Training Center (VSDTC). VSDTC provides counseling services for foreign employment workers, and helps workers enroll in and use online banking services.

Recruitment agencies. A prospective foreign employment worker has two options for migrating legally: (1) through a recruitment agency or (2) on his or her own. Most new workers choose to go through recruitment agencies. Recruitment agencies are regulated by DOFE. Currently, 754 recruitment agencies are registered under DOFE. According to our DOFE data, about 900 agencies helped arrange foreign employment for individuals between 2010 and 2015.

Recruitment agencies rely on their counterparts in destination countries to obtain data on the number and type of workers required. Each recruitment agency submits obtained information to DOFE to verify that it meets the requirements of the FEA and to obtain DOFE's approval to recruit workers. The agency then advertises the employment opportunities through public media channels and individual agents, and recruits workers. Once it selects the workers and obtains the necessary documents (such as a medical report and proof of life insurance), the agency registers the workers with DOFE and obtains employment permits for them.

Initially, a prospective foreign employment worker interacts with an individual agent who represents one or more agencies in his or her locality. The individual agent provides the worker with information on foreign employment opportunities and often helps him or her to obtain necessary documents, such as a passport. After the contract is secured, the worker travels to Kathmandu to sign the necessary papers, pass a medical examination, and obtain required predeparture training on, as relevant, procedures, legal rights, culture, and language at destination. Prior to departure, the worker must pass a document check by the Labor Migration Desk at Kathmandu's Tribhuvan International Airport to ensure that he or she has at least the minimum required documents: (1) a copy of the contract in Nepali providing at least a minimum wage; (2) proof of life insurance; (3) proof of passed medical tests; and (4) an employment permit from DOFE.

Workers can also secure foreign employment without using recruitment agents or agencies. Workers who choose this path are referred to as individual foreign employment workers. To proceed as an individual foreign employment worker, the worker either (1) must have an immediate family member or an employer in the destination country to sponsor his or her foreign employment, or (2) must be renewing his or her contract with the foreign employer for whom the worker previously worked. In 2011–12, DOFE began to allow applications for individual foreign employment permits. In 2012, the Nepal government decided to legalize the status of those who had illegally obtained foreign employment in the past, and DOFE began issuing individual foreign employment permits to such workers. The government also strengthened the process associated with individual foreign employment through the 2013 Directive on the Procedure on Individual Labor Permits.

Both agency-based and individual foreign employment workers have access to grievance redressal mechanisms provided by DOFE and FET. However, DOFE handles grievances of agency-based foreign employment workers only. Grievance redressal mechanisms have been improving for DOFE and FET, but only a very small number of workers register cases with either of them—and that figure continues to fall. Between 2012 and 2015, DOFE resolved only 19 percent of cases against recruitment agencies and only 13 percent of cases against individual agents. Public data are currently unavailable on the nature of cases that are settled by DOFE; nor are details available on the actual amounts paid to complainants. However, data show that the average settlement amount is less than 20 percent of the amount claimed and that, for most cases, it takes more than one year to reach a settlement (Paoletti et al. 2014; ILO 2016). In contrast to DOFE, FET's performance has been improving, with the organization settling 50 percent of cases by the end of fiscal 2014/15.[3]

Although in principle the Nepal government has the laws and institutions to provide for safe and gainful foreign employment for migrant workers, in practice, it faces several challenges. The institutional arrangements are geared toward ensuring safe employment through premigration checks and training provided by DOFE, FEPB, and VSDTC. FEPB and labor attachés provide support to Nepalese foreign employment workers at their destinations, and workers can register their grievances with DOFE and FET. Furthermore, recent legislative changes that increase the focus on ensuring safe migration for individual foreign employment workers reflect the responsiveness of the system to changing ground realities. However, many of the institutions engaged in the foreign employment process remain underfunded and understaffed. Inefficiencies in grievance redressal services likely discourage workers from taking their issues to DOFE or FET. These inefficiencies are potentially due in part to understaffing and underfunding in the two organizations.

Potential inefficiencies in the foreign employment process

Figure 5.8 summarizes the process followed by the worker to obtain foreign employment. Foreign employment workers who secure contracts through recruitment agencies tend to do so with the assistance of local individual recruitment agents. Recruitment agencies are mostly registered in Kathmandu, and have a limited number of local branches. These local branches can be opened after obtaining approval from DOFE. In 2014, the government halted the process of registering and opening local branches. As a result, according to Paoletti et al. (2014), there were only 47 legal local branches belonging to 35 agencies in 2014.

Agencies use registered and unregistered individual agents to identify workers for recruitment. Workers may not have a good way to signal their ability or reliability to the recruitment agency. They also may have little reliable information on the process for foreign employment. This limits them to working through an individual agent. Individual agents usually come from the same communities as workers and are thus well placed to assess the qualities of the worker. Supporting this conjecture, Paoletti et al. (2014) report that agencies tend to prefer workers whom individual agents send them as opposed to workers who approach the agency on their own.

The widespread use of individual agents is substantiated by 2015 KNOMAD migration cost data and 2009 NMS data. All workers who obtained their jobs through recruitment agencies made payments to local individual agents. Less than 5 percent of foreign employment workers stated that they sought help directly from a recruitment agency.

Few data are available on the number of registered and unregistered agents, and the data that are available often appear contradictory. For example, the DOFE website listed 693 agents as of February 2015, whereas pravasipath.com (an online migration rights awareness project of Humanity United) states that in 2015 only 1,800 of almost 100,000 agents were registered. Furthermore, to our knowledge, no studies exist that examine the worker–individual agent marketplace and the conditions and processes through which workers and individual agents interact; the individual agent–agency marketplace and the conditions and process through which agents and agencies interact; or the interaction among individual agents, such as how they share or split market territory. That workers tend to interact with individual agents to secure foreign employment would be less a source for concern if the worker-agent market was competitive and transparent, if there were efficient ways to obtain credible information on agent and agency reputations, and if formal grievance redressal systems for workers were efficient and effective. There is little evidence of these aspects as well.

One reason that agencies tend to use unregistered agents is that agent registration costs can be prohibitively expensive for both agencies and agents. Agencies must pay a deposit of about US$2,000 to DOFE for each registered agent. The agency has the right to ask the agent to repay up to US$700 of this sum, making registration an expensive proposition for the agent as well. Once registered with one agency, the agent cannot work with any other agency. Another reason agencies use unregistered agents is that DOFE imposes only a small penalty for using unregistered agents. In addition, workers have no way to file claims against agencies that use unregistered individual agents, which lowers agencies' risk associated with using them.

FIGURE 5.8

Path of the foreign employment worker

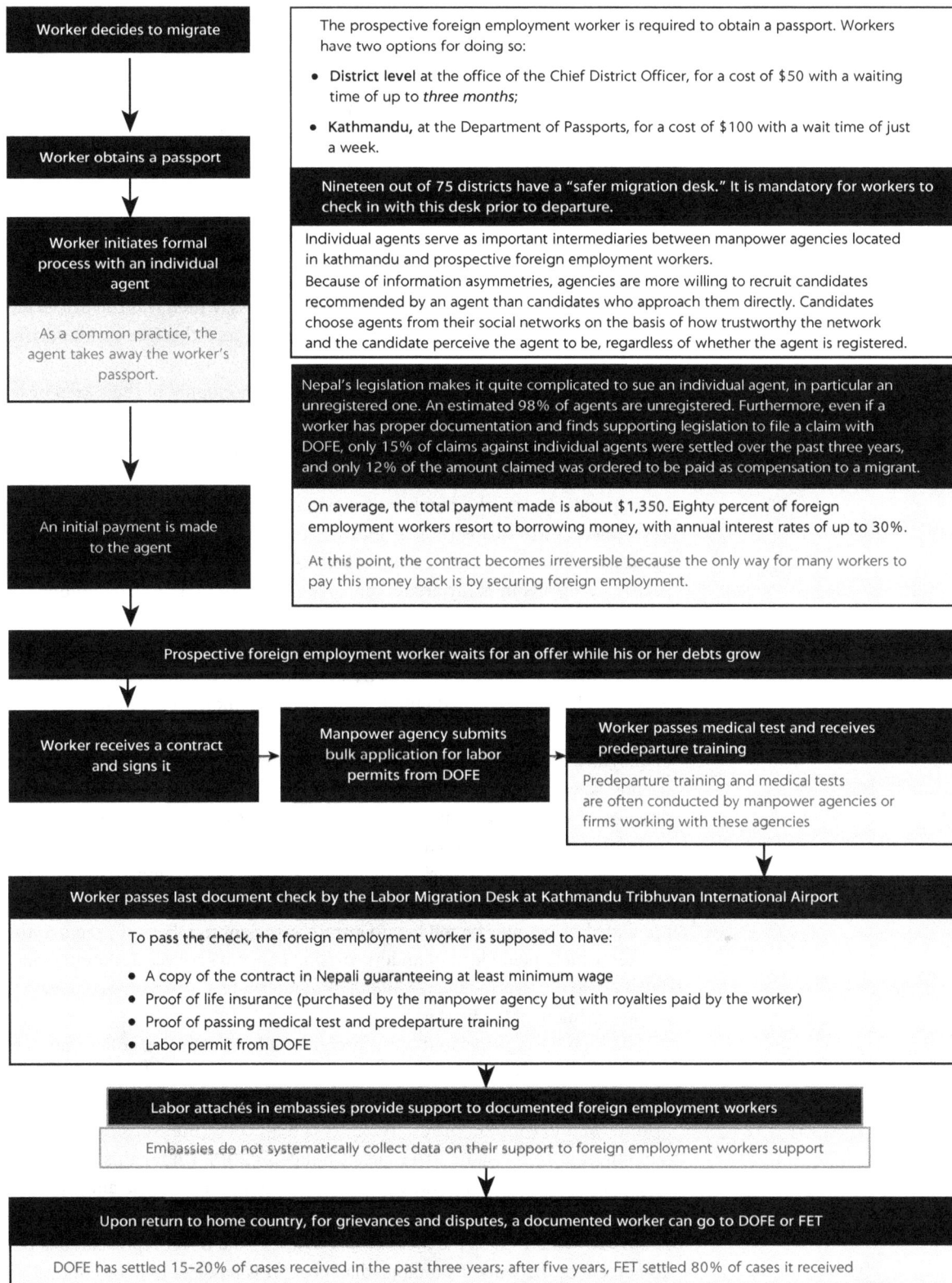

Worker decides to migrate	The prospective foreign employment worker is required to obtain a passport. Workers have two options for doing so:
	• **District level** at the office of the Chief District Officer, for a cost of $50 with a waiting time of up to *three months*;
Worker obtains a passport	• **Kathmandu,** at the Department of Passports, for a cost of $100 with a wait time of just a week.
	Nineteen out of 75 districts have a "safer migration desk." It is mandatory for workers to check in with this desk prior to departure.
Worker initiates formal process with an individual agent	Individual agents serve as important intermediaries between manpower agencies located in kathmandu and prospective foreign employment workers.
	Because of information asymmetries, agencies are more willing to recruit candidates recommended by an agent than candidates who approach them directly. Candidates choose agents from their social networks on the basis of how trustworthy the network and the candidate perceive the agent to be, regardless of whether the agent is registered.
As a common practice, the agent takes away the worker's passport.	Nepal's legislation makes it quite complicated to sue an individual agent, in particular an unregistered one. An estimated 98% of agents are unregistered. Furthermore, even if a worker has proper documentation and finds supporting legislation to file a claim with DOFE, only 15% of claims against individual agents were settled over the past three years, and only 12% of the amount claimed was ordered to be paid as compensation to a migrant.
An initial payment is made to the agent	On average, the total payment made is about $1,350. Eighty percent of foreign employment workers resort to borrowing money, with annual interest rates of up to 30%.
	At this point, the contract becomes irreversible because the only way for many workers to pay this money back is by securing foreign employment.

Prospective foreign employment worker waits for an offer while his or her debts grow

Worker receives a contract and signs it	**Manpower agency submits bulk application for labor permits from DOFE**	**Worker passes medical test and receives predeparture training**
		Predeparture training and medical tests are often conducted by manpower agencies or firms working with these agencies

Worker passes last document check by the Labor Migration Desk at Kathmandu Tribhuvan International Airport

To pass the check, the foreign employment worker is supposed to have:

- A copy of the contract in Nepali guaranteeing at least minimum wage
- Proof of life insurance (purchased by the manpower agency but with royalties paid by the worker)
- Proof of passing medical test and predeparture training
- Labor permit from DOFE

Labor attachés in embassies provide support to documented foreign employment workers

Embassies do not systematically collect data on their support to foreign employment workers support

Upon return to home country, for grievances and disputes, a documented worker can go to DOFE or FET

DOFE has settled 15–20% of cases received in the past three years; after five years, FET settled 80% of cases it received

Sources: Calculations based on data from Pravasi Path, http://pravasipath.com/; Shrestha 2017a; Paoletti et al. 2014; ILO 2016; Department of Foreign Employment, Government of Nepal.
Note: DOFE = Department of Foreign Employment; FEPB = Foreign Employment Promotion Board; FET = Foreign Employment Tribunal.

The high prices paid by workers for agent services suggest that the market may not be competitive. Given the large number of agencies and unregistered agents, basic economic theory would suggest that competition among agents would drive agent prices down to the cost of the transaction for the agent. There is little evidence that agent prices have declined over time. A comparison of the costs of migration, as recorded in the 2009 NMS and the 2015 KNOMAD databases, shows that the median price paid by the worker to obtain employment in Qatar declined by about NPR 10,000—from a median of about NPR 100,000 in 2009 to a median of NPR 90,000 in 2015. Furthermore, both the 2009 and 2015 median prices are substantially higher than the government-mandated price of NPR 70,000 for Middle Eastern destinations. Only 25 percent of foreign employment workers surveyed in 2015 paid the mandated price or less. Furthermore, in the 2015 data, virtually no worker reported paying the local agent NPR 10,000 or less, which was the price ceiling for agents mandated by the government before the free visa and free ticket policy.

Agents may gain market power by having a monopoly in their area or by engaging in collusive behavior with other agents. This market power can result in higher agent prices. To our knowledge, there are currently no studies of the structure and dynamics of the agency market, and what these imply for agent prices. Unless the number of registered agents is increased, the recent government push to ensure that foreign employment workers use registered agents may have the unintended effect of increasing the market power of registered agents in many areas, and, given their limited number, potentially driving up prices.

The market may fail to weed out bad agents and agencies, which can add to market inefficiency. In the 2015 KNOMAD database, 37 percent of workers reported that they learned about foreign employment opportunities from a relative and 80 percent of those said they had to pay a local agent to secure employment. Paoletti et al. (2014) indicate that agents are often close relatives or friends, so workers may opt to suppress grievances to avoid damaging community ties. Thus, bad agents and agencies can continue to survive and operate with their reputations untarnished.

Although high agency prices may be due to an uncompetitive market, the competitive price may actually exceed the price mandated by the government. Mandated prices may be too low to attract sufficient numbers of agents to the market, which would lead to underprovision of agent services. Enforcing mandated prices or lowering them could in fact undermine the worker-agent market to the detriment of the worker.

The high costs associated with foreign employment are a policy concern. High costs can lead foreign employment workers to take on large amounts of debt early in the process, which in turn may make them more accepting of fraud or unfavorable contract terms. To address high costs, the Nepal government announced a free visa and free ticket policy in 2015. Under this policy, the employer should bear the full cost of the migrant worker's visa and travel. It remains unclear what effect this policy will have on the worker's costs. According to 2015 KNOMAD data, the median cost of a visa and ticket represented about 40 percent of the worker's total median cost.[4] It is possible that, by controlling visa and ticket costs but not other costs, the policy could have the unintended effect of increasing worker payments to agents because agents would have more consumer surplus available from the worker to extract as payment.

Foreign employment trends

In the remaining subsections, we discuss patterns in and correlates of trends in foreign employment flows for Nepalese male workers only (the female foreign employment outflow represents only 5 percent of the total outflow). Note that, although we refer to the statistics as representing workers, to be precise, they are employment permit statistics (because a worker can obtain multiple employment permits over time, the number of unique workers would be less than the number of employment permits issued). Also note that our full data period is January 2010–May 2016 for statistics related to agency-based foreign employment outflow and September 2011–May 2016 for statistics related to individual foreign employment outflow.

Ninety-six percent of agency-based foreign employment workers and 85 percent of individual foreign employment workers went to four destinations: Malaysia, Qatar, Saudi Arabia, and the United Arab Emirates. Prior to 2015, Middle Eastern countries were the second-most-popular destination after Malaysia for agency-based foreign employment workers, and the most popular destination for individual foreign employment workers (see figure 5.9). Qatar was the top destination among Middle Eastern countries for agency-based foreign employment workers; when numbers declined in 2015, Saudi Arabia took its place as No. 1. Among individual foreign employment workers, Qatar has consistently remained the top destination through the years.

Effects of macroeconomic factors in Nepal and destination countries on foreign employment flow

The main Middle Eastern destination countries are largely dependent on oil exports. Oil prices experienced a drastic decline in the second half of 2014, falling from US$100 per barrel in August 2014 to about US$50 per barrel in January 2015.[5] This decline negatively affected economic growth in these countries. Except for Becker et al. (2005), who find that macroeconomic deterioration in the Russian Federation depressed migration from Kazakhstan to Russia, international evidence is lacking on the effect of negative shocks in destination countries on labor migration.

Table 5.3 reports regression results for the relationship of international oil prices, quarterly gross domestic product (GDP) growth rates at destination, and annual GDP growth rates in Nepal, all lagged, with agency-based and individual foreign employment outflow to Malaysia, Qatar, and Saudi Arabia (the top three destinations). International oil prices are positively associated with both agency-based and individual foreign employment outflow from Nepal.

GDP growth rates in Qatar and Saudi Arabia are negatively associated with agency-based and individual foreign employment outflow from Nepal. This result differs from Shrestha (2017a), who finds that the growth in the numbers of foreign employment workers going to Middle Eastern countries and Malaysia between 2001 and 2010–11 is positively associated with growth in the construction and manufacturing sectors (as proxied by the growth in carbon dioxide emissions from these sectors) in these destination countries.

Many destination country employers find foreign employment workers especially attractive because the employers can easily hire and fire such workers. In addition, foreign employment workers are under legal contract to a particular employer. Thus, reforms to laws that govern foreign employment in destination

FIGURE 5.9

Top destinations of male foreign employment workers

a. Agency-based outflow in 2011–15

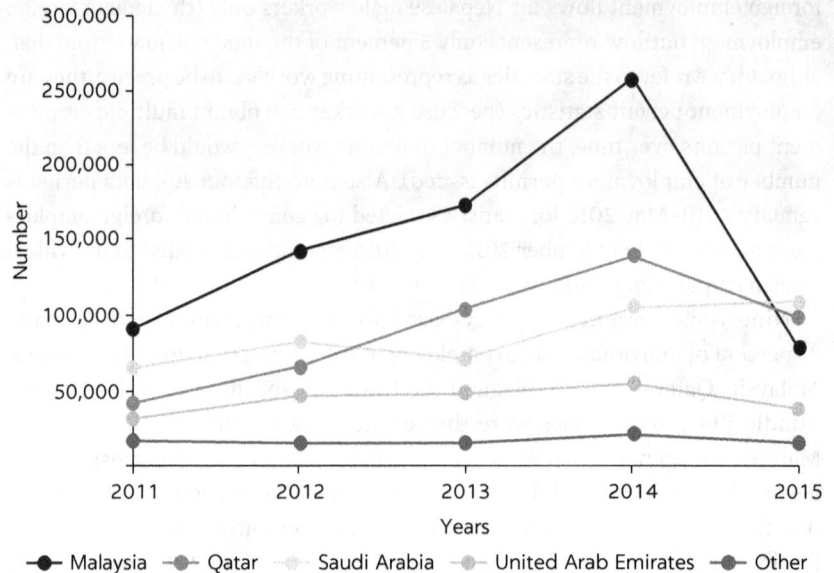

b. Individual outflow in 2012–2015

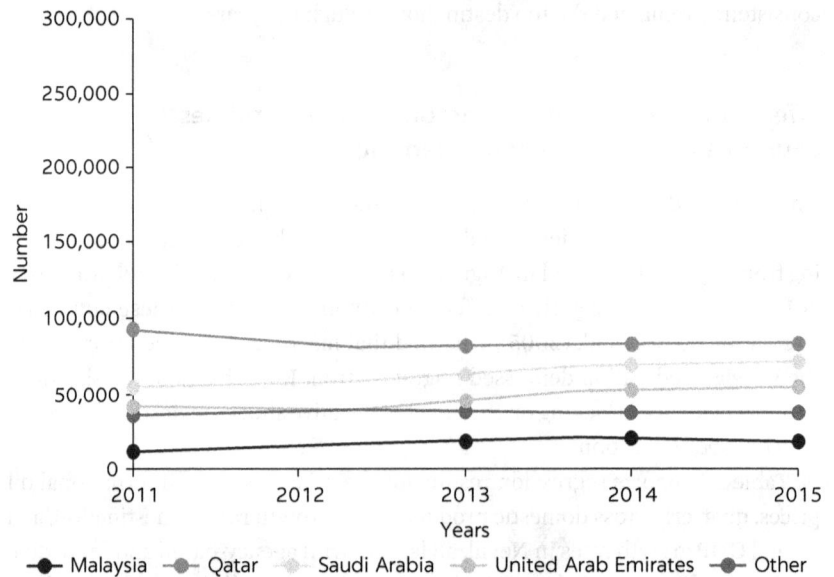

Source: Calculations based on data from the Department of Foreign Employment, Government of Nepal.

Middle Eastern countries may have had different effects on new and repeat foreign employment workers. For example, in 2011, the United Arab Emirates began to allow foreign employment workers to change employers, a departure from the traditional *kafala* system that tied the worker to his or her employer without any possibility of change, and that made the employer the worker's legal guardian. Naidu, Nyarko, and Wang (2016) find that the reform led to higher earnings for incumbent foreign employment workers and a decrease in demand for new foreign employment workers. Qatar passed a similar law in December 2016.

TABLE 5.3 **Macroeconomic determinants of male foreign employment worker outflow**

Quarterly data from January 2013 to December 2015

	LOGGED QUARTERLY FOREIGN EMPLOYMENT OUTFLOW BY HOME DISTRICT AND DESTINATION			
	AGENCY-BASED OUTFLOW		INDIVIDUAL-BASED OUTFLOW	
	(1)	(2)	(3)	(4)
Logged lagged annual GDP growth rate in Nepal	−2.540*** (0.09)	0.201* (0.09)	−0.421*** (0.10)	0.432*** (0.08)
Logged lagged quarterly GDP growth rate at destination	−0.154*** (0.02)	−0.595*** (0.02)	0.161*** (0.01)	−0.106*** (0.02)
Malaysia × logged lagged quarterly GDP growth rate at destination	0.936*** (0.10)	1.478*** (0.07)	−1.723*** (0.12)	0.05 (0.05)
Logged lagged quarterly oil price	n.a.	2.811*** (0.07)	n.a.	0.601*** (0.07)
Malaysia × logged lagged quarterly oil price	n.a.	−0.0807*** (0.02)	n.a.	−0.239*** (0.02)
District dummies	Yes	Yes	Yes	Yes
Observations	1,345	1,121	1,300	1,087
R^2 statistic	0.85	0.92	0.87	0.91

Sources: Estimated using data from the Department of Foreign Employment, Government of Nepal; World Development Indicators Database; and the Global Economic Monitor Commodities Database.

Note: n.a. = not applicable. Dependent variable is logged quarterly outflow of male foreign employment workers from a given district to a particular destination starting from January 2013 to December 2015. The estimations are limited to the top three destinations (Malaysia, Qatar, and Saudi Arabia) that account for close to 85 percent of total male foreign employment outflow in that period. Quarterly gross domestic product (GDP) growth rates in destination countries and average quarterly oil prices are lagged by two quarters. Average quarterly oil price is constructed from data on monthly crude oil, average spot price of Brent, Dubai, and West Texas Intermediate, equally weighed. Standard errors are reported in parentheses.
*$p < 0.1$, **$p < 0.05$, ***$p < 0.01$.

Malaysia was the top destination country for agency-based foreign employment workers until 2015, with an increase in numbers from 2011 through 2014. However, the country has ranked behind Qatar, Saudi Arabia, the United Arab Emirates, and other countries (taken together) with respect to the number of individual foreign employment workers (see figure 5.10). The sharp difference in the levels of agency-based and individual foreign employment flows to Malaysia may be due in part to the low wages offered to foreign employment workers. Malaysia offers the lowest wages out of the top destination countries. The median monthly wage for foreign employment workers in Malaysia is US$60 lower than the next-lowest median wage among the main destination Middle Eastern countries (Qatar, Saudi Arabia, and the United Arab Emirates). Thus, foreign employment workers may be less inclined to return to Malaysia and may seek employment elsewhere. The low repeat flow (reflected in the number of Nepalese workers renewing their foreign employment permits for Malaysia) may also be due to Malaysian regulations aimed at discouraging long-term employment of low-skilled foreign employment workers. The Malaysian government views foreign employment inflows to be a stopgap measure for domestic labor shortages (Devadason and Meng 2014).

Foreign employment flows from Nepal to Malaysia dropped sharply in 2015 (see figure 5.10). The trend may be due to efforts by the Malaysian government to adhere to its 2009 promise to drastically reduce the number of labor migrants by 2015. The trend may also be due a sharp decline in the value of

FIGURE 5.10

Monthly male foreign employment flows to Malaysia versus other foreign employment destinations, January 2014–April 2016

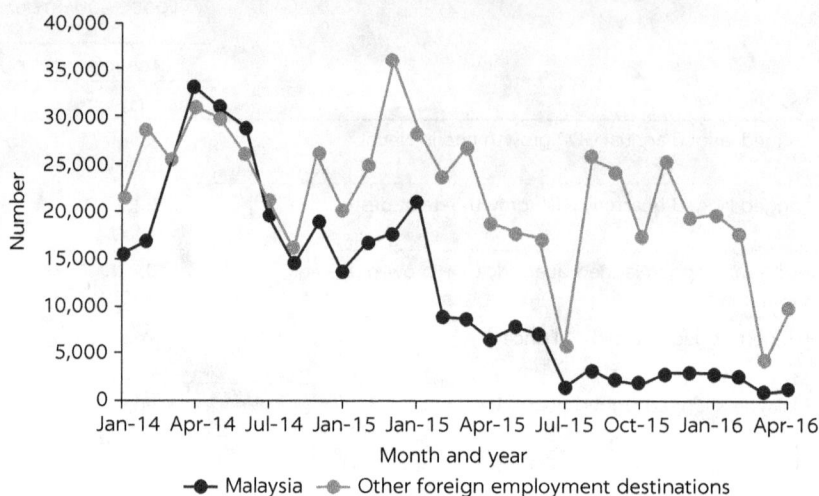

Source: Calculations based on data from the Department of Foreign Employment, Government of Nepal.

the Malaysian currency between mid-2014 and mid-2015, which would have made the country a less attractive foreign employment destination for Nepalese workers (Shrestha 2017c).

Effect of the 2015 earthquake in Nepal on foreign employment outflow

Nepal experienced a severe earthquake with a magnitude of 7.8 to 8.1 on April 25, 2015, which caused extensive damage and loss.[6] The potential effect of this earthquake on foreign employment outflow is theoretically ambiguous. Foreign employment outflow may have fallen because workers decided to remain in Nepal to help their households and communities recover from the earthquake. Foreign employment outflow may also have fallen because workers had greater difficulty in raising the funds needed to migrate, or because the arrangements for securing foreign employment (for example, recruitment agency operations) may have been disrupted by the earthquake. On the other hand, outflow may have risen if workers used foreign employment as an economic coping strategy.

Table 5.4 reports regression results for the effect of the earthquake on foreign employment outflow to the top three destinations of Malaysia, Qatar, and Saudi Arabia, under a difference-in-differences framework (before and after the earthquake, and between worst-affected districts and other districts). We find that the earthquake had a negative effect on agency-based foreign employment outflow, controlling for district of origin and lagged values for GDP growth rates in destination countries and in Nepal. Agency-based foreign employment flows may have been negatively affected because workers were unable to make the needed payments to recruitment agencies, and because the earthquake disrupted the recruitment agencies' operations. Individual foreign employment flows would have been free of these constraints.

TABLE 5.4 **Effect of the 2015 earthquake on male foreign employment worker outflow**

Quarterly data from January 2013 to December 2015

	LOGGED QUARTERLY FOREIGN EMPLOYMENT OUTFLOW BY HOME DISTRICT AND DESTINATION	
	AGENCY-BASED OUTFLOW	INDIVIDUAL-BASED OUTFLOW
	(1)	(2)
Post-earthquake	0.168***	−0.131***
	(0.03)	(0.03)
Earthquake-affected district	2.133***	2.850***
	(0.04)	(0.04)
Earthquake-affected district × post-earthquake	−0.173**	0.07
	(0.05)	(0.05)
District dummies	Yes	Yes
Observations	1,121	1,087
R^2 statistic	0.92	0.91

Sources: Estimated using data from the Department of Foreign Employment, Government of Nepal; World Development Indicators Database; and the Global Economic Monitor Commodities Database.
Note: Dependent variable is logged quarterly outflow of male foreign employment workers from a given district to a particular destination starting from January 2013 to December 2015. The estimations are limited to the top three destinations (Malaysia, Qatar, and Saudi Arabia) that account for close to 85 percent of total male foreign employment outflow in that period. Regressions control for lagged gross domestic product growth rates at destination and in Nepal, lagged international oil prices, and district. Earthquake-affected districts are the 14 districts that are considered to be the heaviest hit: Bhaktapur, Dhading, Dolakha, Gorkha, Kathmandu, Kavrepalanchowk, Lalitpur, Makwanpur, Nuwakot, Okhladunga, Ramechhap, Rasuwa, Sindhuli, and Sindupalchowk. Standard errors are reported in parentheses.
$*p < 0.1, **p < 0.05, ***p < 0.01.$

EFFECTS OF MALE YOUTH LABOR MIGRATION ON THE LABOR OUTCOMES OF REMAINING YOUTH HOUSEHOLD MEMBERS

What are the effects of labor migration on the labor outcomes of youth who have not migrated? Given the extent of labor migration and the potential interdependency of labor choices of household members in Nepal, labor migration can affect the labor outcomes of household members who remain at home. In addition, a large outflow of male youth can have aggregate labor market effects at home.

Labor supply

According to standard theory, the overall effect of labor migration on the labor supply of nonmigrating members of the migrant's household is ambiguous (for brevity, we refer to these nonmigrant household members as "stayers"). There are at least two pathways through which labor migration could affect the labor outcomes of stayers, with opposite effects. A first pathway is the receipt of remittances by households. In our sample, 81 percent of labor migrants sent remittances to their households. The standard model of labor-leisure choice predicts that individuals receiving remittances will increase their consumption of leisure and decrease their labor supply, because household nonlabor income increases through remittances (an income effect).

As a second pathway, labor migration can create a need to substitute for the labor of migrants to compensate for forgone income (a disruption effect). If the labor of stayers and the labor of out-migrants are substitutes, stayers may increase their labor supply. In addition, a large outflow of migrants can have aggregate labor market effects at home. In particular, a reduction in aggregate labor supply can increase aggregate wages in the local labor market, increasing the price of leisure for stayers. Stayers may then choose to increase their labor supply (a substitution effect). For households observing both the income effect and the disruption effect or substitution effect, the net effect of labor migration on the labor supply of stayers is ambiguous. In addition, households may initially have to finance the costs of migration of their members, a particularly important concern for labor migration to external destinations other than India. As a result, stayers may have to increase labor supply to pay for these costs.

Rigorous international evidence on the effects of migration on home outcomes is mixed. De Brauw and Giles (2012) find for China that labor migration from rural areas is associated with increases in the total labor supplied to productive activities and the amount of land per capita managed by remaining household members. Examining the effect of remittances on household labor supply in rural Mexico, Amuedo-Dorantes and Pozo (2006) find that male labor supply does not change but female labor supply declines. Examining the effect of remittances on household labor supply in El Salvador, Acosta (2006) finds that female labor supply declines.

The available evidence for Nepal is also mixed. Using 2003–04 NLSS data, Lokshin and Glinskaya (2009) find that male out-migration has a negative effect on household female labor force participation. Using household data from two districts, Maharjan, Bauer, and Knerr (2013) find that male out-migration has a positive effect on female employment, especially on female agricultural employment. Using 2010–11 NLSS data, Phadera (2016) finds that out-migration has a positive effect on wage employment by female household members, and a negative effect on the labor supply of male household members. Finally, using population census data from 2001 and 2010 to construct village-level statistics, Shrestha (2017d) finds that an increase in the village out-migration rate is associated with an increase in the village labor force participation rate. The result appears to be driven by increases in nonagricultural employment by women and agricultural employment by men. Combining population census and 2010–11 NLSS data, Shrestha also finds that a higher village out-migration rate is associated with higher wages. The result appears to be driven by higher wages for women and higher wages in agriculture. The mixed results are likely due in part to differing samples, instrumental variable strategies, and units of treatment (for example, household members versus village residents). They also likely reflect the challenge of identifying and estimating the effects of labor out-migration using observational data.

Here, we examine the effect of whether a household has a male youth member who is a labor migrant (our main "treatment" indicator) on the labor outcomes of female and male youth stayers. A labor migrant is defined here to be an individual who was a labor migrant at the time the 2010-11 NLSS was administered to the household. There are few observations for female labor migrants, and hence they are excluded from the treatment indicator. We also examine the effects of alternative household-level treatment indicators, namely whether the household had a male youth labor migrant who (1) sent remittances, (2) had migrated internally, (3) had migrated to India, or (4) had migrated to another external destination.

As discussed in the section titled "Correlates of Youth Labor Migration," we find that youth labor migrants systematically differ from youth nonmigrants. Consequently, we expect that stayers in households with labor migrants may differ from stayers in households without labor migrants. The poor overlap in the distribution of characteristics of these two groups of households can make estimates of the effects of male youth labor migration on stayer outcomes imprecise and sensitive to the choice of specification. To obtain an optimal subsample, we use the approach of Crump et al. (2009), discarding any observations with extreme predicted probabilities of male youth labor migration from the household. The approach does not bias the estimates because the optimal subsample depends on the joint distribution of characteristics and household labor migration status and not on the distribution of outcomes. The approach also can greatly improve the precision of the estimates. However, given the data, the method does not allow us to interpret these associations (which we refer to as "effects") as causal.

We estimate the effect of male youth labor migration on stayers in two stages. In the first stage, we (1) estimate regressions of whether the household has a male youth labor migrant, using an extensive set of household and community characteristics; (2) predict the household probabilities of having a male youth labor migrant; and (3) following the general optimal rule suggested by Crump et al. (2009), retain only households with predicted probabilities between 0.1 and 0.9. Implementing this procedure results in trimming about 16 percent of households from the sample. Sample sizes for the outcome regressions for stayers are still large after the trimming. In the second stage, we estimate the effect of having a male youth labor migrant on the labor outcomes of stayers in the trimmed sample, separately for female and male youth stayers, controlling for individual, household, and community characteristics.

Tables 5.5 and 5.6 present regression results for the effects of male youth labor migration on the labor outcomes of female and male youth stayers, respectively. Table 5.7 presents the regression results of male youth labor migration on school enrollment and years of schooling for children ages 5–15 years in the household. All statistics are based on 2010–11 NLSS data.

We find that male youth labor migration has negative effects on the likelihood of employment for female and male youth stayers, but the effects are insignificant. Male youth labor migration also has negative effects on hours worked for female and male youth stayers, but only the effect of –11 percent for female youth stayers is significant. Looking at the alternative treatment indicators, we find that male youth labor migration to external destinations other than India has significant negative effects on the likelihood of employment of –34 percentage points for male youth stayers and –21 percentage points for female youth stayers. Male youth migration coupled with remittances has significant negative effects on hours worked of –12 percent for male youth stayers and –13 percent for female youth stayers.

Looking at participation in noneconomic activities, male youth labor migration has a significant positive effect of 8 percentage points on the likelihood of noneconomic participation by male youth stayers, with the effect appearing to

TABLE 5.5 **Effects of male youth labor migration on female youth stayers, trimmed sample, 2010–11**

Least squares and binomial logit estimations, average marginal effects

INDICATOR	EMPLOYED	CONDITIONAL ON EMPLOYMENT						CONDITIONAL ON NEA	
		WAGE EMPLOYED	SELF-EMPLOYED IN AG.	EMPLOYED IN INDUSTRY	EMPLOYED IN SERVICES	LOG HOURS WORKED	LOG WAGE EARNINGS	ENGAGED IN NEA	LOG HOURS IN NEA
	(1)	(2)	(3)	(4)	(5)	(6)	(7)	(8)	(9)
a. Main household-level treatment indicator									
Household has male youth labor out-migrant(s)	-0.103	-0.012	0.018	0.002	0.008	-0.109**	0.085	0.013	-0.042
	(0.080)	(0.020)	(0.020)	(0.015)	(0.017)	(0.047)	(0.053)	(0.010)	(-0.030)
b. Alternative household-level treatment indicators									
Has male youth labor out-migrant(s) sending remittances	-0.066	-0.018	0.018	-0.003	0.016	-0.134***	0.101*	0.006	-0.024
	(0.085)	(0.021)	(0.022)	(0.014)	(0.016)	(0.051)	(0.057)	(0.010)	(0.032)
Has male youth labor out-migrant(s) to internal des.	0.115	-0.009	0.024	0.002	0.002	-0.073	0.071	0.012	0.049
	(0.114)	(0.026)	(0.027)	(0.019)	(0.021)	(0.055)	(0.077)	(0.013)	(0.042)
Has male youth labor out-migrant(s) to India	-0.008	-0.007	0.033	-0.009	-0.079**	-0.079	0.008	0.012	-0.162***
	(0.125)	(0.033)	(0.036)	(0.025)	(0.032)	(0.073)	(0.082)	(0.013)	(0.051)
Has male youth labor out-migrant(s) to other external des.	-0.206*	-0.025	-0.003	0.010	0.035	-0.083	0.160	0.009	0.043
	(0.110)	(0.027)	(0.028)	(0.019)	(0.024)	(0.060)	(0.102)	(0.012)	(0.043)
Observations	4,446	2,040	2,040	2,040	2,040	2,040	645	4,446	1,969

Source: Estimates using data from the 2010–11 Nepal Living Standards Survey (NLSS).

Note: Ag. = agriculture; des. = destination; NEA = noneconomic activity. A youth labor migrant is defined as an individual ages 16–34 years who was absent from the household for labor reasons at the time the 2010–11 NLSS was administered to the household and who has the intention to return, as reported by the household. The propensity score trimmed sample only includes observations with predicted values between 0.1 and 0.9 in a household-level male youth labor migration binomial logit regression. All outcome regressions control for the individual's age, marital status, schooling status, education level, and ethnicity/caste; whether the individual has a chronic illness or disability; whether the individual was ill in the last month; whether the individual is poor; community amenities and access to roads; the share of household heads employed in agriculture in the primary sampling unit (PSU); and region identifiers. Robust standard errors, clustered at the PSU level, are reported in parentheses. All estimates are adjusted for sampling weights.

*p < 0.1, **p < 0.05, ***p < 0.01.

TABLE 5.6 **Effects of male youth labor migration on male youth stayers, trimmed sample, 2010–11**

Least squares and binomial logit estimations, average marginal effects

| INDICATOR | EMPLOYED | WAGE EMPLOYED | CONDITIONAL ON EMPLOYMENT | | | | | CONDITIONAL ON NEA | |
| | | | SELF-EMPLOYED IN AG. | EMPLOYED IN INDUSTRY | EMPLOYED IN SERVICES | LOG HOURS WORKED | LOG WAGE EARNINGS | ENGAGED IN NEA | LOG HOURS IN NEA |
	(1)	(2)	(3)	(4)	(5)	(6)	(7)	(8)	(9)
a. Main household-level treatment indicator									
Household has male youth labor out-migrant(s)	-0.172 (0.114)	-0.01 (0.032)	0.011 (0.026)	0.017 (0.027)	-0.021 (0.029)	-0.075 (0.049)	0.063 (0.065)	0.081*** (0.024)	-0.016 (0.081)
b. Alternative household-level treatment indicators									
Has male youth labor out-migrant(s) sending remittances	-0.105 (0.125)	-0.046 (0.033)	0.054** (0.027)	0.014 (0.028)	-0.053* (0.031)	-0.123** (0.056)	0.073 (0.075)	0.109*** (0.027)	0.008 (0.086)
Has male youth labor out-migrant(s) to internal des.	-0.001 (0.16)	-0.013 (0.043)	-0.020 (0.033)	0.049 (0.034)	0.017 (0.033)	-0.193*** (0.066)	0.020 (0.085)	0.065* (0.035)	0.172* (0.102)
Has male youth labor out-migrant(s) to India	0.087 (0.207)	0.001 (0.048)	0.025 (0.038)	0.013 (0.042)	-0.089* (0.049)	0.017 (0.097)	0.121 (0.094)	0.030 (0.040)	-0.319*** (0.122)
Has male youth labor out-migrant(s) to other external des.	-0.341** (0.171)	0.022 (0.052)	0.017 (0.043)	0.024 (0.041)	-0.035 (0.041)	0.059 (0.073)	0.039 (0.093)	0.072** (0.036)	0.089 (0.126)
Observations	2,341	1,318	1,318	1,318	1,318	1,318	688	2,341	792

Source: Estimated using data from the 2010–11 Nepal Living Standards Survey.

Note: Ag. = agriculture; des. = destination; NEA = noneconomic activity. A youth labor migrant is defined to be an individual ages 16–34 years who was absent from the household for labor reasons at the time the 2010–11 NLSS was administered to the household and has the intention to return, as reported by the household. The propensity score trimmed sample only includes observations with predicted values between 0.1 and 0.9 in a household-level male youth labor migration binomial logit regression. All outcome regressions control for the individual's age, marital status, schooling status, education level, and ethnicity/caste; whether the individual has a chronic illness or disability; whether the individual was ill in the last month; whether the individual is poor, community amenities and access to roads; the share of household heads employed in agriculture in the primary sampling unit (PSU); and region identifiers. Robust standard errors, clustered at the PSU level, are reported in parentheses. All estimates are adjusted for sampling weights.

*p<0.1, **p<0.05, ***p<0.01.

TABLE 5.7 **Effects of male youth labor migration on household child's education, trimmed sample, 2010–11**

Ordinary least squares and binomial logit estimations, average marginal effects

INDICATOR	SCHOOL ENROLLMENT	YEARS OF SCHOOLING
	(1)	(2)
a. Main household level-treatment indicator		
Household has male youth labor out-migrant(s)	0.011 (0.010)	0.104* (0.053)
b. Alternative household-level treatment indicators		
Has male youth labor out-migrant(s) sending remittances	0.023* (0.012)	0.101* (0.055)
Has male youth labor out-migrant(s) to internal destinations	0.002 (0.017)	0.082 (0.079)
Has male youth labor out-migrant(s) to India	0.001 (0.014)	0.088 (0.086)
Has male youth labor out-migrant(s) to other external destinations	0.021 (0.016)	0.049 (0.082)
Observations	6,745	

Source: Estimated using data from the 2010–11 Nepal Living Standards Survey (NLSS).
Note: A youth labor migrant is defined as an individual ages 16–34 years who was absent from the household for labor reasons at the time the 2010–11 NLSS was administered to the household and who has the intention to return, as reported by the household. The propensity score trimmed sample only includes observations with predicted values between 0.1 and 0.9 in a household-level male youth labor migration binomial logit regression. Child is defined as an individual ages 5–15. Child-level regressions control for age, age squared, gender, presence of a disability or health problem, consumption quintiles, the share of household heads employed in agriculture in the primary sampling unit (PSU), household head's education, household size, ethnicity, community amenities index, amount of travel time to paved road, and whether a natural disaster occurred in the community in the past four years. Robust standard errors, clustered at the primary sampling unit level, are reported in parentheses. All estimates are adjusted for sampling weights.
$*p < 0.1, **p < 0.05, ***p < 0.01$.

be driven by remittances. Male youth labor migration to India has significant negative effects on hours in noneconomic activities of –32 percent for male youth stayers and –16 percent for female youth stayers. The collective evidence suggests that cutbacks in labor supply occur in economic and noneconomic activities by youth stayers.

Sector and type of employment

Labor migration could affect the allocation of labor supply by stayers across types of employment (Amuedo-Dorantes and Pozo 2006). One way is through the disruption effect discussed previously, in particular when the household runs an enterprise. Eighty-five percent of labor migrants originate in rural areas, where self-employment in agriculture is prevalent, representing 61 percent of total rural employment. The disruption effect can produce a labor shortage in household enterprises. If the skills of stayers are a substitute for those of labor migrants, stayers may increase their labor supply to household enterprises.

We find that male youth labor migration does not appear to have effects on the likelihoods of wage employment, self-employment in agriculture, employment in industry, or employment in services, either for male or female youth stayers. Looking at the alternative treatment indicators, male youth labor migration to India has significant negative effects on the likelihood of employment in services for female and male youth stayers. Male youth labor migration combined with remittances has a significant positive effect of 5 percentage points on the likelihood of self-employment in agriculture for male youth stayers.

Wage earnings

Male labor migration can affect the labor earnings of stayers. Migration out of rural areas decreases local labor supply. Keeping labor demand fixed, a decrease in labor supply can increase aggregate wages. We find that the effects on wage earnings for female and male youth stayers are positive (9 percent and 6 percent, respectively), but insignificant. The direction of the effects we find is in line with what Shrestha (2017d) documents.

Children's education

Previous studies suggest that labor migration can influence the education investment decision for children in the household, mainly by providing extra household income to cover children's school expenditures and by reducing the need for child labor. Acosta (2006) and Yang (2008) find for El Salvador and the Philippines, respectively, that remittances reduce child labor and increase child school enrollment. Evidence for Nepal suggests that remittances are positively associated with children's education. Using 1995–96 NLSS data, Bansak and Chezum (2009) find that remittances have a positive effect on children's school enrollment, particularly for young boys. Using data for the Sainik Basti settlement in western Nepal, Thieme and Wyss (2005) find that migration is associated with higher education attainment by children. Using 2010–11 NLSS data, Shrestha (2017d) finds that migration to Malaysia and Middle Eastern countries has a positive effect on girls' school enrollment.

Whereas the effect of male youth labor migration on the likelihood of school enrollment by household children is small and insignificant, male youth labor migration combined with remittances to the household has a positive effect of 2 percentage points on the likelihood of child school enrollment. Although none of the effects is significant, the effect on child school enrollment is larger for male youth labor migration to external destinations compared to the effects for migration to India and to internal destinations. Male youth labor migration also has a positive effect of 0.1 additional year of schooling for household children. The effect that male youth labor migration combined with remittances has on years of schooling is of the same magnitude. Here, although again none of the effects are significant, the effects of male youth migration to India and to internal destinations are larger than the effect of male youth migration to other external destinations. To summarize, it appears that male youth labor migration has positive effects on the education of household children, mediated through remittances to the household.

YOUTH LABOR MIGRANTS WHO HAVE RETURNED

What is the incidence of returning (or the rate of return) from labor migration for youth, and what are the labor outcomes at home of returned youth labor migrants? A returned youth labor migrant (or "returnee") is defined to be a youth household member who had migrated for labor for at least two consecutive months in the five years before the 2010–11 NLSS was administered to the household but who is present in the household at the time of the survey. Seventeen percent of male youth were returnees, whereas 1 percent of female youth were returnees. Given the negligible percentage of female youth returnees, we restrict the analysis to male youth returnees only.

Share of youth labor migrants who have returned

Figure 5.11 shows the share of male returnees among male youth who migrated for labor in the five years before the 2010–11 NLSS was administered. In total, 29 percent returned. The rate of return differs by destination type, specifically between India (41 percent) and other destinations (21 percent for internal destinations and 24 percent for other external destinations). The higher rate of return for male youth labor migrants to India is consistent with the view that labor migration to India tends to be seasonal in nature, or is used as a temporary coping strategy by households during times of economic distress (WFP 2008).

The rate of return suggests that temporary labor migration is extensive. However, the high rate may be an artifact of the data, given that the NLSS defines household absentees as individuals who are temporarily absent from the household but are expected by the household to return. Those household members who have migrated for labor and are not expected to return would not be accounted for in the estimation, and thus the estimated rate may be upwardly biased.

FIGURE 5.11

Percent of returned male youth labor migrants, by destination type

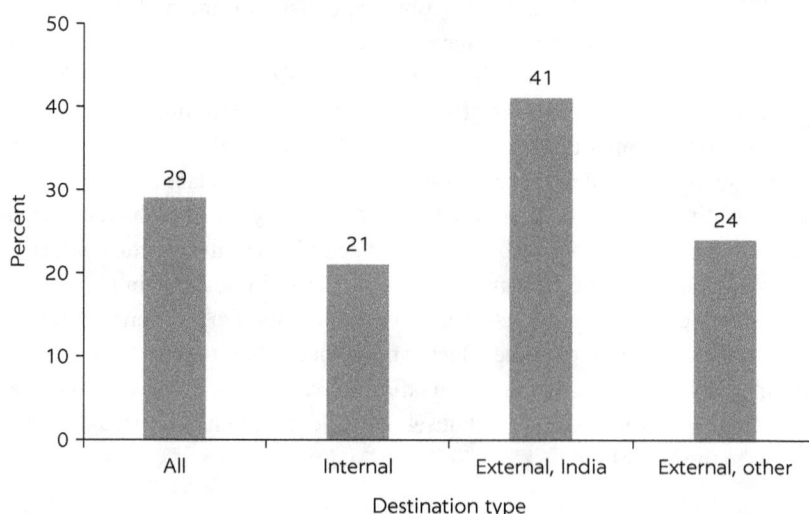

Source: Estimated using data from the 2010–11 Nepal Living Standards Survey (NLSS).
Note: A returned youth labor migrant is defined as an individual ages 16–34 years who migrated for labor in the five years before the 2010–11 NLSS was administered to the household, but was present in the household at the time of the survey. The percentages reported in the figure are estimated shares of returned youth labor migrants out of youth who migrated for labor in the five years before the 2010–11 NLSS was administered. All estimates are adjusted for sampling weights.

Home labor outcomes of male youth labor migrants who have returned

The international literature is thin on the labor outcomes of migrant workers once they return home. Evidence from low- and middle-income countries suggests that returning from international migration is associated with higher wages at home. Reinhold and Thom (2013) find that the labor market experience accumulated by Mexican migrants in the United States increases their earnings upon returning home. Similarly, Wahba (2015) finds that temporary international migration by Egyptian workers results in a wage premium upon return. A few studies examine the occupational choices of returned labor migrants, in particular with respect to entrepreneurship and self-employment (Mesnard 2004; Dustmann and Kirchkamp 2002; McCormick and Wahba 2001). These studies find that returned labor migrants are more likely to become employers and self-employed workers compared to nonmigrants, and that savings accumulated by a migrant at destination is an important factor.

Comparing the labor outcomes of youth returnees back home to those of youth nonmigrants is complicated by the double selectivity of returning (migration self-selection and return self-selection). To adjust for these differences in characteristics between returned labor migrants and nonmigrants, we trim the sample using the approach of Crump et al. (2009) discussed in the previous section. On the basis of this approach, we trim out 33 percent of observations. Given that we are also interested in comparing the labor outcomes of nonmigrants to those of returnees from the three destination types, we repeat the trimming exercise with each appropriate subsample. The subsample of returnees from internal destinations has a small number of observations.[7] Hence, the results from comparing the labor outcomes of nonmigrants to those of returnees from internal destinations should be viewed with caution.

Table 5.8 presents the average labor outcomes of male youth nonmigrants, and the difference in average labor outcomes for male youth returnees, in the relevant trimmed samples. Returnees are 12 percentage points less likely to be employed than nonmigrants. Conditional on working, returnees work 15 percent fewer hours on average, are 9 percentage points more likely to be self-employed in agriculture, and are 6 percentage points less likely to be engaged in services than nonmigrants.

The overall results are driven by returnees from external destinations. Labor market integration appears to be weaker for returnees from other external destinations (that is, other than India) than other returnees. Returnees from other external destinations are 23 percentage points less likely to be employed than nonmigrants. Conditional on working, such returnees are 24 percentage points less likely to be wage employed, are 10 percentage points less likely to be engaged in services, and work 25 percent fewer hours on average than nonmigrants. The weak labor market integration of returnees from other external destinations may be because these returnees expect to migrate for labor again soon. Our data do not allow us to distinguish between those whose return is temporary and those whose return is more permanent.

The outcomes for returnees may be poorer than those for nonmigrants because the former recently returned and therefore may not have had sufficient time to reintegrate into the local labor market. We investigate whether the labor outcomes of recent returnees (those who returned less than a year ago) differ from the outcomes of returnees who have been back home for a longer period.

TABLE 5.8 **Labor outcomes of returned labor migrants relative to nonmigrants, male youth, trimmed sample, 2010–11**

Ordinary least squares and binomial logit estimations, average marginal effects

			CONDITIONAL ON EMPLOYMENT				CONDITIONAL ON WAGE EMPLOYMENT
	EMPLOYED	WAGE EMPLOYED	SELF-EMPLOYED IN AG.	EMPLOYED IN INDUSTRY	EMPLOYED IN SERVICES	LOG HOURS WORKED	LOG WAGE EARNINGS
	(1)	(2)	(3)	(4)	(5)	(6)	(7)
Return migrant	-0.122***	-0.041	0.088***	0.036	-0.95***	-0.149***	-0.036
	(0.025)	(0.033)	(0.031)	(0.023)	(0.026)	(0.051)	(0.099)
a. By time of return							
Returned in the past year	-0.152***	-0.037	0.096**	-0.005	-0149**	-0.245***	-0.099
	(0.034)	(0.051)	(0.043)	(0.039)	(0.060)	(0.094)	(0.112)
Returned over a year ago	-0.095***	-0.052	0.088**	-0.007	-0.084**	-0.108***	-0.026
	(0.028)	(0.038)	(0.035)	(0.032)	(0.036)	(0.054)	(0.084)
b. By return destination							
From internal destinations	-0.056	0.075	-0.048	0.126***	-0.044	-0.058	-0.016
	(0.053)	(0.063)	(0.050)	(0.039)	(0.054)	(0.123)	(0.104)
From India	-0.072**	0.085**	0.082**	0.020	-0.034	-0.133**	-0.093
	(0.034)	(0.036)	(0.040)	(0.030)	(0.037)	(0.065)	(0.103)
From other external destinations	-0.225***	-0.236***	0.210***	-0.014	-0.096**	-0.245***	0.105
	(0.034)	(0.063)	(0.049)	(0.039)	(0.043)	(0.090)	(0.178)
Observations	1,383	1,000	1,000	1,000	1,000	1,000	357

Source: Estimated using data from the 2010–11 Nepal Living Standards Survey (NLSS).

Note: A returned labor migrant is defined as an individual ages 16–34 years who migrated for labor for at least two consecutive months in the five years before the 2010–11 NLSS was administered to the household, but was present in the household at the time of the survey. The propensity score trimmed sample only includes observations with predicted values between 0.1 and 0.9 in a household-level labor migration logit regression. All outcome regressions control for the individual's age, marital status, schooling status, education level, and ethnicity/caste; whether the individual has a chronic illness or disability; whether the individual was ill in the last 30 days; whether the individual is poor; community amenities and access to roads; the share of household heads employed in agriculture in the primary sampling unit (PSU); and region identifiers. Robust standard errors, clustered at the PSU level, are reported in parentheses. Estimates are adjusted for sampling weights.

*p<0.1, **p<0.05, ***p<0.01.

We find that recent returnees are 15 percentage points less likely to be employed than nonmigrants, while other returnees are 10 percentage points less likely to be employed. Both differences with nonmigrants are statistically significant. Also, recent returnees work 25 percent fewer hours on average than nonmigrants (who work on average 37 hours a week), whereas other returnees work 11 percent fewer hours on average than nonmigrants. The differences with nonmigrants are statistically significant for both types of returnees. In sum, the labor supply of returnees, at both the intensive and extensive margins, is significantly lower than for nonmigrants, even for returnees who have been back home for a relatively long period.

CONCLUSION

Standard economic theory posits that earnings differentials between home and potential destination influence the labor migration decision. Youth in Nepal tend to leave more agricultural communities, presumably for remunerative employment opportunities elsewhere. A large majority of labor migrants are wage-employed in services, whereas a large share of youth who did not migrate for labor is self-employed in agriculture. Low household income is an important correlate of labor migration to India, suggesting that poorer households may use such labor migration as a strategy to cope with chronic economic distress or temporary income shortfalls, such as during the agricultural slack season. The predominance of India as a labor migration destination among poorer households may also be due to financial constraints because migration to India is relatively low cost compared to the cost of migration to other external destinations. Additionally, the low, fixed cost of labor migration to India makes circular or seasonal migration more affordable, which may explain the higher return rate observed for labor migrants to India.

Further analysis of the gains and costs of internal and external labor migration for Nepalese youth would benefit from the systematic collection of representative data on labor migrants at destination, including data on labor earnings, working and living conditions, and contract and employer characteristics. Such data could be gathered from cross-sectional surveys conducted at main destinations of labor migrants, or from panel data in which Nepalese youth are tracked over time (with continued tracking at destination for those who migrate).

Although Nepal has laws and institutions to regulate the foreign employment process for external destinations other than India, there are indications that the process is not sufficiently safe, efficient, or economical for workers. The design of sound interventions to improve the foreign employment process will require primary data and diagnostic research on several, interrelated issues. These include (1) the characteristics, motives, and practices of individual agents; (2) the structure, workings, and evolution of the worker-individual agent market, and likewise for the agent-agency market, with a focus on how information on the quality of workers, agents, and agencies is exchanged and how service prices are set—and what these imply for the welfare of workers, agents, and agencies; (3) the search and matching process that workers follow to link with an agent and, in turn, an agency; (4) the perceptions that workers hold about the gains and risks of seeking foreign employment through agents and agencies; (5) the efficiency and effectiveness of interventions to train workers for foreign employment; and (6) the efficiency and effectiveness of formal grievance redressal mechanisms.

On the basis of available documentation, data, and analysis, we find that Nepal's management of the foreign employment process could benefit from efforts to (1) improve the performance of formal grievance redressal systems for workers, (2) make the agent market more open and competitive, (3) provide crucial information to prospective workers on the migration process and related expected costs and benefits, and (4) detect, punish, and debar agents and agencies that engage in fraudulent or exploitative transactions with workers.

The evidence suggests that some groups are much less likely to migrate for labor, which indicates low gains, or high barriers or costs, for these groups. The low rates of labor migration by female youth to external and internal destinations are particularly striking. Globally, female labor migration has been increasing. However, the risk of abuse and exploitation is perceived to be higher for female than male labor migrants. This concern accounts in part for the low rate of female labor migration from Nepal to external destinations. Some bilateral labor agreements between Nepal and destination countries explicitly restrict female labor migration to prevent abuses. Female youth labor migration rates to India and to internal destinations also remain very low, despite the absence of formal restrictions. Thus, there is a need to better understand the factors, both drivers and barriers, associated with female labor migration.

Our analysis of returned labor migrants shows that integration into the home labor market appears to be weak. This may be due to constraints on, or choices made by, the returned labor migrant. More investigation is required to develop interventions to effectively leverage returned labor migrants' work experience, financial capital, labor skills, and other competencies they may have acquired at destination. One way to gather data on the labor outcomes of returnees would be through a more detailed module in household sample surveys, one that directly questions household members who have returned from external and internal labor migration.

Reintegration programs may help returned labor migrants obtain productive, remunerative employment at home. One of the more comprehensive programs is the Overseas Foreign Worker Reintegration Program in the Philippines. The program provides services and assistance to the labor migrant and his or her family through the entire cycle—that is, from prior to departure, to destination, through the worker's time at destination, and upon the worker's return—to help him or her reintegrate into the home community and labor market. Labor market reintegration services include skill training, credit, and guidance for self- or wage-employment activities (Go 2012). Some programs have aimed to better recognize the skills and competencies that labor migrants acquire at destination. Rigorous evidence is lacking on the effectiveness of such reintegration programs in general.

It may be worth considering policies and programs that aim to increase the gains and reduce the costs of labor migration, tailored by destination type (internal, India, and other external). Presently, labor migrants to internal destinations or to India tend to find employment at destination through informal channels, whereas labor migrants to other external destinations tend to use private recruitment agencies to find employment at destination. The government could facilitate by providing prospective labor migrants with regular, reliable, and relevant information on employment opportunities at destination, through easily accessible channels such as mobile phone-based portals. At the same time, it could provide prospective employers at destination with information on prospective labor migrants. Evidence for Nepal shows that labor migrants adjust their beliefs and decisions according to information about employment risks and conditions at destination (Shrestha 2017b). Similarly, evidence from the Philippines indicates that information gathered at fairs organized for rural workers to obtain domestic or international employment influences decisions on type and location of employment (Beam 2016).

Government facilitation could also take the form of small cash transfers to incentivize labor migration. Even transfers of a relatively small amount of money have been shown to facilitate labor migration and raise household welfare in Bangladesh (Bryan, Chowdhury, and Mobarak 2014). Such facilitation may help socioeconomically disadvantaged groups overcome information, skill, or financial constraints to labor migration, potentially boosting the efficiency and equity gains from labor migration.

NOTES

1. As an exception, foreign employment worker recruitment for the Republic of Korea is handled by the Nepal Ministry of Labor and Employment, and private recruitment agencies are not allowed to engage in this activity.
2. Landholding households on average own 0.7 hectare of agricultural land.
3. As a caveat, the statistic does not provide information on (1) the length of time it takes for many cases to be settled (some end up being carried over for years); (2) the outcomes of the settled cases (the tribunal does not make this information public); and (3) whether the settlements were in fact adhered to by the parties, given the tribunal's limited enforcement capacity (Paoletti et al. 2014).
4. However, only 12 percent of respondents knew the airfare, and fewer than 10 percent knew the visa cost.
5. Data in this section are from the International Monetary Fund's Regional Economic Outlook page: see http://www.imf.org/external/pubs/ft/survey/so/2016/car042516c.htm.
6. The country also experienced several aftershocks, including one with a magnitude of 7.3, on May 12, 2015.
7. Trimmed sample sizes for the analysis: (1) analysis of all returnees: 418 returnees and 1,298 stayers; (2) analysis of returnees from internal destinations: 75 returnees and 1,298 stayers; (3) analysis of returnees from India: 198 returnees and 1,298 stayers; (4) analysis of returnees from other external destinations: 145 returnees and 1,298 stayers.

REFERENCES

Acosta, Pablo. 2006. "Labor Supply, School Attendance, and Remittances from International Migration: The Case of El Salvador." Policy Research Working Paper 3903, World Bank, Washington DC.

Amuedo-Dorantes, Catalina, and Susan Pozo. 2006. "Migration, Remittances, and Male and Female Employment Patterns." *American Economic Review* 96 (2): 222–26.

Bansak, Cynthia, and Brian Chezum. 2009. "How Do Remittances Affect Human Capital Formation of School-Age Boys and Girls?" *American Economic Review* 99 (2): 145–48.

Beam, Emily A. 2016. "Do Job Fairs Matter? Experimental Evidence on the Impact of Job-Fair Attendance." *Journal of Development Economics* 120 (C): 32–40.

Becker, Charles M., Erbolat N. Musabek, Ai-Gul S. Seitenova, and Dina S. Urzhumova. 2005. "The Migration Response to Economic Shock: Lessons from Kazakhstan." *Journal of Comparative Economics* 33 (1): 107–32.

Bhandari, Prem. 2004. "Relative Deprivation and Migration in an Agricultural Setting of Nepal." *Population and Environment* 25 (5): 475–99.

Bryan, Gharad, Shyamal Chowdhury, and Ahmed Mushfiq Mobarak. 2014. "Under-Investment in a Profitable Technology: The Case of Seasonal Migration in Bangladesh." *Econometrica* 82 (5): 1671–1748.

Crump, Richard, Joseph Hotz, Guido Imbens, and Oscar Mitnik. 2009. "Dealing with Limited Overlap in Estimation of Average Treatment Effects." *Biometrika* 96 (1): 187–99

De Brauw, Alan, and John Giles. 2012. "Migrant Labor Markets and the Welfare of Rural Households in the Developing World: Evidence from China." Discussion Paper 6765, Institute for the Study of Labor, Bonn.

Devadason, Evelyn. S., and Chan W. Meng. 2014. "Policies and Laws Regulating Migrant Workers in Malaysia: A Critical Appraisal." *Journal of Contemporary Asia* 44 (1): 19–35.

Dustmann, Christian, and Oliver Kirchkamp. 2002. "The Optimal Migration Duration and Activity Choice after Remigration." *Journal of Development Economics* 67 (2): 351–72.

Gaurab, K. C. 2014. "The Cultural and Economics Imaginaries of Migration." Research Paper 5, Center for the Study of Labour and Mobility, Kathmandu.

Go, Stella P. 2012. *The Philippines and Return Migration: Rapid Appraisal of the Return and Reintegration Policies and Service Delivery*. Manila: International Labour Organization.

Government of Nepal. 2011. *Nepal Living Standards Survey 2010/11: Statistical Report, Volume 1.* Kathmandu: Central Bureau of Statistics, Government of Nepal.

ILO (International Labour Organization). 2016. *Labour Migration for Employment: A Status Report for Nepal, 2014/15*. Kathmandu: International Labour Organization.

Lokshin, Michael, and Elena Glinskaya. 2009. "The Effect of Male Migration on Employment Patterns of Women in Nepal." *World Bank Economic Review* 23 (3) 481–507.

Maharjan Amina, Seigfried Bauer, and Beatrice Knerr. 2013. "Migration for Labor and Its Impact on Farm Production in Nepal." Working Paper IV, Center for the Study of Labor and Mobility, Kathmandu.

Massey, Douglas S., William G. Axinn, and Dirgha J. Ghimire. 2010. "Environmental Change and Out-Migration: Evidence from Nepal." *Population and Environment* 32 (2–3): 109–36.

McCormick, Barry, and Jackeline Wahba. 2001. "Overseas Work Experience, Savings and Entrepreneurship Amongst Return Migrants to LDCs." *Scottish Journal of Political Economy* 48 (2): 164–78.

Mesnard, Alice. 2004. "Temporary Migration and Capital Market Imperfections." *Oxford Economic Papers* 56 (2): 242–62.

Naidu, Suresh, Yaw Nyarko, and Shing-Yi Wang. 2016. "Monopsony Power in Migrant Labor Markets: Evidence from the United Arab Emirates." *Journal of Political Economy*, 124 (6): 1735–92.

Paoletti, Sarah, Eleanor Taylor-Nicholson, Bandita Sijapati, and Bassina Farbenblum. 2014. *Migrant Workers' Access to Justice at Home: Nepal*. New York: Open Society Foundation.

Phadera, Lokendra. 2016. "International Migration and Its Effect on Labor Supply of the Left-Behind Household Members: Evidence from Nepal." Paper prepared for the 2016 Annual Meeting of the Agricultural and Applied Economics Association, Boston, July 31–August 2.

Regmi, Madhav, Krishna Paudel, and Deborah Williams. 2014. "Push and Pull Factors Associated with Migration in Nepal: An Economic Perspective." Paper presented at the Agricultural and Applied Economics Association Annual Meeting, Minneapolis, July 27–29.

Reinhold, Steffen, and Kevin Thom. 2013. "Migration Experience and Earnings in the Mexican Labor Market." *Journal of Human Resources* 48 (3): 768–820.

Sharma, Sanjay, Shibani Pandey, Dinesh Pathak, and Bimbika Sijapati-Basnett. 2014. *State of Migration in Nepal*. Kathmandu: Center for the Study of Labor and Mobility.

Shrestha, Maheshwor. 2017a. "Push and Pull: A Study of International Migration from Nepal." Policy Research Working Paper 7965, World Bank, Washington, DC.

——. 2017b. "Death Scares: How Potential Work-Migrants Infer Mortality Rates from Migrant Deaths." Policy Research Working Paper 7946, World Bank, Washington, DC.

——. 2017c. "Get Rich or Die Tryin': Perceived Earnings, Perceived Mortality Rate and the Value of a Statistical Life of Potential Work-Migrants from Nepal." Policy Research Working Paper 7945, World Bank, Washington, DC.

——. 2017d. "The Impact of Large-Scale Migration on Poverty, Expenditures, and Labor Market Outcomes in Nepal." Policy Research Working Paper 8232, World Bank, Washington, DC.

Shrestha, Sundar, and Prem Bhandari. 2007. "Environmental Security and Labor Migration in Nepal." *Population and Environment* 29 (1): 25–38.

Sjaastad, Larry. 1962. "The Costs and Returns of Human Migration." *Journal of Political Economy* 70 (4, supplement): 80–93.

Thieme, Susan, and Simone Wyss. 2005. "Migration Patterns and Remittance Transfer in Nepal: A Case Study." *International Migration* 43 (5): 59–98.

Wahba, Jackline. 2015. "Selection, Selection, Selection: Labor Market Impact of Return." *Journal of Population Economics* 28 (3): 535–63.

World Bank. 2011. *Large-Scale Migration and Remittance in Nepal: Issues, Challenges and Opportunities.* Report No. 55390-NP. Washington DC: World Bank.

WFP (World Food Programme). 2008. *Passage to India: Migration as a Coping Strategy in Times of Crisis in Nepal.* Kathmandu: World Food Program.

Yang, Dean. 2008. "International Migration, Remittances and Household Investment: Evidence from Philippine Migrants' Exchange Rate Shocks." *Economic Journal* 118 (528): 591–630.

6 Youth Labor Skill Training

DHUSHYANTH RAJU

INTRODUCTION

One of the main ways that the Nepal government intervenes in the labor market is by training workers.[1] The country's preference for training supply is reportedly motivated by at least three reasons. First, training is seen as appropriate, given the relatively low level of human capital acquisition in Nepal. As one measure, the average education attainment among individuals ages 16–34 years in 2010–11 was eight years. Second, training has attributes that make it attractive from both technical and political angles: it is visible, tangible, seemingly straightforward to design and administer, and relatively uncontentious (for example, in contrast to welfare programs). Third, international donors have driven the development of the country's training system and the expansion of training supply by providing funds and technical assistance (ADB 2004, 2013a; World Bank 2011, 2017). As a result, training has increased substantially in Nepal since its emergence over four decades ago and is now extensive.

Although training represents an important intervention in Nepal's labor and development space, little systematic empirical research exists on training in the country, such as on the drivers and barriers to training demand and supply, or on the labor market effects of training. The existing literature on the topic is mainly composed of basic descriptions of the structure and status of the training system, as presented in project documents of international donors (see, for example, ADB 2013a, 2013b; and World Bank 2011, 2017), or of statistical profiles of training providers and recipients based on administrative data in government reports (see, for example, Government of Nepal 2010).

In this study, we conduct a descriptive analysis of mainly formal, off-the-job training among youth. Youth is defined as individuals ages 16–34 years. Formal off-the-job training is defined as training through short-term training courses, or through vocational education tracks that confer a Technical School Leaving Certificate (TSLC) or a technical diploma.

We investigate several questions:

- What is the incidence (or rate) of training in Nepal, and how does it compare to rates in other countries in South Asia?
- How do training rates differ by the individual's gender, age, schooling status, and education attainment?
- How do training rates differ spatially, that is, between urban and rural areas, and among major regions in Nepal?
- What types of training do recipients obtain?
- How do training recipients differ from nonrecipients?
- Is training associated with employment and earnings outcomes?
- What are the levels, patterns, and correlates of interest in training?

To answer these questions, we use data from the 2008 Nepal Labour Force Survey (NLFS) and the 2013 Nepal School-to-Work Transition Survey (SWTS). Both household sample surveys are representative for Nepal and its six major regions. The NLFS is the latest available survey with data on whether the individual obtained any formal off-the-job training. It has a large sample size and data on a number of potentially relevant individual and household covariates. In comparison, the SWTS, to its advantage, gathered data on whether employed workers obtained on-the-job training. However, it gathered data only on whether the individual obtained off-the-job training through TSLC/technical diploma programs; it has a small sample size; and it has data on a small number of potentially relevant covariates. The SWTS also did not gather data from individuals older than age 29. Consequently, our analysis of training is mostly based on NLFS data.

In 2008, 10 percent of youth had obtained formal off-the-job training at some point. In 2013, a total of 6 percent of individuals ages 16–29 years obtained training through TSLC/technical diploma programs at some point, a substantial increase from 1.3 percent in 2008. In addition, in 2013, 10 percent of individuals ages 16–29 years obtained on-the-job training over the preceding year.

Training rates are higher for youth than nonyouth (ages 35–54 years), for urban residents than rural ones, and for individuals who have obtained at least a School Leaving Certificate (SLC). (The certificate is given to those who pass a national exam at the end of grade 10.) Gender differences in training rates are small, whereas differences between regions in Nepal are large. Training rates for Nepal tend to be higher than for Bangladesh, India, or Pakistan.

The fields with the greatest participation by female training recipients are basic computing and dressmaking/tailoring, whereas basic computing training has the most male recipients. Short-term training predominates; the median length of training is three months for rural recipients and six months for urban ones.

Training recipients are on average older, more educated, and more likely to be attending school. They tend to come from wealthier households and from traditionally advantaged ethnic or caste communities in the country, such as Brahmin/Chhetri or Newar. Urban training recipients are also less likely to come from the Terai and more likely to come from the Kathmandu Valley and the Hills. Those who obtained training in basic computing appear to be more advantaged in terms of education, wealth, and caste or ethnic affiliation than those who obtained training in other fields.

We examine the effects of training on various employment margins and wage earnings, adjusting for the individual's selection into training on the basis of essentially multiple regressions fitted to cross-sectional, observational data. In general, for women, training is associated with higher likelihoods of employment, wage work, and nonfarm work. Whether training effects for women are significant varies by selected sociodemographic and training subgroups, namely schooling status, education attainment, rural versus urban residence, short-term training versus TSLC/technical diploma programs, and training in basic computing versus other fields. For men, training does not appear to be associated with the examined employment margins. In addition, whether training effects are significant for men varies little for any of the examined sociodemographic and training subgroups.

In general, we do not find that training is positively associated with wage earnings for either gender. This finding contrasts with evidence from relatively rigorous evaluations by Chakravarty et al. (2015) and Bhatta et al. (2017), who find that selected short-term training interventions had significant positive effects on the labor earnings of socioeconomically disadvantaged groups in Nepal. We recognize that our empirical approach to identifying effects is weak. Notwithstanding, among other nonmethodological explanations, we posit that the general absence of effects on wage earnings that we find indicates that skills (on their own) may not be the main binding constraint on labor market success for disadvantaged individuals. It may (additionally) be a lack of financial and physical capital to invest in income-generating activities, as suggested by evidence from some recent evaluations of training and self-employment programs in other low-income countries (Blattman, Fiala, and Martinez 2014; Hicks et al. 2015) and by SWTS data for self-employed workers in Nepal.

Interest in training is high: 40 percent of youth express interest in obtaining training. Interest is particularly high in areas outside the Kathmandu Valley. For those interested in training, dressmaking/tailoring and basic computing garner the most interest among women, whereas men are most interested in basic computing. Other fields with significant interest include farming and livestock management and hairdressing/beautician services for women, and farming and livestock management, manufacturing and repair, and driving for men. In contrast to patterns for those who received training, interest in training is higher among younger and less wealthy individuals. Interest in training is also higher among those who have already obtained training, and among those already employed. Those already trained tend to be interested in training in the same field, which may signal demand for upskilling. Unemployed workers tend to view their education as relevant but inadequate and to view higher education and training through TSLC/technical diploma programs, training in computing, and on-the-job apprenticeships as useful for obtaining work.

The remaining sections of the chapter are organized as follows: The next section presents background information on the formal, off-the-job training system in Nepal. The subsequent section discusses the data and samples for the analysis. Then the next three sections, respectively, present results on the levels, patterns, and correlates of training; the effects of training on labor market outcomes; and the levels, patterns, and correlates of interest in training, as well as on worker perceptions of training in relation to employment. The final section concludes by discussing the implications of our findings for training research and policy, with respect to effectiveness, efficiency, and equity.

NEPAL'S TRAINING SYSTEM

Nepal has offered formal training programs for workers for more than four decades. Tribhuvan University, the country's first university, has provided training in engineering, agriculture, livestock, forestry, and medicine since the late 1960s. The first independent technical institute was established in 1980 (ADB 2015).

The Nepal government has passed a number of major policies on training over the years. These include the Council for Technical Education and Vocational Training (CTEVT) Act of 1989 (amended in 1993), the National Technical and Vocational Education and Training Sectoral Policy of 1999, the Technical Education and Vocational Training and Skills Development Policy of 2007, and the Nepal Technical and Vocational Education and Training Policy of 2012. As a primary goal, all these policies call for a major expansion of training supply. Other government policies, plans, and documents—such as the National Planning Commission's periodic development plans and the Ministry of Youth and Sports' National Youth Policy of 2015 and Youth Vision 2025—also call for expanding training supply and see training as a critical instrument for improving the country's economy (ADB 2015; Government of Nepal 2015a, 2015b, 2017; World Bank 2017).

In a pivotal move, the government in 1989 established CTEVT to formulate policies and plans and to coordinate, supply, and assure the quality of training. CTEVT has its own technical institutes, and it also accredits private technical institutes (ADB 2015).

Nepalese workers have three main training options: (1) programs that confer a TSLC, (2) programs that confer a technical diploma, and (3) short-term training courses or events that confer a training completion certificate. CTEVT and private technical institutes offer TSLC/technical diploma programs. A few community secondary schools also offer TSLC programs, which are managed by CTVET.

Short-term training courses are offered by various providers, including CTEVT and private technical institutes, departments under different government ministries, industry associations, nongovernmental organizations, and civil society organizations (ADB 2015; World Bank 2011, 2017). Government entities that offer short-term training courses include

- Directorates of Agricultural Training and Animal Health under the Ministry of Agricultural Development;
- Nepal Academy of Science and Technology;
- Nepal Academy of Tourism and Hotel Management under the Ministry of Culture, Tourism, and Civil Aviation;
- Local Development Training Academy under the Ministry of Federal Affairs and Local Development;
- Youth and Small Entrepreneur Self-Employment Fund under the Ministry of Finance;
- Department of Cottage and Small Industries and the Cottage and Small Industry Development Committee under the Ministry of Industry;
- Vocational Skills Development Training Directorate under the Ministry of Labor and Employment;
- Ministry of Peace and Reconstruction;
- Mechanical Training Center under the Department of Roads, Ministry of Physical Infrastructure and Transport;

- Cottage and Small Industry Development Board; and
- Industrial Enterprise Development Institute.

For entry into TSLC programs, individuals must have completed grade 10 or passed the SLC exam, which is a national academic exam that students take at the end of grade 10. For grade 10 completers, programs are 29 months long, whereas for SLC holders, programs are either 15 or 18 months long. For entry into technical diploma programs, individuals must have obtained the SLC. These programs are typically three years long. The main TSLC/technical diploma programs are in the fields of agriculture, engineering, and health (ADB 2015; World Bank 2011, 2017).

For entry into short-term training courses, individuals must be at least age 16. Other than that, entry qualifications differ greatly. Some training courses do not require any academic qualifications, whereas some others require completing grade 8 or certification in lower-level training (World Bank 2017). Short-term training courses typically range in length from a few days to 10 months (ADB 2015).

Irrespective of how their skills were acquired, individuals can choose to get certified by taking occupational skill tests administered by the National Skills Testing Board (NSTB) under CTEVT.

Training has expanded substantially over time (ADB 2004, 2013a, 2013b, 2015; World Bank 2011, 2017). In 2009–10, some 25,000 individuals participated in TSLC/technical diploma programs, and another 60,000 individuals participated in short-term training courses. In comparison, in the early 2000s, the estimated annual enrollment capacity in all training programs and courses was 50,000. Between 2000 and 2010, the number of short-term training courses grew from 45 to more than 225. The number of private technical institutes increased from less than a handful in 1990 to more than 100 in 2000, and to more than 400 in 2010. Individuals tested and certified by NSTB increased almost tenfold over the late 2000s.

Much of the country's developments and activities in the training space have been driven by significant, sustained financial and technical support from international donors, mainly the Asian Development Bank (ADB), the Swiss Agency for Development and Cooperation (SDC), and the World Bank, starting as far back as the early 1990s (ADB 2015; World Bank 2017).

Nepal's training system is perceived to perform poorly. Project documents by international donors report that training is marked by insufficient and inequitable access, poor quality, and low market relevance. These issues are thought to be linked to poor capacity to deliver training. As suggestive evidence of issues with training quality and relevance, a 2012 labor demand survey of a sample of employers in construction, service, and manufacturing subsectors found that only about one-half of employers viewed TSLC/technical diploma holders as adequately prepared (ADB 2013a). What is more, the issues with training appear to be chronic (for example, compare the description of the issues in ADB 2004 to that in ADB 2013b).

Initiatives have been introduced at different levels aimed at improving the supply of training. They have included

- Offering training to administrators, instructors, and assessors;
- Developing course curricula;
- Constructing or rehabilitating facilities;
- Purchasing machinery, equipment, and materials for courses;

- Conducting rapid labor demand assessments;
- Hiring training providers through a competitive bidding process;
- Contracting providers to offer training on vocational and life skills, post-training services such as job counseling and placement services, and training in hard-to-reach villages through a community-based model; and
- Paying providers for their services partly conditional on training-recipient employment and minimum earning requirements (ADB 2013a, 2013b; World Bank 2011, 2017).

Initiatives have also been introduced to encourage demand for training. They have included

- Providing free or subsidized training; and
- Providing stipends, scholarships, and transportation benefits conditional on minimum attendance and learning requirements.

Traditionally disadvantaged groups—such as women, the poor, or members from the Dalit community—receive preferential treatment (benefit from affirmative action) in terms of admission into training programs and eligibility for training program benefits (ADB 2013a, 2013b; World Bank 2011, 2017).

DATA

Our main data source is the 2008 NLFS (Government of Nepal 2009). The household survey is representative at the national level, as well as for six regions within the country (Kathmandu Valley, urban Hills, urban Terai, rural Hills, rural Terai, and Mountains). With respect to training, the NLFS asked questions on whether the individual obtained any formal off-the-job training, through either short-term training courses or TSLC/technical diploma programs, as well as what field the training was in and how long it took. The survey also asked whether the individual is interested in training and, if yes, what specific field he or she is interested in. All the training questions are separate questions in the education module, and they were posed to individuals ages 14 years and above.

The NLFS is the latest available survey with data on total formal off-the-job training. The survey also has other advantages, such as its large sample size and its data on a number of potentially relevant individual and household covariates.

Our secondary data source is the 2013 Nepal SWTS (Serriere and CEDA 2014). This household survey is representative at the national level, and for the same six regions as the NLFS. Only individuals ages 15–29 years were interviewed. With respect to training, the SWTS included technical education at the secondary and postsecondary levels—that is, TSLC/technical diploma programs—as response options to questions on the current level of education for those attending school or the highest level of education for those who have completed their schooling. The SWTS also asked questions about on-the-job training in the last year to employed workers (39 percent of individuals), and views on the value of education and training to unemployed workers (9 percent of individuals).[2] However, our analysis using the SWTS data is limited because of the survey's small sample size and less extensive data on potentially relevant individual and household covariates.

As an important caveat, both the NLFS and SWTS gathered training data only from individuals residing in the household at the time of the respective survey. Nepal has experienced substantial labor migration, mostly by young men, to other countries and regions such as India, Malaysia, and the Middle East. Eighteen percent of Nepalese young men (and 1 percent of young women) were absent from their households and employed in other countries, according to the 2010–11 Nepal Living Standards Survey. Reflecting this, the estimated sex ratio for individuals ages 15–34 years—based on 2011 National Population Census data—is 85 men per 100 women (Government of Nepal 2012). As chapter 5 shows, young men who are present in households systematically differ in characteristics from young men who are absent. Thus, our analysis of training for young men who are present may be biased relative to all young Nepalese men.

PATTERNS AND CORRELATES OF TRAINING

Training rates

The 2013 SWTS data show that 6 percent of individuals ages 16–29 years obtained training through TSLC/technical diploma programs. The rates of such training are comparable between urban and rural residents. Using data on training length in the 2008 NLFS, we indirectly estimate the share of individuals ages 16–29 years who obtained training through TSLC/technical diploma programs to be 1.3 percent. Thus, it appears that the rate of training through these tracks increased approximately fourfold over the five-year period from 2008 to 2013. The large increase is consistent with the increase in training enrollment (capacity) presented in the section titled "Nepal's Training System."

SWTS data also show that 10 percent of employed workers ages 16–29 years report that they received on-the-job training in the last year. Another 5 percent of employed workers report that they obtained off-the-job training, mainly in vocational trades, basic computing, and basic business and accounting. The on-the-job training rate for employed workers is higher in rural than urban areas (11 percent versus 7 percent). On-the-job training rates appear to be similar between wage and self-employed workers.

On the basis of NLFS data, we find that 10 percent of youth (ages 16–34 years) obtained formal off-the-job training. In the rest of this section, we examine training patterns using these data.

Patterns in training rates

Figure 6.1 shows training rates, separately for youth and nonyouth (ages 35–54 years) age cohorts. For Nepal, the training rate is 10 percent for youth and 6 percent for nonyouth. Training rates among youth range from 6 percent for rural women to 21 percent for urban men, whereas among nonyouth they range from 3 percent for rural women to 13 percent for urban men.

Multiple factors may explain the difference in training rates between youth and nonyouth. On the supply side, training supply has increased over time. Thus, current youth enjoy a higher supply than the nonyouth did when they were younger. Training supply also often by design targets youth. On the demand side, those who are making the transition from school to work or who are seeking greater labor market returns by shifting between work activities tend to be

FIGURE 6.1

Training rates, by gender and by urban versus rural, 2008

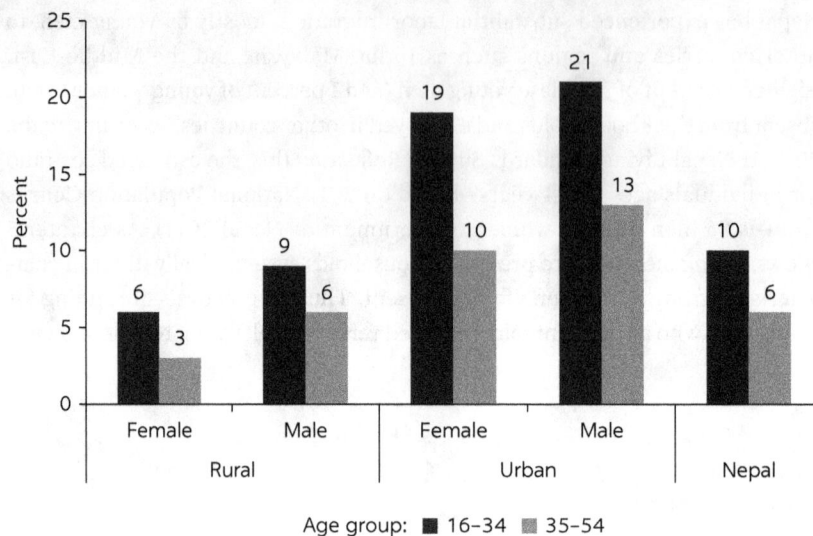

Source: Estimated using 2008 Nepal Labour Force Survey data.
Note: All estimates are adjusted for sampling weights.

youth, and they are more likely to seek training than those who have stable work, who tend to be nonyouth.

Youth training rates are markedly higher in urban areas than rural ones. For example, for women, the youth training rate is 19 percent in urban areas and 6 percent in rural areas. Youth training rates are slightly lower for women than men. For example, in rural areas, the youth training rate is 6 percent for women and 9 percent for men. In the rest of this section, all statistics are for youth only.

Figure 6.2 compares youth training rates in Nepal to rates for three other South Asia countries: Bangladesh, India, and Pakistan. The data for India and Pakistan allow us to construct identical training indicators to those for Nepal, specifically whether or not the individual ever obtained any formal off-the-job training. The data for Bangladesh allow us to construct a training indicator only for whether or not the individual obtained any formal off-the-job training *in the last year*. The period-limited indicator for Bangladesh would work in favor of Nepal exhibiting higher rates. In contrast, the data for India and Pakistan are more recent than for Nepal, which would work against Nepal exhibiting higher rates if training markets have expanded in all countries.

With these caveats in mind, we find that training rates for Nepal are mostly higher than for other countries. At the country level, the training rate for Nepal (10 percent) is slightly higher than for Bangladesh and Pakistan (8 percent each), and considerably higher than for India (3 percent). In each of the gender-by-location subgroups, the rates for Nepal are either highest or second highest relative to the other countries. The contrast is most notable for urban women: Nepal has the highest rate at 19 percent, followed next by Bangladesh, with a rate less than half Nepal's, at 9 percent.

Figure 6.3 shows training rates across regions in Nepal. The most striking pattern is the higher rates in urban regions than rural ones. For example,

FIGURE 6.2

Training rates for Nepal versus other South Asian countries, individuals ages 16–34 years

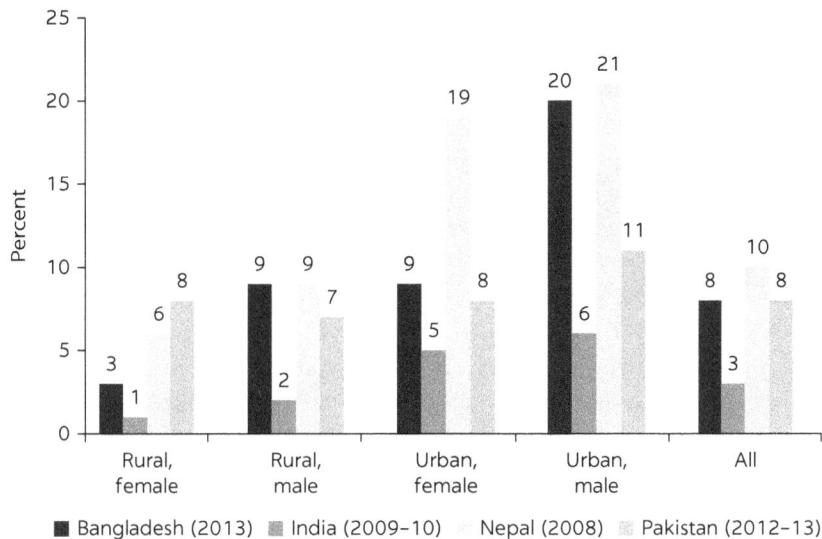

Source: Estimated using labor force survey data for Nepal (2008), Bangladesh (2013), and Pakistan (2012–13), and data from India's National Sample Survey, 66th round (2009–10).
Note: All estimates are adjusted for sampling weights.

FIGURE 6.3

Training rates, by region, individuals ages 16–34 years, 2008

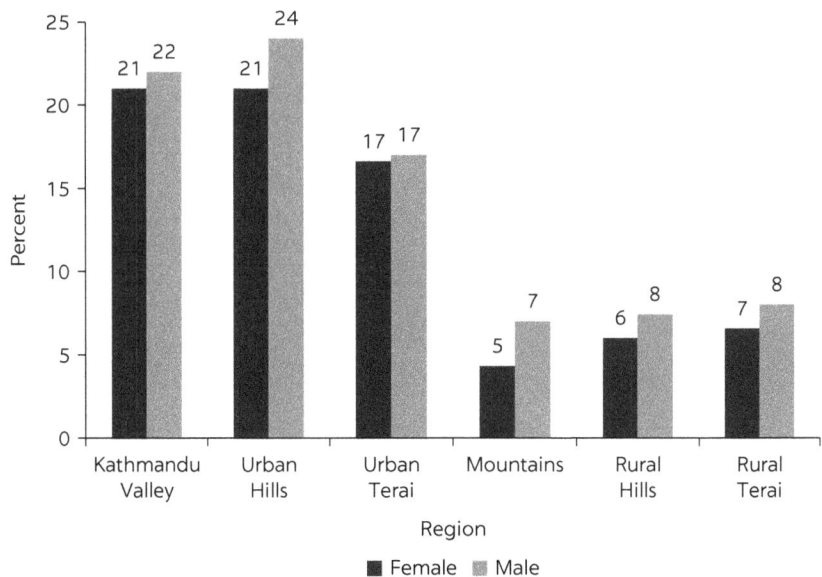

Source: Estimated using 2008 Nepal Labour Force Survey data.
Note: All estimates are adjusted for sampling weights.

for women, training rates range from 17 percent to 21 percent in urban regions, compared to 5 percent to 7 percent in rural regions. Among urban regions, rates in the Terai are lower than in the Kathmandu Valley and the Hills. For example, for women, it is 17 percent in the Terai compared to 21 percent in the Kathmandu Valley and the Hills.

Figure 6.4 shows training–age profiles. Figure 6.5 shows training–schooling status (panel a) and training–education attainment profiles (panel b). We treat the profiles as reflecting the "timing" of training uptake in relation to age, schooling status, and education attainment. The profiles are imperfect, however, because information on these variables was not captured in relation to the timing of training but only as of the time of the survey.

The training–age profiles display a weak, inverted-U shape. Training rates rise with age over the late teens and early twenties before falling over the late twenties and early thirties. This pattern is more discernible in the urban profiles. Training rates are higher for those who are attending school than for those who have completed their schooling. The rates range from 9 percent for rural women to 26 percent for urban men who are attending school, whereas they range from 6 percent for rural women to 18 percent for urban men who have completed their schooling. The training–education attainment profiles display a convex shape. Training rates are flat at relatively low levels, and then rise sharply when individuals have obtained the SLC.

Multiple factors may explain this pattern of change in the training–education attainment profiles. On the supply side, entry into at least TSLC/technical diploma programs requires that the individual has completed grade 10 or obtained the SLC. On the demand side, individuals may seek training upon leaving school in order to improve their labor market prospects. The rate of school exits increases sharply upon completing grade 10, obtaining the SLC, or completing grade 12 (intermediate education).

FIGURE 6.4

Training–age profiles, 2008

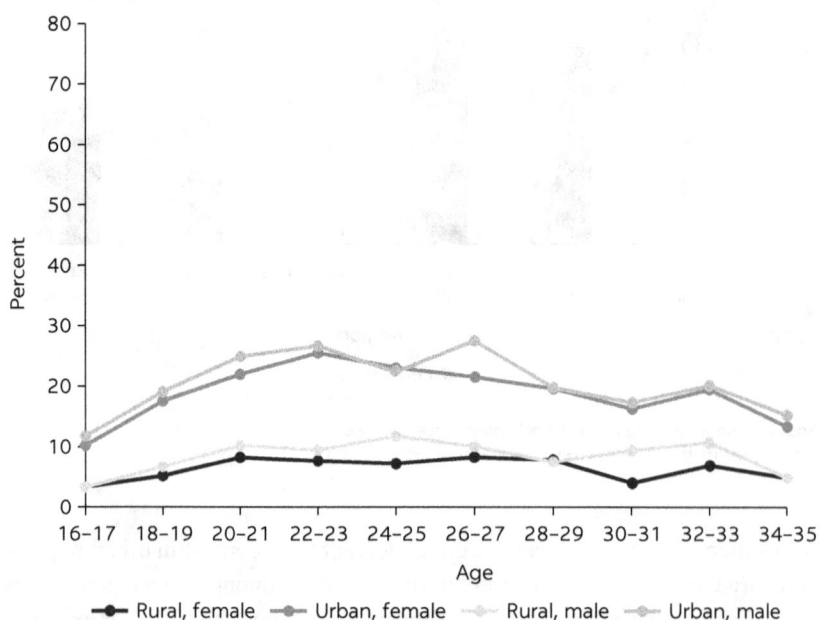

Source: Estimated using 2008 Nepal Labour Force Survey data.
Note: All estimates are adjusted for sampling weights.

FIGURE 6.5

Training-education profiles, individuals ages 16–34 years, 2008

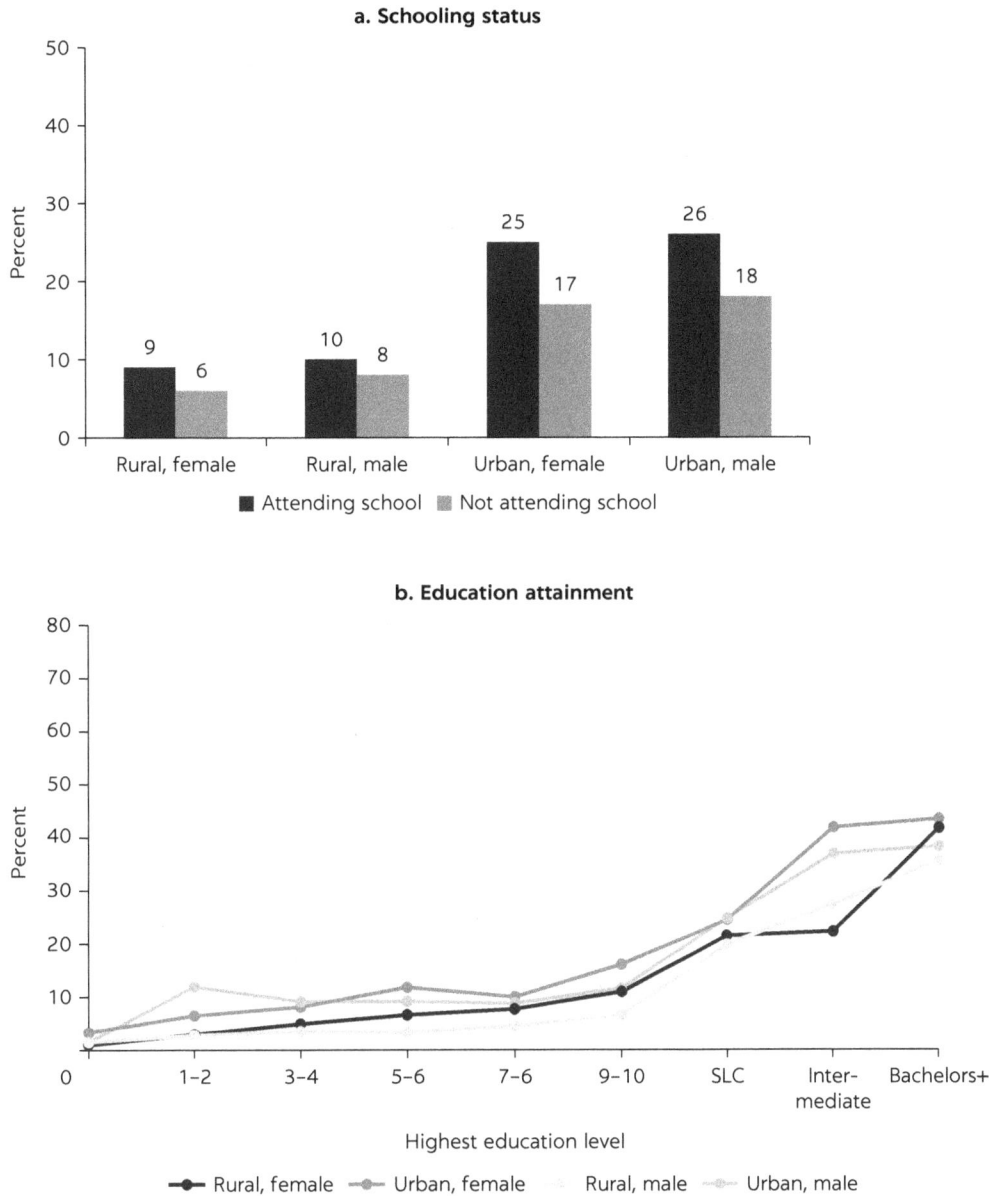

a. Schooling status

b. Education attainment

Source: Estimated using 2008 Nepal Labour Force Survey data.
Note: SLC = School Learning Certificate. All estimates are adjusted for sampling weights.

Training fields

Which fields are the most popular among training recipients? Table 6.1 reports the distribution of recipients by training field.[3] In urban areas, the most common field is basic computing (38 percent for female recipients and 57 percent for male recipients), followed by dressmaking/tailoring for female recipients (30 percent), and other service fields (such as food service, hotel service, tourism, and security) for male recipients (10 percent). In rural areas, the most common field for female recipients is dressmaking/tailoring (48 percent),

TABLE 6.1 **Distribution of training fields, individuals ages 16–34 years, 2008**

Percent

FIELD	RURAL		URBAN	
	FEMALE	MALE	FEMALE	MALE
	(1)	(2)	(3)	(4)
Teaching	6	4	3	2
Handicrafts	7	3	5	3
Fine and performing arts	0	0	2	2
Business and accounting	1	1	2	2
Basic computing	20	37	38	57
Health services	9	9	7	5
Construction	1	13	0	5
Dressmaking/tailoring	48	0	30	0
Small manufacturing and repair	1	10	1	7
Agriculture and livestock management	4	8	2	1
Driving and motor vehicle operation	0	11	0	8
Hairdressing/beautician services	3	0	8	0
Other service trades	1	5	2	10
Observations	426	353	1,272	1,198

Source: Estimated using 2008 Nepal Labour Force Survey data.
Note: All estimates are adjusted for sampling weights.

followed by basic computing (20 percent). As in urban areas, the most common field for male recipients in rural areas is basic computing (37 percent). However, the field distribution in rural areas is less skewed than in urban areas for male recipients. In rural areas, 13 percent of male recipients obtained training in construction, 11 percent in driving, 10 percent in small manufacturing and repair, and 9 percent in health care services.

Table 6.2 reports summary statistics for selected characteristics of recipients and their training by field. Generally consistent with traditional patterns of gender-dominated occupations, women made up most of the recipients of training in teaching, handicrafts, dressmaking/tailoring, and hairdressing/beautician services, whereas men made up most of the recipients of training in construction, small manufacturing and repair, driving, and other service fields. The majority of recipients of training in basic computing were attending school at the time of the survey, whereas the majority of recipients of training in other fields had completed their schooling. Recipients of training in teaching, basic computing, and health services are more likely to have obtained the SLC than recipients of training in other fields. These patterns generally hold for both rural and urban areas.

Short-term training, defined as training lasting less than 12 months, is the norm. With the exception of urban and rural recipients of training in health services and urban recipients of training in the fine and performing arts, the vast majority of recipients across fields obtained short-term training. The median length of training is typically one or three months across fields for rural

TABLE 6.2 **Characteristics of training recipients, by field, individuals ages 16–34 years, 2008**

FIELD	RURAL					URBAN				
	PERCENT FEMALE	PERCENT ATTENDING SCHOOL	PERCENT OBTAINED SLC	PERCENT SHORT-TERM COURSES	MEDIAN TRAINING LENGTH	PERCENT FEMALE	PERCENT ATTENDING SCHOOL	PERCENT OBTAINED SLC	PERCENT SHORT-TERM COURSES	MEDIAN TRAINING LENGTH
	(1)	(2)	(3)	(4)	(5)	(6)	(7)	(8)	(9)	(10)
Teaching	63	36	89	98	4	65	21	88	90	6
Handicrafts	76	6	21	100	3	68	23	43	92	6
Fine and performing arts	100	0	100	100	1	51	25	71	55	9
Business and accounting	43	25	43	100	1	48	34	84	96	2
Basic computing	39	72	94	91	3	41	73	95	92	3
Health services	54	19	60	46	15	63	40	86	33	15
Construction	12	13	37	91	3	9	29	54	84	6
Dressmaking/tailoring	91	8	19	94	3	90	14	38	95	3
Small manufacturing and repair	8	10	41	83	3	17	23	54	81	6
Agriculture and livestock management	40	12	40	85	1	58	28	58	85	1
Driving and motor vehicle operation	3	1	11	97	3	2	8	28	94	3
Hairdressing/beautician services	94	19	42	93	6	99	26	71	92	6
Other service fields	16	18	28	86	3	18	25	72	85	3

Source: Estimated using 2008 Nepal Labour Force Survey data.
Note: SLC = School Leaving Certificate. Short-term courses are defined as training of less than 12 months; training of one month or less was rounded up to one month. All estimates are adjusted for sampling weights.

recipients, whereas it is typically three or six months across fields for urban recipients. Training is longest in health care services, with a median length of 15 months. This is consistent with the length of TSLC programs to become a Community Medical Assistant, Lab Assistant, or Auxiliary Nurse Midwife, which last either 15 or 18 months. Training is shortest in basic business and accounting, and fine and performing arts for rural recipients, and in agriculture and livestock management for both rural and urban recipients, with a median length of one month or less.

Characteristics of training recipients

How do training recipients differ from nonrecipients? Table 6.3 reports pairwise differences in mean individual and household characteristics between nonrecipients and recipients. With respect to demographic characteristics, among urban women, recipients are less likely to be the household head or the head's spouse and more likely to be the child or grandchild of the household head than nonrecipients. Recipients are on average older and are less likely to be married than nonrecipients. Among men, recipients are less likely than nonrecipients to be born in the Village Development Committee or urban municipality where they reside; alternatively put, recipients are more likely than nonrecipients to be migrants. Among urban women, recipients are more likely than nonrecipients to be born in the Village Development Committee or urban municipality where they reside.

With respect to education, recipients are much more likely than nonrecipients to be attending school. In addition, they are, on average, much more educated than nonrecipients. The higher mean education attainment of recipients is also evident when we look at the share that has obtained the SLC.

With respect to household characteristics, among urban women, recipients are more likely than nonrecipients to come from households with absent members. Recipients are more likely than nonrecipients to come from households that have a benefactor from outside the household. Recipients are, on average, substantially wealthier than nonrecipients. Recipients differ from nonrecipients in terms of religion and caste and ethnic composition: they are more likely than nonrecipients to be Hindu and to come from the Brahmin/ Chhetri or Newar communities, and they are less likely than nonrecipients to come from the Terai middle caste and from the Dalit, Janajati, Muslim, and other caste communities.

Finally, with respect to location, among urban women, recipients are more likely to come from the Kathmandu Valley, and less likely to come from the Terai, than nonrecipients. Among urban men, recipients are more likely to come from the Hills, and less likely to come from the Terai, than nonrecipients.

The differences in mean characteristics between recipients and nonrecipients may themselves vary, depending on the training field. To examine if this is the case, we decompose training into main fields—specifically basic computing, dressmaking/tailoring, and all other fields—for female recipients and into basic computing and all other fields for male recipients. Table 6.4 reports pairwise differences in mean characteristics between recipients trained in a specific field (to whom we refer as "trainees" for short) and nonrecipients of training in any field ("nontrainees").

TABLE 6.3 **Differences in mean characteristics for training, recipients versus nonrecipients, individuals ages 16–34 years, 2008**

	RURAL				URBAN			
	FEMALE		MALE		FEMALE		MALE	
CHARACTERISTIC	NONRECIPIENTS MEAN	RECIPIENTS DIFF.	NONRECIPIENTS MEAN	RECIPIENTS DIFF.	NONRECIPIENTS MEAN	RECIPIENTS DIFF.	NONRECIPIENTS MEAN	RECIPIENTS DIFF.
	(1)	(2)	(3)	(4)	(5)	(6)	(7)	(8)
Rel. to head: Head	0.388	0.004	0.307	0.035	0.442	-0.068***	0.311	-0.018
Rel. to head: Spouse	0.282	-0.040*	0.007	0.005	0.310	-0.071***	0.022	-0.002
Rel. to head: Son/daughter (in law)	0.548	0.015	0.606	-0.052	0.451	0.045**	0.509	-0.010
Rel. to head: Grandchild	0.014	-0.007*	0.019	0.007	0.015	0.015*	0.018	0.000
Rel. to head: Other relative	0.044	-0.005	0.059	0.013	0.074	0.013	0.125	0.025
Age	23.67	0.571***	23.31	1.310***	24.03	0.320	23.59	0.420*
Married	0.749	-0.086***	0.565	-0.012	0.663	-0.130***	0.440	-0.077***
Born in present VDC/municipality	0.418	0.006	0.842	-0.127***	0.341	0.037*	0.470	-0.047**
Attending an academic institution	0.161	0.076***	0.277	0.068**	0.300	0.112***	0.387	0.129***
Education (in years)	3.859	4.281***	6.278	3.306***	7.075	3.349***	8.661	2.431***
Passed SLC	0.157	0.380***	0.282	0.448***	0.441	0.367***	0.553	0.304***
Household has absentee(s)	0.492	0.014	0.325	-0.270	0.304	0.044***	0.195	0.026
Household has benefactor	0.038	0.030**	0.032	0.042**	0.055	0.025**	0.067	0.035**
Household asset index	-0.192	0.758***	-0.176	0.672***	1.310	0.544***	1.405	0.515***
Hindu	0.856	0.034**	0.848	0.039*	0.844	0.056***	0.848	0.039***

continued

TABLE 6.3, *continued*

CHARACTERISTIC	RURAL				URBAN			
	FEMALE		MALE		FEMALE		MALE	
	NONRECIPIENTS MEAN	RECIPIENTS DIFF.	NONRECIPIENTS MEAN	RECIPIENTS DIFF.	NONRECIPIENTS MEAN	RECIPIENTS DIFF.	NONRECIPIENTS MEAN	RECIPIENTS DIFF.
	(1)	(2)	(3)	(4)	(5)	(6)	(7)	(8)
Brahmin/Chhetri	0.306	0.167***	0.286	0.126***	0.375	0.117***	0.370	0.137***
Terai middle castes	0.121	−0.047***	0.139	−0.220	0.078	−0.031***	0.101	−0.049***
Dalit	0.130	−0.589***	0.121	−0.051***	0.075	−0.046***	0.072	−0.058***
Newar	0.036	0.059***	0.039	0.039**	0.144	0.058***	0.151	0.010
Janajati	0.340	−0.067**	0.349	−0.062**	0.279	−0.071***	0.249	−0.020
Muslim	0.047	−0.038***	0.043	−0.020**	0.035	−0.022***	0.043	−0.020***
Other castes	0.020	−0.015***	0.022	−0.010*	0.014	−0.005	0.015	0.001
Kathmandu Valley	n.a.	n.a.	n.a.	n.a.	0.326	0.039*	0.394	0.040
Urban Terai	n.a.	n.a.	n.a.	n.a.	0.440	−0.060**	0.423	−0.077***
Urban Hills	n.a.	n.a.	n.a.	n.a.	0.234	0.021	0.183	0.037**
Rural Terai	0.508	0.039	0.523	0.037	n.a.	n.a.	n.a.	n.a.
Rural Hills	0.416	−0.018	0.396	−0.024	n.a.	n.a.	n.a.	n.a.
Mountains	0.076	−0.021	0.803	−0.013	n.a.	n.a.	n.a.	n.a.

Source: Estimated using 2008 Nepal Labour Force Survey data.

Note: n.a. = not applicable; SLC = School Leaving Certificate; VDC = Village Development Committee. Columns 1, 3, 5, and 7 report means for nonrecipients; Columns 2, 4, 6, and 8 report the difference in means between recipients and nonrecipients. Inference based on robust standard errors clustered at the primary sampling unit level.
*$p < 0.1$, **$p < 0.05$, ***$p < 0.01$.

TABLE 6.4 **Differences in mean characteristics between nonrecipients and recipients, by field, individuals ages 16–34 years, 2008**

CHARACTERISTIC	FEMALE				MALE		
	MEAN	DIFFERENCE FROM MEAN FOR NO TRAINING			MEAN	DIFFERENCE FROM MEAN FOR NO TRAINING	
	NO TRAINING	BASIC COMPUTING	DRESSMAKING/ TAILORING	OTHER FIELDS	NO TRAINING	BASIC COMPUTING	OTHER FIELDS
	(1)	(2)	(3)	(4)	(5)	(6)	(7)
Rel. to head: Head	0.396	−0.225***	0.062**	0.072**	0.308	−0.121***	0.124***
Rel. to head: Spouse	0.286	−0.204***	0.013	0.008	0.010	0.001	0.008
Rel. to head: Son/daughter (in law)	0.533	0.138***	−0.038	−0.053*	0.587	0.053*	−0.145***
Rel. to head: Grandchild	0.014	0.023**	−0.009***	−0.003	0.019	0.013	−0.003
Rel. to head: Other relative	0.049	0.063***	−0.012	−0.010	0.072	0.042***	0.025
Age	23.72	−2.288***	1.376***	1.841***	23.36	−1.156***	2.764***
Married	0.736	−0.457***	0.047**	−0.065**	0.540	−0.326***	0.145***
Born in present VDC/municipality	0.406	0.102***	−0.053**	−0.017	0.769	−0.239***	−0.123***
Attending an academic institution	0.182	0.571***	−0.090***	0.022	0.298	0.411***	−0.122***
Education (in years)	4.346	7.366***	3.139***	4.395***	6.748	4.930***	2.265***
Passed SLC	0.200	0.787***	0.205***	0.455***	0.335	0.641***	0.288***
Household has absentee(s)	0.463	−0.057*	0.035	−0.053	0.300	−0.007	−0.055**
Household has benefactor	0.041	0.041**	0.033**	0.023	0.039	0.083***	0.017
Household asset index	0.035	1.670***	0.688***	0.930***	0.136	1.480***	0.523***

continued

TABLE 6.4, *continued*

CHARACTERISTIC	FEMALE				MALE		
	MEAN	DIFFERENCE FROM MEAN FOR NO TRAINING			MEAN	DIFFERENCE FROM MEAN FOR NO TRAINING	
	NO TRAINING	BASIC COMPUTING	DRESSMAKING/ TAILORING	OTHER FIELDS	NO TRAINING	BASIC COMPUTING	OTHER FIELDS
	(1)	(2)	(3)	(4)	(5)	(6)	(7)
Hindu	0.854	0.058***	0.037**	0.028	0.848	0.044**	0.035**
Brahmin/Chhetri	0.316	0.257***	0.100***	0.169***	0.303	0.251***	0.066**
Terai middle castes	0.114	-0.097***	-0.032*	-0.036*	0.131	-0.076***	-0.014
Dalit	0.121	-0.093***	-0.067***	-0.044**	0.111	-0.091***	-0.043***
Newar	0.052	0.127***	0.085***	0.047***	0.061	0.074***	0.033**
Janajati	0.331	-0.146***	-0.033	-0.094***	0.329	-0.122***	-0.021
Muslim	0.045	-0.031***	-0.042***	-0.030***	0.043	-0.023***	-0.018**
Other castes	0.019	-0.017***	-0.011**	-0.012*	0.020	-0.013***	-0.002
Kathmandu Valley	0.049	0.177***	0.030***	0.098***	0.078	0.166***	0.052***
Urban Terai	0.066	0.114***	0.061***	0.076***	0.084	0.096***	0.032***
Urban Hills	0.035	0.103***	0.041***	0.058***	0.036	0.068***	0.046***
Rural Terai	0.431	-0.197***	0.003	-0.135***	0.420	-0.160***	-0.039
Rural Hills	0.353	-0.133***	-0.108***	-0.088***	0.318	-0.125***	-0.081***
Mountains	0.065	-0.065***	-0.026*	-0.009	0.064	-0.044***	-0.010

Source: Estimates based on 2008 Nepal Labour Force Survey data.
Note: SLC = School Leaving Certificate; VDC = Village Development Committee. Inference based on robust standard errors clustered at the primary sampling unit level.
***p<0.01, **p<0.05, *p<0.1.

Trainees in basic computing appear to differ from trainees in other fields. As an extreme illustration, trainees in basic computing and nontrainees exhibit significant differences in individual characteristics—such as relationship to the household head, age, marital status, and education—that are in the *opposite* direction of significant differences between trainees in other fields and nontrainees. Specifically, relative to nontrainees, trainees in basic computing are less likely to be the household head and more likely to be children of the head of the household, are on average younger, and are more likely to be attending school. In contrast, relative to nontrainees, trainees in other fields are more likely to be the household head and less likely to be children of the household head, are on average older, and are either just as likely as, or less likely than, nontrainees to be attending school. Trainees in basic computing are less likely to be married than nontrainees, whereas female trainees in dressmaking/tailoring and male trainees in other fields are more likely to be married.

LABOR MARKET EFFECTS OF TRAINING

Analytical approach

Has training improved labor market outcomes for recipients? To our knowledge, Nepal lacks credible evidence on the effects of training from widely representative data. Chakravarty et al. (2015) and Bhatta et al. (2017) offer two relatively rigorous evaluations of selected short-term training interventions in Nepal, although the findings are likely not generalizable. Chakravarty et al. evaluate a small-scale variant of an existing training initiative undertaken by an international nongovernmental organization in partnership with the government. The intervention offered one- to three-month-long training in a few selected fields (for example, dressmaking/tailoring, construction, electrical work), targeted to young women and other traditionally disadvantaged groups. On the basis of a difference-in-differences strategy (before versus after the intervention, qualifying versus nonqualifying applicants), the study finds that the intervention had significant positive effects on employment, hours worked, and earnings for qualifying applicants within a year after the training. Bhatta et al. evaluate public vouchers for short-term private training offered to traditionally disadvantaged groups in the Kathmandu Valley. The vouchers were randomly assigned to a sample of marginally eligible candidates. The study finds significant positive effects for voucher recipients on employment, hours worked, and earnings within a year after the training.

Generally, the collective, rigorous international evidence on the effects of training programs on youth employment or earnings is promising but inconclusive. Tripney and Hombrados (2013) conduct a meta-evaluation of youth training programs in low- and middle-income countries, and Kluve et al. (2016) conduct a meta-evaluation of youth employment programs, looking at training programs separately. Both studies find that training programs have significant positive aggregate effects. In their meta-evaluation of active labor market programs globally, Card, Kluve, and Weber (2015) find that the aggregate effect of training programs targeted at youth is smaller than that for untargeted training programs. All three meta-evaluations additionally find substantial variability in effect sizes across included evaluation studies, and that large shares of (if not most) evaluation studies have insignificant results. McKenzie (2017) reviews only experimental evaluations of training and other active labor market interventions in low- and middle-income countries. The study finds that training interventions tend to have positive effects on the likelihood of employment and mean earnings that are either small or insignificant, although the interventions tend to have significant, relatively large, positive effects on the likelihood of formal employment.

Here, using NLFS data, we examine whether training obtained by the individual is associated with

- Employment;
- Employment that is primarily wage employment (as opposed to self-employment), which we call wage work;
- Employment that is primarily nonagricultural employment (as opposed to agricultural employment), which we call nonfarm work; and
- Hours-adjusted earnings from the worker's wage employment activities, which we call wage earnings.

The outcome measures in the second, third, and fourth bullets are conditional on employment. Although of interest as an outcome, data on incomes or profits from self-employment activities were not gathered in the NLFS.

As noted earlier, training recipients systematically differ from nonrecipients in characteristics such as age, marital status, education, household economic status, caste, and region of residence. The poor overlap in the distribution of characteristics between recipients and nonrecipients can make estimates imprecise and sensitive to the choice of specification. To arrive at an optimal subsample, we use the approach suggested by Crump et al. (2009) and Imbens (2015) to discard observations with extreme predicted probabilities of training. The approach does not bias the estimates because the optimal subsample depends on the joint distribution of characteristics and training status and not on the distribution of outcomes. Discarding observations with extreme predicted probabilities can also greatly improve the precision of the estimates.

We estimate the effects of training in two stages. In the first stage, we (1) estimate gender-specific regressions of whether the individual obtained training, (2) predict the individual probabilities of having obtained training, and (3) following the general optimal rule suggested by Crump et al. (2009), retain only individuals with predicted probabilities between 0.1 and 0.9. Performing this stage, we trim out 17 percent of recipients and 63 percent of nonrecipients from the full sample for the training receipt regression for women, and 13 percent of recipients and 52 percent of nonrecipients from the full sample for the training receipt regression for men. Sample sizes for the outcome regressions are still large after the trimming.

Recipients and nonrecipients in the trimmed samples are more similar than in the full samples (see table 6A.1). Differences in mean characteristics are substantially smaller in the trimmed samples relative to the corresponding full samples, and the differences between means for many characteristics lose significance in the trimmed samples.

In the second stage, we estimate gender-specific regressions of the effects of training only for individuals in the trimmed samples, controlling for all the characteristics we examine in table 6.3. Standard errors in all regressions are clustered at the primary sampling unit (PSU) level, to account for potential correlation between individuals within the same PSU.

Although we discuss the estimated effects of training for only the trimmed female and male samples, we also estimate regressions for the full female and male samples. The full-sample regression results are reported in appendix tables 6A.2–6A.5. Note that our selected method provides arguably well-estimated associations between training and outcomes of interest, which we sometimes refer to as "effects." However, given the data, the method does not allow us to interpret these associations as causal. Also note that the associations are not representative of all recipients, but only those recipients who survived the trimming step.

Delving further, we additionally investigate the variation in the effects of training by selected sociodemographic subgroups: school attendance status, education attainment (completed grade 10 or less, passed the SLC only, completed at least intermediate education), and area of residence (rural or urban).[4] We also investigate the variation in the effects of training by selected training characteristics: type of training (short-term courses or TSLC/technical diploma programs), which we determined indirectly using information on the length of training; and major training field (basic computing and other fields for men, and basic computing, dressmaking/tailoring, and other fields for women). We examine whether the effects differ across subgroups as well as whether a given subgroup-specific effect is significant. In discussing the results, we focus on the latter.

Although we attempt to adjust for selection into training, we do not adjust for selection into the various sociodemographic and training-related subgroups. The training and schooling decisions may be jointly determined, as may be training and residence decisions. The decision to obtain training may be influenced by the type or length of training. The subgroup analysis may then be a source of bias. Thus, the results should be interpreted as suggestive at best.

Effects for women

Table 6.5 reports estimated average marginal effects (AMEs) of training for women. Training is associated with an increase in the likelihood of employment of 6 percentage points, or 10 percent in relative terms. Training is also associated with increases in the likelihoods of wage work of 5 percentage points (31 percent) and nonfarm work of 16 percentage points (46 percent). However, training does not appear to be associated with wage earnings.[5]

Table 6.5 also reports training effects interacted with schooling status, education attainment, and area of residence for women. Whether training effects are significant appears to differ by sociodemographic groups. With respect to schooling status, training is associated with increases in the likelihoods of employment (9 percentage points) and nonfarm work (17 percentage points) for those who have completed school, and increases in the likelihoods of wage work of 7 percentage points and nonfarm work of 11 percentage points for those attending school. With respect to education attainment, training is associated with an increase in the likelihood of nonwage work of 21 percentage points for those who have not obtained the SLC; increases in the likelihood of employment of 6 percentage points, the likelihood of wage work of 7 percentage points, and the likelihood of nonfarm work of 16 percentage points for those who have obtained the SLC only; and an increase in the likelihood of employment of 9 percentage points for those

TABLE 6.5 **Training effects for females ages 16–34 years, overall and by schooling level and location, trimmed sample, 2008**

	EMPLOYMENT	WAGE WORK	NONFARM WORK	LOG WAGE EARNINGS
	(1)	(2)	(3)	(4)
Training	0.061***	0.045**	0.156***	0.013
	(0.020)	(0.019)	(0.026)	(0.066)
a. Heterogeneous effects, by schooling status				
Training (β_1)	0.093***	0.032	0.171***	−0.077
	(0.025)	(0.022)	(0.031)	(0.077)
Training × attending school (β_2)	−0.076**	0.041	−0.057	0.239*
	(0.036)	(0.037)	(0.048)	(0.144)
$\beta_1+\beta_2>0$; p–value	0.558	0.020	0.005	0.177
b. Heterogeneous effects, by education attainment				
Training (β_1)	0.039	0.045	0.209***	−0.128
	(0.037)	(0.036)	(0.038)	(0.148)
Training × passed SLC only (β_2)	0.021	0.028	−0.048	0.223
	(0.046)	(0.051)	(0.053)	(0.218)
Training × Intermediate or higher (β_3)	0.048	−0.031	−0.164***	0.154
	(0.049)	(0.044)	(0.056)	(0.168)
$\beta_1+\beta_2>0$; p–value	0.053	0.032	0.000	0.520
$\beta_1+\beta_3>0$; p–value	0.003	0.615	0.345	0.746
c. Heterogeneous effects, by location				
Training (β_1)	0.072***	0.035	0.129***	−0.083
	(0.018)	(0.023)	(0.028)	(0.061)
Training × rural (β_2)	−0.018	0.006	0.027	0.153
	(0.039)	(0.036)	(0.043)	(0.139)
$\beta_1+\beta_2>0$; p–value	0.117	0.141	0.000	0.568
Observations	5,332	2,803	2,814	622

Source: Estimates based on 2008 Nepal Labour Force Survey data.

Note: SLC = School Leaving Certificate. Wage work and nonfarm work are conditional on employment, and log wage earnings are conditional on wage work. Employment, wage work, and nonfarm work regressions are estimated as logit based on maximum likelihood, and log wage earnings regressions are estimated based on least squares. All regressions control for the individual's relation to the head of household, age, marital status, current schooling status, education attainment in years, a standardized index of household consumptive assets, and region identifiers. The regressions also control for whether the individual obtained the SLC; what his or her caste is; whether the individual's household has a private benefactor; and whether the individual's household has an absentee member. The propensity-score trimmed sample only includes observations with predicted values between 0.1 and 0.9 in a training-receipt logit regression. Robust standard errors, clustered at the primary sampling unit level, are reported in parentheses. All estimates are adjusted for sampling weights.
*p < 0.1, **p < 0.05, ***p < 0.01.

who have completed at least intermediate education. With respect to area of residence, training is associated with increases in the likelihood of employment of 7 percentage points and the likelihood of nonfarm work of 13 percentage points for urban residents, and an increase in the likelihood of nonfarm work of 16 percentage points for rural residents. Training does not appear to be associated with wage earnings for any of the sociodemographic groups, with the exception of those attending school, for whom training is associated with an increase in wage earnings of 24 percent.

Table 6.6 reports training effects separately by type and length of training subgroups for women. Training through short courses is associated with increases in the likelihoods of employment of 6 percentage points, wage work of 4 percentage points, and nonfarm work of 14 percentage points. Training through TSLC/technical diploma programs is associated with an increase in the likelihood of nonfarm work of only 15 percentage points.

Training in basic computing is associated with an increase in the likelihood of nonfarm work of only 10 percentage points. Training in dressmaking/tailoring is associated with increases in the likelihoods of employment of 6 percentage points and nonfarm work of 16 percentage points. Training in dressmaking/tailoring does not appear to be associated with the likelihood of wage work. Dressmaking/tailoring tends to be a self-employment activity for Nepalese women: 71 percent of female youth engaged in dressmaking/tailoring are self-employed, according to NLFS data. Training in other fields is associated

TABLE 6.6 **Training effects for females ages 16–34 years, by training length and field, trimmed sample, 2008**

	EMPLOYMENT	WAGE WORK	NONFARM WORK	LOG WAGE EARNINGS
	(1)	(2)	(3)	(4)
a. Heterogeneous effects, by training type				
Short training courses (β_1)	0.057***	0.042**	0.142***	0.015
	(0.021)	(0.020)	(0.028)	(0.071)
TSLC/tech. dip. programs (β_2)	0.041	0.023	0.153**	−0.009
	(0.062)	(0.042)	(0.078)	(0.123)
$\beta_1 = \beta_2$; p-value	0.817	0.546	0.989	0.654
b. Heterogeneous effects, by training field				
Basic computing (β_1)	0.014	0.042	0.103**	0.136
	(0.028)	(0.027)	(0.044)	(0.105)
Dressmaking/tailoring (β_2)	0.057*s	−0.005	0.159***	−0.058
	(0.032)	(0.029)	(0.039)	(0.128)
Other fields (β_3)	0.123***	0.081***	0.186***	−0.047
	(0.034)	(0.028)	(0.040)	(0.076)
$\beta_1 = \beta_2$; p-value	0.271	0.223	0.312	0.218
$\beta_1 = \beta_3$; p-value	0.008	0.275	0.130	0.105
$B_2 = \beta_3$; p-value	0.117	0.024	0.610	0.941
Observations	5,332	2,803	2,814	622

Source: Estimates based on 2008 Nepal Labour Force Survey data.
Note: TSLC/tech. dip. programs = Technical School Leaving Certificate / technical diploma programs. Wage work and nonfarm work are conditional on employment, and log wage earnings are conditional on wage work. Employment, wage work, and nonfarm work regressions are estimated as logit based on maximum likelihood, and log wage earnings regressions are estimated based on least squares. All regressions control for the individual's relation to the head of household, age, marital status, current schooling status, education attainment in years, a standardized index of household consumptive assets, and region identifiers. The regressions also control for whether the individual obtained the SLC; which caste he or she belongs to; whether the individual's household has a private benefactor; and whether the individual's household has an absentee member. The propensity-score trimmed sample only includes observations with predicted values between 0.1 and 0.9 in a training-receipt logit regression. Robust standard errors, clustered at the primary sampling unit level, are reported in parentheses. All estimates are adjusted for sampling weights.
*p<0.1, **p<0.05, ***p<0.01.

with increases in the likelihoods of employment of 12 percentage points, wage work of 8 percentage points, and nonfarm work of 19 percentage points. The mean effect of training on wage earnings is insignificant, irrespective of the type or major field of training.

Effects for men

Tables 6.7 and 6.8 report estimated AMEs of training for men. The structure of the tables mirrors tables 6.5 and 6.6 for women, respectively. Training does not appear to be associated with any outcome for men.

In terms of training effects interacted with sociodemographic groups, training does not appear to be associated with any outcome for those who have completed their schooling, or those who have obtained the SLC only or with less schooling. Training also does not appear to be associated with any outcome for rural or urban residents as groups. For those who are attending school, training is associated with increases in the likelihood of wage work by 14 percentage points and the likelihood of nonfarm work by 8 percentage points. For those who have completed at least intermediate education, training is associated with an increase in the likelihood of employment by 5 percentage points.

In terms of training effects by type and length of training subgroups, training through short-term courses is associated with an increase in the likelihood of wage work by 5 percentage points. Training through TSLC / technical diploma programs is associated with an increase in the likelihood of employment of 8 percentage points, and with a 15 percent increase in wage earnings. Neither training in basic computing nor training in other fields appears to be associated with any outcome.

Plausible explanations

In general, we find that training is associated with shifts in employment for women, along both extensive and intensive margins, but not so for men. In general, we do not find that training is associated with higher wage earnings for either gender.

At least two competing explanations may account for the general absence of an effect of training on wage earnings. First, the lack of skills may be a binding constraint on local labor market success; but the obtained training fails to improve skills. Second, the obtained training improves skills, but only relaxing the skills constraint is not sufficient for labor market success.

Recent evidence from other low-income countries suggests that financial capital constraints may be dominant. On the basis of an experimental evaluation, Hicks et al. (2015) find that cash vouchers given to out-of-school youth for training in vocational education institutions increase training but do not, in general, lead to an increase in employment and earnings, measured variously. The study also reports that interviews with training students indicate that the lack of financial capital for self-employment activities serves as a barrier to the effective use of training. Also on the basis of an experimental evaluation, Blattman, Fiala, and Martinez (2014) find that cash grants given to poor youth groups in Uganda to pay for training and business start-up costs lead to higher investments in training and business assets, and higher employment and earnings measured

TABLE 6.7 **Training effects for males ages 16–34 years, by schooling level and location, trimmed sample, 2008**

	EMPLOYMENT	WAGE WORK	NONFARM WORK	LOG WAGE EARNINGS
	(1)	(2)	(3)	(4)
Training	0.000	0.038	0.026	–0.016
	(0.020)	(0.026)	(0.028)	(0.057)
a. Heterogeneous effects, by schooling status				
Training (β_1)	–0.010	–0.010	–0.006	0.004
	(0.036)	(0.030)	(0.036)	(0.072)
Training × attending school (β_2)	0.014	0.142***	0.084	–0.061
	(0.043)	(0.051)	(0.052)	(0.113)
$\beta_1+\beta_2>0$; *p*–value	0.839	0.002	0.046	0.520
b. Heterogeneous effects, by education attainment				
Training (β_1)	–0.065	0.021	–0.043	0.065
	(0.064)	(0.059)	(0.073)	(0.147)
Training × obtained SLC only (β_2)	0.033	0.003	0.087	–0.168
	(0.064)	(0.073)	(0.079)	(0.189)
Training × intermediate or higher (β_3)	0.110	0.034	0.065	–0.056
	(0.072)	(0.064)	(0.083)	(0.151)
$\beta_1+\beta_2>0$; *p*–value	0.247	0.561	0.232	0.397
$\beta_1+\beta_3>0$; *p*–value	0.075	0.109	0.616	0.895
c. Heterogeneous effects, by location				
Training (β_1)	0.005	0.040	0.036	–0.087
	(0.019)	(0.025)	(0.030)	(0.066)
Training × rural (β_2)	–0.009	–0.020	–0.024	0.116
	(0.038)	(0.049)	(0.044)	(0.113)
$\beta_1+\beta_2>0$; *p*–value	0.892	0.619	0.724	0.759
Observations	4,739	3,041	3,041	1,225

Source: Estimates based on 2008 Nepal Labour Force Survey data.
Note: SLC = School Leaving Certificate. Wage work and nonfarm work are conditional on employment, and log wage earnings are conditional on wage work. Employment, wage work, and nonfarm work regressions are estimated as logit based on maximum likelihood, and log wage earnings regressions are estimated based on least squares. All regressions control for the individual's relation to the head of household, age, marital status, current schooling status, education attainment in years, a standardized index of household consumptive assets, and region identifiers. Regressions also control for whether the individual obtained the SLC; which caste he or she belongs to; whether the individual's household has a private benefactor; and whether the individual's household has an absentee member. The propensity-score trimmed sample only includes observations with predicted values between 0.1 and 0.9 in a training-receipt logit regression. Robust standard errors, clustered at the primary sampling unit level, are reported in parentheses. All estimates are adjusted for sampling weights.
*p < 0.1, **p < 0.05, ***p < 0.01.

variously, with most of the grant funds used to buy business tools, materials, and supplies.

Suggestive evidence indicates that financial capital constraints may be important for labor market success in Nepal. The SWTS asked self-employed workers to name the most important issue they face in undertaking their activities. Among individuals ages 16–29 years, in rural areas, the lack of financial capital is the most commonly reported issue, at 27 percent; in urban areas, it is the second-most-commonly reported issue, at 16 percent (the most commonly reported issue is intense market competition, at 46 percent). Other response

TABLE 6.8 **Training effects for males ages 16–34 years, by training length and field, trimmed sample, 2008**

	EMPLOYMENT	WAGE WORK	NONFARM WORK	LOG WAGE EARNINGS
	(1)	(2)	(3)	(4)
a. Heterogeneous effects, by training type				
Short training courses (β_1)	−0.013	0.050*	0.004	−0.037
	(0.021)	(0.030)	(0.032)	(0.061)
TSLC/tech. dip. programs (β_2)	0.081**	−0.059	0.096	0.146*
	(0.034)	(0.056)	(0.061)	(0.082)
$\beta_1 = \beta_2$; p-value	0.045	0.032	0.423	0.370
b. Heterogeneous effects, by training field				
Basic computing (β_1)	−0.007	0.039	0.040	−0.111
	(0.022)	(0.034)	(0.038)	(0.083)
Other fields (β_2)	0.015	0.038	0.016	0.065
	(0.031)	(0.031)	(0.035)	(0.064)
$\beta_1 = \beta_2$; p-value	0.497	0.974	0.619	0.067
Observations	4,739	3,041	3,041	1,225

Source: Estimated using 2008 Nepal Labour Force Survey data.

Note: TSLC/tech. dip. programs = Technical School Leaving Certificate / technical diploma programs. Wage work and nonfarm work are conditional on employment, and log wage earnings are conditional on wage work. Employment, wage work, and nonfarm work regressions are estimated as logit based on maximum likelihood, and log wage earnings regressions are estimated based on least squares. All regressions control for the individual's relation to the head of household, age, marital status, current schooling status, education attainment in years, a standardized index of household consumptive assets, and region identifiers. The regressions also control for whether the individual obtained the SLC; which caste he or she belongs to; whether the individual's household has a private benefactor; and whether the individual's household has an absentee member. The propensity-score trimmed sample only includes observations with predicted values between 0.1 and 0.9 in a training-receipt logit regression. Robust standard errors, clustered at the primary sampling unit level, are reported in parentheses. All estimates are adjusted for sampling weights.
*p<0.1, **p<0.05, ***p<0.01.

options to the question included "poor quality staff" and "lack of business expertise." Treating these other response options as signifying inadequate labor skills, only about 11 percent of rural or urban self-employed workers report skills to be an issue.

Notwithstanding the general result of a lack of a training's effect on wage earnings for either gender, the differential results by gender of the training effects on employment are consistent with those from the evaluation of short-term training in Nepal by Chakravarty et al. (2015). Their evaluation results also differ by gender. For men, they find that the intervention has significant positive effects on the likelihoods of nonfarm work and work in the field in which they were trained, that it does not have significant effects on the likelihood of employment or on work hours, and that the significance of the positive effect on labor earnings depends on their specific earnings measure. In contrast, for women, they find that the intervention has significant positive effects on all of the study's labor market measures.[6]

The differing results we find between men and women are also consistent with evidence from meta-evaluations, such as of youth employment programs globally (Kluve et al. 2016), youth training programs in low- and middle-income countries (Tripney and Hombrados 2013), and active labor market programs globally (Card, Kluve, and Weber 2015). These evaluations find larger aggregate effects for women than for men, although the aggregate effects for women are not always statistically different from those for men.[7]

We posit three explanations for the differential employment effects by gender. First, the most common training for men is in basic computing, and we find that the effects of basic computing tend to be insignificant for both genders. This suggests that training in basic computing may often be for nonwork reasons. Second, given that our analysis data were collected when the labor migration flow of Nepalese men to other countries was already substantial, the trained men in the analysis sample—in other words, trained men *in* Nepal—may be negatively selected relative to all trained men, and thus the effects of training for this sample may be biased toward zero. Third, the trained men in the analysis sample may have obtained training to work in external labor markets, and decided to wait for, or actively seek, external work opportunities instead of seeking local labor market success. One explanation that we discount is that the results for men may be due to ceiling constraints: the rates of employment, wage work, and nonfarm work are well below 100 percent for untrained men.

INTEREST IN, AND PERCEPTIONS OF, TRAINING

Training desire rates

We examine NLFS data on the individual's stated preference for training—specifically, whether the individual desires training and, if so, what particular training field he or she desires. Estimates of training desire rates based on these questions presumably overstate the extent of effective demand for training (that is, the rate of individuals who are willing to obtain training and able to incur any costs, including opportunity costs, of training).

Figure 6.6 shows training desire rates, separately for youth and nonyouth cohorts. There appears to be extensive interest in training among youth in Nepal. The training desire rate for youth is 39 percent, and less than half that

FIGURE 6.6

Training desire rates, by gender and by urban versus rural, 2008

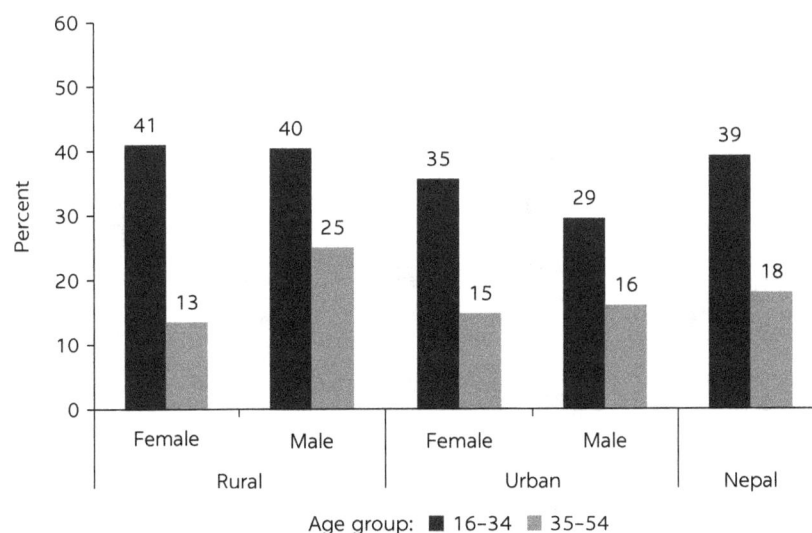

Source: Estimated using 2008 Nepal Labour Force Survey data.
Note: All estimates are adjusted for sampling weights.

much for nonyouth, at 18 percent. Youth training desire rates range from a low of 29 percent for urban men to a high of 41 percent for rural women. Youth training desire rates appear to be higher in rural than urban areas. For example, for female youth, the training desire rate is 41 percent in rural areas, whereas it is 35 percent in urban areas. Youth training desire rates are comparable between women and men in rural areas, and higher for women than men in urban areas. In the rest of the section, unless noted, all statistics are restricted to youth.

Figure 6.7 contrasts training desire rates for Nepal in 2008 with those for Bangladesh in 2013, the only other country from the region for which we found comparable questions in a recent national labor force survey. Training desire rates for Nepal are strikingly similar to those for Bangladesh. At the country level, the desire rate is 39 percent for Nepal compared to 37 percent for Bangladesh. Training desire rates are also similar between the two countries for all the gender-by-location subgroups.

Figure 6.8 shows training desire rates across regions within Nepal. Interest in training by women and men is especially extensive in regions outside the Kathmandu Valley. For example, for women, training desire rates range from 35 percent (rural Hills) to 47 percent (urban Terai) outside the Kathmandu Valley, whereas it is 19 percent in the Kathmandu Valley.

Figure 6.9 shows training desire age profiles. In general, training desire rates are higher among individuals in their early twenties than individuals in their late twenties or early thirties. Figure 6.10 shows training desire schooling status profiles (panel a) and training desire education attainment profiles (panel b). Training desire rates for those attending school are either higher than or similar to the rates for those who have completed their schooling. Training desire rates for rural women and men jump for those who have obtained the SLC only or completed at least intermediate education. We do not observe a similar pattern for urban women and men.

FIGURE 6.7

Training desire rates, Nepal versus Bangladesh, individuals ages 16–34 years

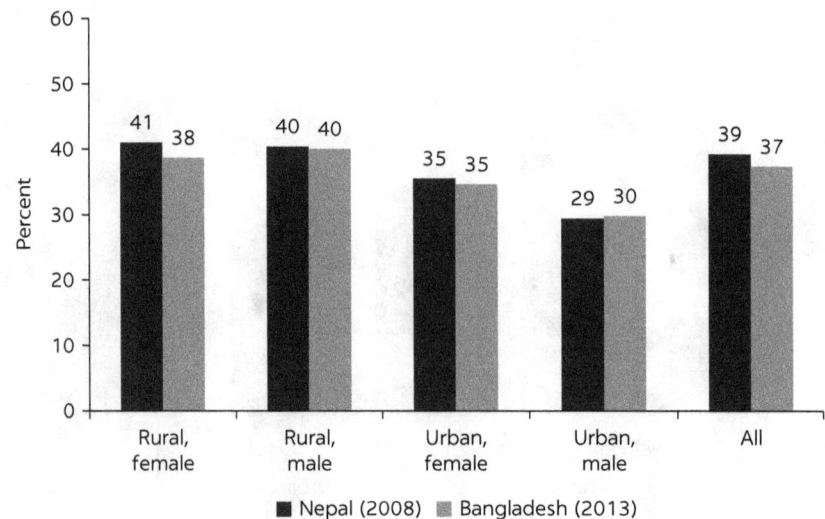

Sources: Estimated using data from the 2008 Nepal Labour Force Survey and the 2013 Bangladesh Labour Force Survey.
Note: All estimates are adjusted for sampling weights.

FIGURE 6.8

Training desire rates, by region, individuals ages 16–34 years, 2008

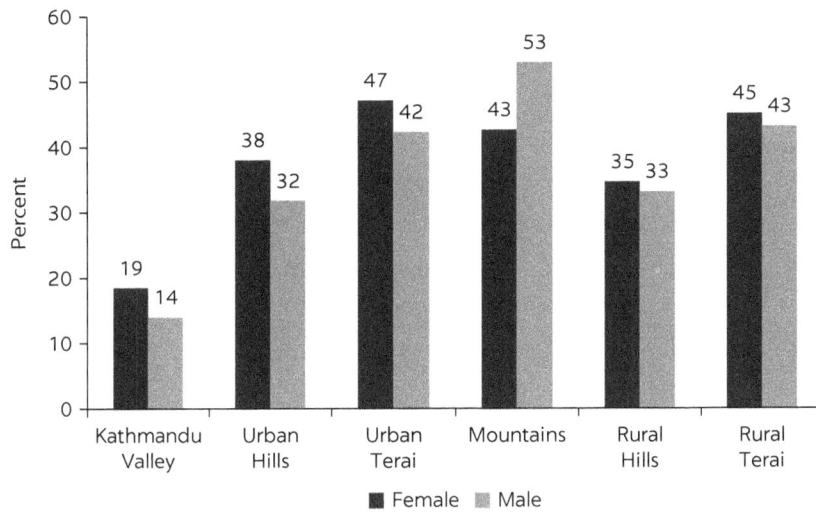

Source: Estimated using 2008 Nepal Labour Force Survey data.
Note: All estimates are adjusted for sampling weights.

FIGURE 6.9

Training desire age profiles, 2008

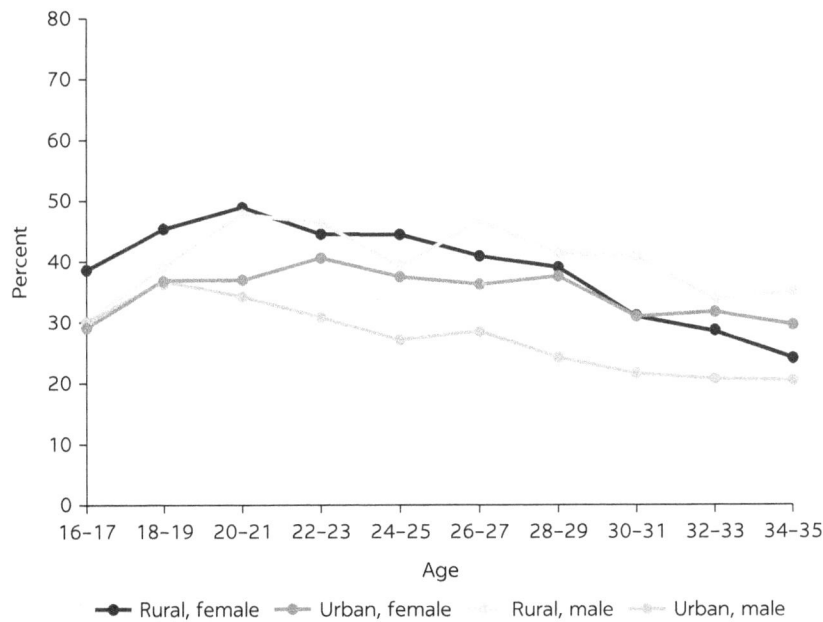

Source: Estimated using 2008 Nepal Labour Force Survey data.
Note: All estimates are adjusted for sampling weights.

FIGURE 6.10

Training desire education profiles, individuals ages 16–34 years, 2008

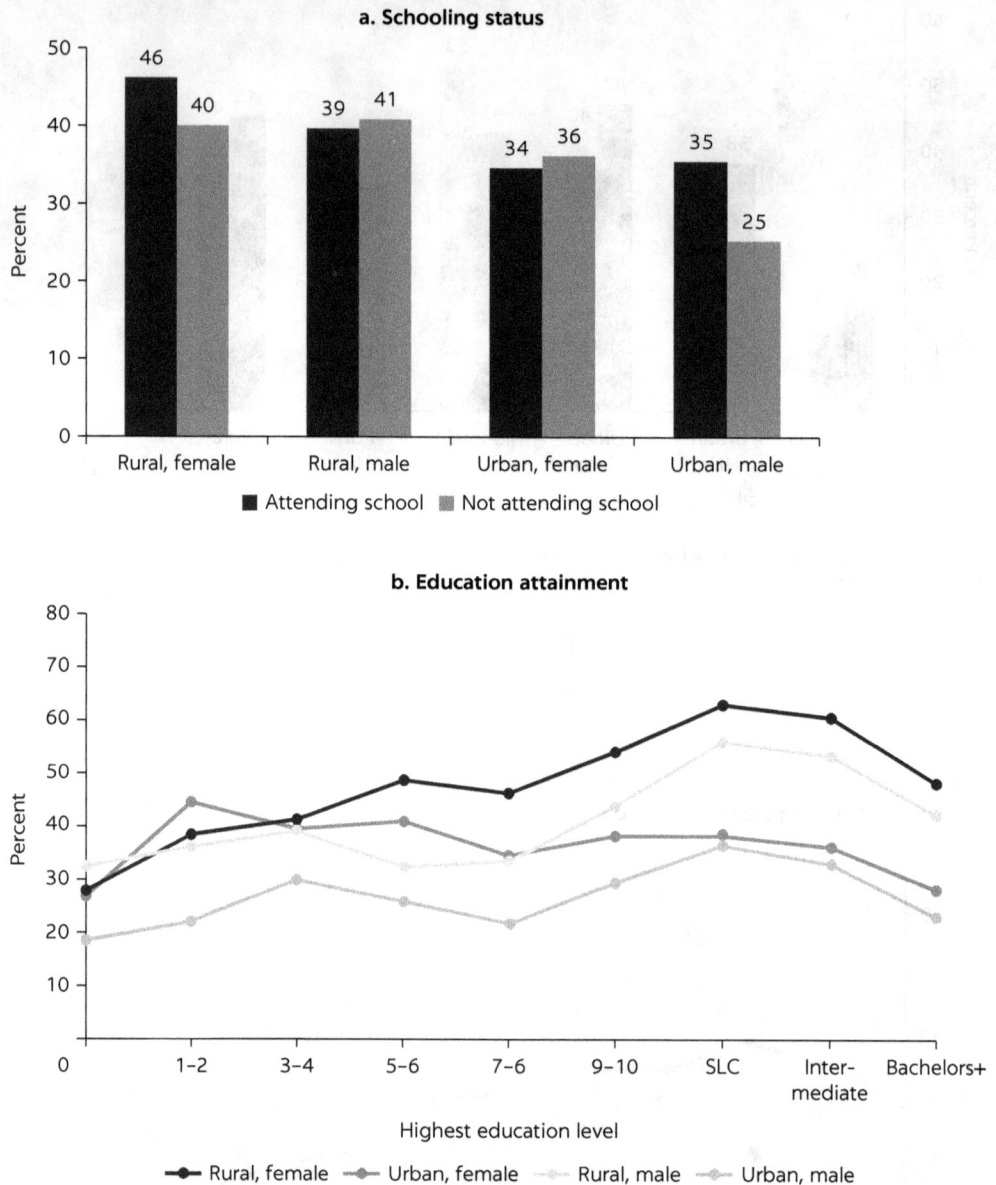

a. Schooling status

■ Attending school ■ Not attending school

b. Education attainment

Highest education level

◆ Rural, female ◆ Urban, female ◆ Rural, male ◆ Urban, male

Source: Estimated using 2008 Nepal Labour Force Survey data.
Note: SLC = School Leaving Certificate. All estimates are adjusted for sampling weights.

Desired training fields

Table 6.9 reports the distribution of desired training fields. Although our wording is loose here, all statistics are for those who express interest in training. Among women, training in dressmaking/tailoring has the highest interest by a large margin; 64 percent of rural women and 47 percent of urban women desire training in it. Interest in training in basic computing and farming/livestock management ranks next among rural women, at 12 percent each, whereas interest in training in basic computing and hairdressing/beautician services ranks next among urban women, at 26 percent and 8 percent, respectively.

TABLE 6.9 **Distribution of desired training fields, individuals ages 16–34 years, 2008**

Percent

	RURAL		URBAN	
FIELD	FEMALE	MALE	FEMALE	MALE
	(1)	(2)	(3)	(4)
Teaching	3	3	4	2
Handicrafts	2	0	4	0
Business and accounting	0	1	1	2
Basic computing	12	27	26	48
Health services	3	1	4	3
Construction	0	12	0	7
Dressmaking/tailoring	64	6	47	3
Small manufacturing and repair	1	13	2	14
Architecture	0	1	0	1
Agriculture and livestock management	12	20	3	4
Driving and motor vehicle operation	0	10	0	9
Hairdressing/beautician services	2	0	8	0
Other service fields	1	6	2	9
Observations	2,606	1,673	2,292	1,666

Source: Estimated using 2008 Nepal Labour Force Survey data.
Note: All estimates adjusted for sampling weights.

Among men, training in basic computing has the highest interest; 48 percent of urban men and 27 percent of rural men desire training in basic computing. Interest in basic computing is followed by interest in training in farming/livestock management (20 percent), manufacturing and repair (13 percent), and construction (12 percent) among rural men, and manufacturing and repair (14 percent), driving (9 percent), and other services fields (9 percent) among urban men.

Characteristics of those who desire training

Table 6.10 reports pairwise differences in mean characteristics between those who desire training versus those who do not. As discussed earlier in the subsection titled "Characteristics of Training Recipients," those who obtained training are on average older and wealthier, and more likely to come from the Kathmandu Valley, than those who did not obtain training. In contrast, those who desire training are on average younger and less wealthy, and more likely to come from the rural or urban Terai, than those who do not desire training.

We also examine whether training desire rates differ according to the individual's training and employment status. Those who desire training are more likely to have obtained training than those who do not desire training. Among rural men and urban women, those who desire training are more likely to be employed than those who do not desire training. Apart from rural women, those who desire training are more likely to be self-employed in agriculture than those who do not desire training. Among rural women, those who desire training are more likely to be wage-employed in services or self-employed in industry than those who do not desire training.

TABLE 6.10 **Differences in mean characteristics, those who desire training versus those who do not, individuals ages 16–34 years, 2008**

CHARACTERISTIC	RURAL				URBAN			
	FEMALE		MALE		FEMALE		MALE	
	DO NOT DESIRE	DESIRE	DO NOT DESIRE	DESIRE	DO NOT DESIRE	DESIRE	DO NOT DESIRE	DESIRE
	MEAN	DIFF.	MEAN	DIFF.	MEAN	DIFF.	MEAN	DIFF.
	(1)	(2)	(3)	(4)	(5)	(6)	(7)	(8)
Rel. to head: Head	0.406	−0.044***	0.301	0.026	0.427	0.009	0.316	−0.033**
Rel. to head: Spouse	0.302	−0.055***	0.009	−0.005	0.307	−0.031*	0.027	−0.018***
Rel. to head: Son/daughter (in law)	0.528	0.052***	0.602	−0.001	0.454	0.012	0.496	0.038
Rel. to head: Grandchild	0.016	−0.008**	0.025	−0.014***	0.022	−0.008	0.018	0.000
Rel. to head: Other relative	0.044	−0.001	0.062	−0.006	0.076	−0.005	0.130	0.003
Age	24.09	−0.946***	23.27	0.403**	24.12	−0.079	24.03	−1.150***
Married	0.757	−0.030**	0.559	0.017	0.629	0.027	0.452	−0.089***
Born in present VDC/municipality	0.431	−0.032**	0.834	−0.006	0.354	−0.018	0.444	0.063**
Attending an academic institution	0.151	0.035***	0.284	−0.008	0.324	−0.014	0.376	0.123***
Education (years)	3.292	2.079***	6.143	1.000***	7.604	0.319	9.032	0.385**
Passed SLC	0.078	0.106***	0.174	0.132***	0.415	0.012	0.487	0.089***
Household has absentee(s)	0.477	0.039***	0.315	0.021	0.286	0.076***	0.182	0.058***
Household has benefactor	0.033	0.019***	0.029	0.016**	0.049	0.030***	0.064	0.027**
Household asset index	−0.189	0.112***	−0.085	−0.086*	1.521	−0.296***	1.623	−0.380***
Hindu	0.846	0.031*	0.831	0.051***	0.834	0.060***	0.841	0.043**
Brahmin/Chhetri	0.277	0.100***	0.246	0.127***	0.385	0.039*	0.379	0.058**
Terai middle castes	0.119	−0.001	0.143	−0.016	0.060	0.031**	0.083	0.024
Dalit	0.131	−0.014	0.121	−0.011	0.064	0.008	0.055	0.021**
Newar	0.046	−0.016**	0.052	−0.022**	0.172	−0.048***	0.178	−0.081***
Janajati	0.356	−0.048**	0.364	−0.053**	0.274	−0.025	0.247	−0.016
Muslim	0.050	−0.014	0.049	−0.014	0.034	−0.008	0.044	−0.009
Other castes	0.021	−0.005	0.025	−0.011	0.012	0.003	0.014	0.002
Got training	0.034	0.079***	0.068	0.058***	0.163	0.093***	0.178	0.123***
Not employed	0.168	−0.009	0.148	−0.038***	0.515	−0.062***	0.345	0.015
Wage employed in agriculture	0.038	−0.019***	0.062	−0.024***	0.010	−0.001	0.011	0.003
Wage employed in industry	0.011	0.002	0.098	−0.016	0.028	−0.004	0.123	−0.018*
Wage employed in services	0.013	0.022***	0.092	−0.001	0.100	−0.016	0.231	−0.046**
Self-employed in agriculture	0.686	−0.029	0.479	0.081***	0.172	0.083***	0.066	0.061***
Self-employed in industry	0.019	0.022***	0.035	0.003	0.033	0.005	0.045	−0.010
Self-employed in services	0.066	0.010	0.089	−0.005	0.143	−0.007	0.180	−0.005
Kathmandu Valley	n.a.	n.a.	n.a.	n.a.	0.424	−0.247***	0.489	−0.290***
Urban Terai	n.a.	n.a.	n.a.	n.a.	0.348	0.219***	0.329	0.264***
Urban Hills	n.a.	n.a.	n.a.	n.a.	0.228	0.027	0.182	0.027
Rural Terai	0.471	0.095***	0.501	0.069**	n.a.	n.a.	n.a.	n.a.
Rural Hills	0.456	−0.101***	0.437	−0.111***	n.a.	n.a.	n.a.	n.a.
Mountains	0.073	0.006	0.062	0.042**	n.a.	n.a.	n.a.	n.a.

Source: Estimated using 2008 Nepal Labour Force Survey data.

Note: n.a. = not applicable; SLC = School Leaving Certificate; VDC = Village Development Committee. Inference is based on robust standard errors clustered at the primary sampling unit level. All estimates adjusted for sampling weights.
*p<0.1, **p<0.05, ***p<0.01.

Relationship between obtained and desired training fields

We found that individuals who desire training are more likely to have obtained training than those who do not desire training. Does the field in which the individual desires training differ from the field in which the individual has already obtained training (which may indicate interest in reskilling), or are the fields the same (which may indicate interest in upskilling)? We explore this question in relation to training in basic computing and dressmaking/tailoring, given that these two fields have by far the highest rates of both interest and receipt.

Panel a of figure 6.11 shows the rates of individuals who desire training in basic computing, separately for those who have received training in basic computing, those who have received training in other fields, and those who have not obtained any training. The majority of those trained in basic computing desire more training in the same field. The rates range from 56 percent for urban women to 82 percent for rural men. Rates for individuals trained in other fields or for individuals who have not obtained training and desire training in basic computing are much lower. For individuals who have not obtained any training, the percentage that desires training in basic computing ranges from 10 percent for rural women to 42 percent for urban men. For individuals trained in other fields, the percentage ranges from 9 percent for rural women to 24 percent for rural men.

Panel b in the same figure presents rates for women who desire training in dressmaking/tailoring, separately for those who have already received training in the same field, those who have received training in other fields, and those who have not obtained any training. There is extensive interest in training for dressmaking/tailoring among women already trained in

FIGURE 6.11

Desire for training in selected fields, conditional on obtained training status, individuals ages 16–34 years, 2008

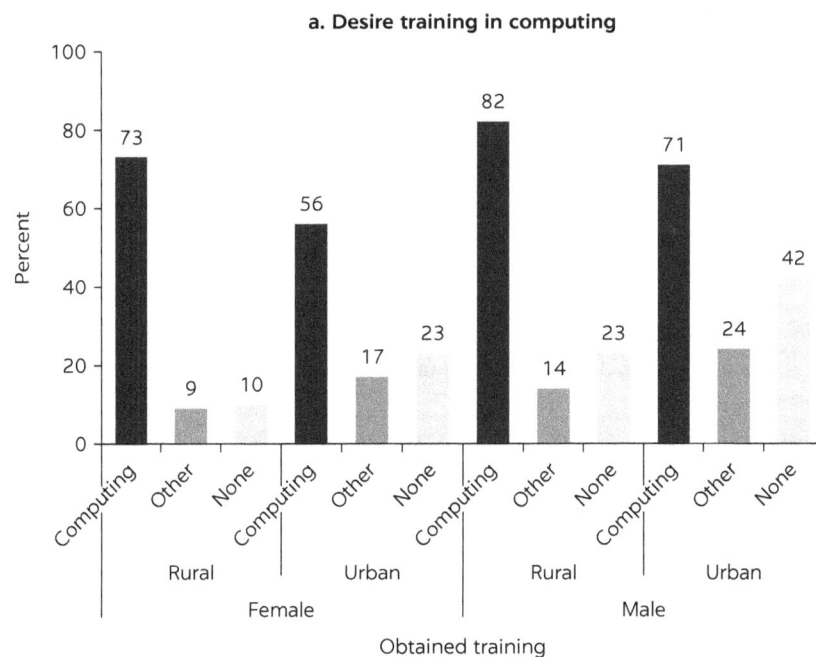

a. Desire training in computing

continued

FIGURE 6.11, continued

b. Desire training in tailoring/dressmaking, women only

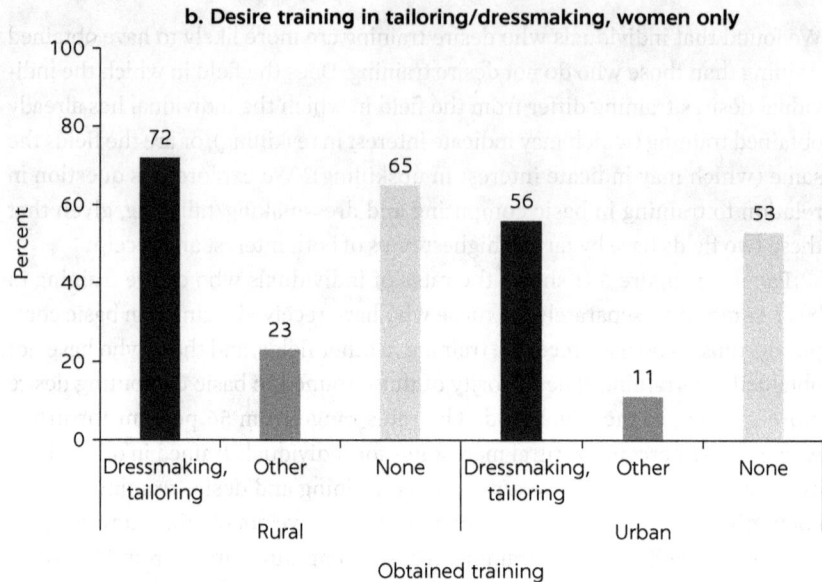

Source: Estimated using 2008 Nepal Labour Force Survey data.
Note: All estimates adjusted for sampling weights.

dressmaking/tailoring, as well as among women who have not obtained any training. For example, 72 percent of rural women already trained in dressmaking/tailoring desire training in the same field, and 65 percent of rural women without any training desire training in dressmaking/tailoring. Interest in training in this field is much lower among those trained in other fields. For example, only 23 percent of rural women trained in other fields desire training in dressmaking/tailoring.

Perceptions of education and training

Using SWTS data, figure 6.12 shows the views held by employed and unemployed workers ages 16–29 years regarding the value of human capital accumulation (collectively, education and training) in finding employment. Fifty-five percent of employed workers report that their education and training are relevant, followed by 26 percent who report that they are underqualified. Nineteen percent of employed workers report that inadequate qualifications were the main difficulty they faced finding employment, second only to inadequate employment opportunities (26 percent).

Among unemployed workers, 33 percent and 32 percent report that insufficient employment opportunities and insufficient qualifications, respectively, are the main difficulties they face in finding employment, followed by insufficient work experience (20 percent). The majority of unemployed workers (78 percent) view their education or training to be useful for finding employment, even if they report that their education or training is insufficient. When asked what type of education or training would be most useful for finding employment, the most common responses are completing secondary or tertiary education (27 percent), training in computing and information technology (27 percent), training in technical institutes (presumably in TSLC/technical diploma programs) (19 percent), and employment apprenticeships (17 percent).

FIGURE 6.12

Perceptions of education and training, individuals ages 16–29 years, 2013

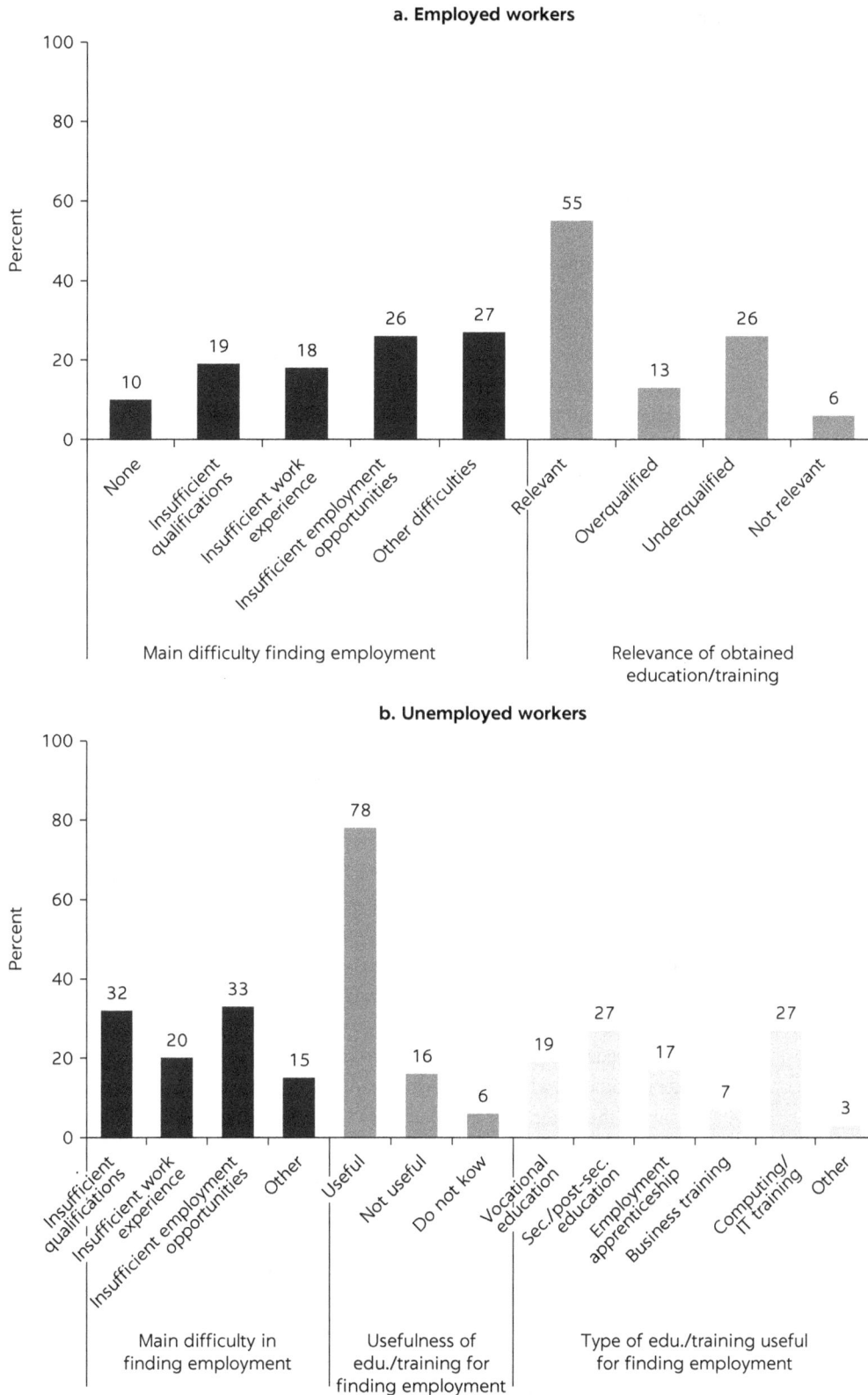

Source: Estimated using 2013 Nepal School-to-Work Transition Survey data.
Note: Edu. = education; IT = information technology; sec. = secondary. Employed workers are defined as those who are engaged in an economic activity for at least one hour in the reference week. Unemployed workers are defined as those who are not employed, were available for work in the reference week, and actively looked for work in the reference month. All estimates adjusted for sampling weights.

CONCLUSION

Under the standard basic model, individuals demand training if the private stream of expected benefits from training (net of costs) is positive. Using labor earnings as the measure of benefits, the evidence we find suggests that the condition may be unmet in Nepal. The problem may lie within the training production function in terms of quantity and quality, which is what most training projects in Nepal have fixed their sights on. Alternatively, it may lie within the labor-earnings production function broadly. That is, the effect of training on labor earnings may depend on factors outside of training, such as the acquisition of financial and physical capital for income-generating activities, an expanding market for skilled labor, and the existing labor market structure. With respect to the labor market structure, if, for example, the wage labor market is characterized by monopsonistic employers, trained workers may obtain lower returns to training, even if it induces higher labor productivity.

In the case of women, even if labor earnings are no greater for training recipients than for nonrecipients, we find that training is associated with a higher likelihood of employment. Employment may be welfare improving for women measured along nonmonetary dimensions, as suggested, for example, by Chakravarty et al. (2015).

Even if a compelling case existed in the past, the rationale for public intervention in the training market for Nepal should be reevaluated because the current landscape is radically different in terms of formal training supply.[8] Without public intervention, will there be a missing market for training, where the price at which private providers are willing to offer training exceeds the price that workers—particularly poorer workers—are willing to pay? If so, what are the sources behind training-market failure? Answers to these questions are vital for designing public interventions that address the specific sources of training-market failure.

We find that a large share of workers, especially poorer workers, report that they are interested in training. However, these workers may still underinvest in training. In general, workers are predicted to underinvest in training for several reasons. They may (1) not be able to afford the costs of training, (2) have high discount rates or be present biased, (3) be averse to riskiness or uncertainty in the returns to training, or (4) face costs in signaling the productivity gain induced by training to employers (Brunello and De Paola 2009). Which reason predominates may differ across workers. Compared to richer workers, the human-capital investment behavior of poorer workers may be more constrained by the noted reasons.

Nepal needs rigorous empirical research to inform the extent and nature of public intervention in the labor market in general and in the training market in particular. In terms of the latter, we note four areas where evidence is missing but where it would be valuable for policy making. The first is to measure the willingness of workers to pay for training as well as the willingness of employers to pay for trained workers, examining the relative importance of different attributes of training and how different attributes are traded off by workers and employers. The second area is to measure perceptions of training and its returns and the risk, uncertainty, and time preferences of the target population for training, and to investigate the associations of perceptions and preferences with training demand. The third is to conduct cost-benefit or cost-effectiveness analyses of public interventions in the training market, where costs are measured comprehensively (that is, covering the direct and indirect costs incurred by training providers, and the explicit and opportunity costs borne by recipients). And the fourth is to investigate employer-provided training, in part to learn what role the government can play in terms of promoting the effectiveness, efficiency, and equity effects of such training.

TABLE 6A.1 **Differences in mean characteristics, training recipients versus nonrecipients, full versus trimmed sample, individuals ages 16–34 years, 2008**

	FEMALE				MALE			
	FULL SAMPLE		TRIMMED SAMPLE		FULL SAMPLE		TRIMMED SAMPLE	
	NONRECIPIENTS	RECIPIENTS	NONRECIPIENTS	RECIPIENTS	NONRECIPIENTS	RECIPIENTS	NONRECIPIENTS	RECIPIENTS
CHARACTERISTIC	MEAN	DIFF.	MEAN	DIFF.	MEAN	DIFF.	MEAN	DIFF.
	(1)	(2)	(3)	(4)	(5)	(6)	(7)	(8)
Rel. to head: Head	0.396	-0.019	0.356	-0.005	0.308	0.014	0.294	-0.012
Rel. to head: Spouse	0.286	-0.046***	0.220	-0.019	0.010	0.005	0.016	-0.003
Rel. to head: Son/daughter (in law)	0.533	0.004	0.554	0.008	0.587	-0.056***	0.554	0.008
Rel. to head: Grandchild	0.014	0.002	0.014	0.006	0.019	0.004	0.021	0.003
Rel. to head: Other relative	0.049	0.009	0.061	0.000	0.072	0.032**	0.108	0.002
Age	23.72	0.558***	23.80	0.346	23.37	1.000***	24.13	-0.069
Married	0.736	-0.123***	0.594	-0.043*	0.540	-0.067***	0.458	-0.059**
Born in present VDC/municipality	0.406	0.000	0.390	0.025	0.769	-0.175***	0.591	-0.036
Attending an academic institution	0.182	0.122***	0.352	0.020	0.298	0.118***	0.458	0.058**
Highest class/degree completed (years)	4.346	4.672***	9.907	0.646***	6.748	3.464***	10.754	0.672***
Obtained the SLC	0.138	0.395***	0.581	0.140***	0.241	0.454***	0.829	0.084***
Household has absentee(s)	0.463	-0.018	0.453	0.007	0.300	-0.034*	0.283	-0.032
Household has benefactor	0.041	0.032***	0.075	0.002	0.039	0.047***	0.066	0.042***
Household asset index	0.035	1.027***	1.141	0.314***	0.136	0.953***	1.083	0.301***
Hindu	0.854	0.040***	0.899	0.014	0.848	0.039***	0.901	-0.005
Brahmin/Chhetri	0.316	0.164***	0.523	0.021	0.303	0.149***	0.483	0.025
Terai middle castes	0.114	-0.051***	0.059	-0.007	0.131	-0.042***	0.091	-0.000
Dalit	0.121	-0.067***	0.035	-0.004	0.111	-0.065***	0.039	-0.018*
Newar	0.052	0.084***	0.128	0.035**	0.061	0.051***	0.121	0.009
Janajati	0.331	-0.083***	0.244	-0.047**	0.329	-0.067***	0.239	-0.021
Muslim	0.045	-0.035***	0.006	0.001	0.043	-0.020***	0.017	0.003
Other castes	0.019	-0.013***	0.004	0.000	0.020	-0.007	0.010	0.001
Kathmandu Valley	0.049	0.091***	0.144	0.032*	0.078	0.103***	0.180	0.028*
Urban Terai	0.066	0.080***	0.137	0.033**	0.084	0.061***	0.138	0.025*
Urban Hills	0.035	0.063***	0.094	0.031**	0.036	0.056***	0.083	0.031***
Rural Terai	0.431	-0.095***	0.342	-0.020	0.420	-0.093***	0.316	-0.006
Rural Hills	0.353	-0.108***	0.250	-0.065***	0.318	-0.101***	0.236	-0.063***
Mountains	0.065	-0.031***	0.033	-0.011*	0.064	-0.025**	0.048	-0.016

Source: Estimated using 2008 Nepal Labour Force Survey data.

Note: SLC = School Leaving Certificate; VDC = Village Development Committee. Columns 1, 3, 5, and 7 report means for training nonrecipients; Columns 2, 4, 6, and 8 report the difference in means between recipients and nonrecipients. The trimmed sample only includes observations with predicted values between 0.1 and 0.9 from a training-receipt logit regression. The training-receipt regressions were estimated separately by gender. Inference based on robust standard errors clustered at the primary sampling unit level. All estimates are adjusted for sampling weights.

*p<0.1, **p<0.05, ***p<0.01.

TABLE 6A.2 **Training effects for females ages 16–34 years, overall, and by schooling level and location, full sample, 2008**

	EMPLOYMENT	WAGE WORK	NONFARM WORK	LOG WAGE EARNINGS
	(1)	(2)	(3)	(4)
Training	0.044***	0.027**	0.105***	−0.033
	(0.014)	(0.011)	(0.016)	(0.066)
a. Heterogeneous effects, by schooling status				
Training (β_1)	0.061***	0.016	0.106***	−0.105
	(0.017)	(0.013)	(0.017)	(0.077)
Training x attending school (β_2)	−0.047*	0.046**	−0.009	0.231
	(0.024)	(0.023)	(0.033)	(0.142)
$\beta_1+\beta_2>0$; p–value	0.491	0.003	0.001	0.308
b. Heterogeneous effects, by education attainment				
Training (β_1)	0.024	0.023	0.120***	−0.057
	(0.020)	(0.016)	(0.018)	(0.109)
Training x obtained the SLC only (β_2)	0.025	0.017	0.003	0.102
	(0.030)	(0.027)	(0.033)	(0.180)
Training x intermediate or higher (β_3)	0.046	−0.024	−0.104***	0.009
	(0.030)	(0.025)	(0.040)	(0.145)
$\beta_1+\beta_2>0$; p–value	0.038	0.058	0.000	0.769
$\beta_1+\beta_3>0$; p–value	0.002	0.990	0.685	0.595
c. Heterogeneous effects, by location				
Training (β_1)	0.056***	0.025*	0.081***	−0.062
	(0.013)	(0.015)	(0.018)	(0.063)
Training x rural (β_2)	−0.027	0.002	0.031	0.042
	(0.024)	(0.020)	(0.025)	(0.119)
$\beta_1+\beta_2>0$; p–value	0.179	0.058	0.000	0.851
Observations	13,184	8,907	8,907	1,098

Source: Estimates using 2008 Nepal Labour Force Survey data.
Note: SLC = School Leaving Certificate. Wage work and nonfarm work are conditional on employment, and log wage earnings are conditional on wage work. Employment, wage work, and nonfarm work regressions are estimated as logit based on maximum likelihood, and log wage earnings regressions are estimated based on least squares. All regressions control for the individual's relation to the head of household, age, marital status, current schooling status, education attainment in years, a standardized index of household consumptive assets, and region identifiers. The regressions also control for whether the individual obtained the SLC; which caste he or she belongs to; whether the individual's household has a private benefactor; and whether the individual's household has an absentee member. Robust standard errors, clustered at the primary sampling unit level, are reported in parentheses. All estimates are adjusted for sampling weights.
*$p<0.1$, **$p<0.05$, ***$p<0.01$.

TABLE 6A.3 **Training effects for females ages 16–34 years, by training length and field, full sample, 2008**

	EMPLOYMENT	WAGE WORK	NONFARM WORK	LOG WAGE EARNINGS
	(1)	(2)	(3)	(4)
a. Heterogeneous effects, by training program length				
Short training courses (β_1)	0.041***	0.026**	0.098***	−0.022
	(0.015)	(0.012)	(0.016)	(0.071)
TSLC/tech. dip. programs (β_2)	0.035	0.007	0.097*	−0.090
	(0.046)	(0.026)	(0.053)	(0.106)
$\beta_1 = \beta_2$; p–value	0.903	0.719	0.902	0.888

continued

TABLE 6A.3, *continued*

	EMPLOYMENT	WAGE WORK	NONFARM WORK	LOG WAGE EARNINGS
	(1)	(2)	(3)	(4)
b. Heterogeneous effects, by training field				
Basic computing (β_1)	0.010	0.045**	0.062*	0.136
	(0.022)	(0.018)	(0.032)	(0.104)
Dressmaking/tailoring (β_2)	0.040*	−0.016	0.104***	−0.155
	(0.021)	(0.018)	(0.021)	(0.130)
Other fields (β_3)	0.086***	0.054***	0.123***	−0.070
	(0.022)	(0.017)	(0.024)	(0.083)
$\beta_1 = \beta_2$; p-value	0.271	0.013	0.247	0.065
$\beta_1 = \beta_3$; p-value	0.008	0.672	0.097	0.059
$B_2 = \beta_3$; p-value	0.117	0.003	0.550	0.589
Observations	13,184	8,907	8,907	1,098

Source: Estimated using 2008 Nepal Labour Force Survey data.
Note: TSLC/tech. dip. programs = Technical School Leaving Certificate / technical diploma programs. Wage work and nonfarm work are conditional on employment, and log wage earnings are conditional on wage work. Employment, wage work, and nonfarm work regressions are estimated as logit based on maximum likelihood, and log wage earnings regressions are estimated based on least squares. All regressions control for the individual's relation to the head of household, age, marital status, current schooling status, education attainment in years, a standardized index of household consumptive assets, and region identifiers. The regressions also control for whether the individual obtained the SLC; which caste he or she belongs to; whether the individual's household has a private benefactor; and whether the individual's household has an absentee member. Robust standard errors, clustered at the primary sampling unit level, are reported in parentheses. All estimates are adjusted for sampling weights.
*$p<0.1$, **$p<0.05$, ***$p<0.01$.

TABLE 6A.4 **Training effects for males ages 16–34 years, overall, and by schooling level and location, full sample, 2008**

	EMPLOYMENT	WAGE WORK	NONFARM WORK	LOG WAGE EARNINGS
	(1)	(2)	(3)	(4)
Training	−0.009	0.082***	0.070***	0.046
	(0.012)	(0.022)	(0.024)	(0.047)
a. Heterogeneous effects, by schooling status				
Training (β_1)	−0.009	0.042*	0.054*	0.035
	(0.019)	(0.023)	(0.028)	(0.054)
Training x attending school (β_2)	0.000	0.175***	0.062	0.054
	(0.024)	(0.044)	(0.049)	(0.108)
$\beta_1+\beta_2>0$; p-value	0.587	0.000	0.005	0.350
b. Heterogeneous effects, by education attainment				
Training (β_1)	−0.044*	0.098***	0.101***	0.082
	(0.023)	(0.030)	(0.035)	(0.065)
Training x obtained the SLC only (β_2)	0.016	−0.090*	−0.058	−0.135
	(0.030)	(0.050)	(0.053)	(0.140)
Training x intermediate or higher (β_3)	0.083***	−0.063	−0.094	−0.078
	(0.029)	(0.048)	(0.064)	(0.091)
$\beta_1+\beta_2>0$; p-value	0.147	0.032	0.000	0.520
$\beta_1+\beta_3>0$; p-value	0.037	0.381	0.897	0.959

continued

TABLE 6A.4, *continued*

	EMPLOYMENT	WAGE WORK	NONFARM WORK	LOG WAGE EARNINGS
	(1)	(2)	(3)	(4)
c. Heterogeneous effects, by location				
Training (β_1)	0.002	0.087***	0.054*	−0.013
	(0.010)	(0.026)	(0.029)	(0.059)
Training x rural (β_2)	−0.023	−0.003	0.019	0.073
	(0.022)	(0.038)	(0.039)	(0.087)
$\beta_1+\beta_2>0$; p-value	0.309	0.004	0.008	0.382
Observations	10,100	7,568	7,568	2,652

Source: Estimates using 2008 Nepal Labour Force Survey data.
Note: SLC = School Leaving Certificate. Wage work and nonfarm work are conditional on employment, and log wage earnings are conditional on wage work. Employment, wage work, and nonfarm work regressions are estimated as logit based on maximum likelihood, and log wage earnings regressions are estimated based on least squares. All regressions control for the individual's relation to the head of household, age, marital status, current schooling status, education attainment in years, a standardized index of household consumptive assets, and region identifiers. The regressions also control for whether the individual obtained the SLC; which caste he or she belongs to; whether the individual's household has a private benefactor; and whether the individual's household has an absentee member. Robust standard errors, clustered at the primary sampling unit level, are reported in parentheses. All estimates are adjusted for sampling weights.
***denotes $p<0.01$, **$p<0.05$, and *$p<0.1$.

TABLE 6A.5 **Training effects for males ages 16–34 years, by training length and field, full sample, 2008**

	EMPLOYMENT	WAGE WORK	NONFARM WORK	LOG WAGE EARNINGS
	(1)	(2)	(3)	(4)
a. Heterogeneous effects, by training program type				
Short training courses (β_1)	−0.016	0.090***	0.052**	0.028
	(0.013)	(0.023)	(0.026)	(0.048)
TSLC/tech. dip. programs (β_2)	0.051*	−0.047	0.115*	0.149
	(0.027)	(0.052)	(0.065)	(0.116)
$\beta_1 = \beta_2$; p-value	0.041	0.150	0.256	0.141
b. Heterogeneous effects, by training field				
Basic computing (β_1)	−0.014	0.099***	0.051	0.011
	(0.015)	(0.033)	(0.038)	(0.088)
Other fields (β_2)	−0.001	0.074***	0.077***	0.060
	(0.018)	(0.024)	(0.029)	(0.051)
$\beta_1 = \beta_2$; p-value	0.560	0.486	0.565	0.616
Observations	10,100	7,568	7,568	2,652

Source: Estimated using 2008 Nepal Labour Force Survey data.
Note: TSLC/tech. dip. programs = Technical School Leaving Certificate / technical diploma programs. Wage work and nonfarm work are conditional on employment, and log wage earnings are conditional on wage work. Employment, wage work, and nonfarm work regressions are estimated as logit based on maximum likelihood, and log wage earnings regressions are estimated based on least squares. All regressions control for the individual's relation to the head of household, age, marital status, current schooling status, education attainment in years, a standardized index of household consumptive assets, and region identifiers. The regressions also control for whether the individual obtained the SLC; which caste he or she belongs to; whether the individual's household has a private benefactor; and whether the individual's household has an absentee member. Robust standard errors, clustered at the primary sampling unit level, are reported in parentheses. All estimates are adjusted for sampling weights.
***denotes $p<0.01$, **$p<0.05$, and *$p<0.1$.

NOTES

1. The other two main ways are extensive public sector employment and the provision of permits to Nepalese for short-term, contract labor migration to countries with which Nepal has bilateral labor agreements.
2. Employed is defined as engaged in an economic activity for at least one hour in the reference week. Unemployed is defined as not employed, available to work in the reference week, and having actively searched for work in the reference month.
3. Training fields are constructed as follows. Individual responses were coded using the 1997 International Standard Classification of Education (ISCED) fields for training. With the exception of four detailed fields (*computer science, dressmaking/tailoring, driving and motor vehicle operation,* and *hairdressing/beautician work*) that had reasonable numbers of observations, detailed fields were aggregated to the broad field level. Given their similarity, the broad field of *engineering* was combined with the broad field of *other craft, trade, and industrial.* Broad fields with less than 1 percent of observations each were eliminated. Instead of using ISCED's broad field names, we sometimes named the field on the basis of the detailed field in it with the highest percent of observations. For example, instead of using the broad field name of *fine and applied arts,* we named it "handicrafts"; instead of using the broad field name of *agriculture, forestry, and fisheries,* we named it "farming and livestock management." Discussions with training providers indicate that the computer science observations are largely tantamount to basic computer and Internet use. Thus, we named this field "basic computing."
4. All training of 12 months or more is classified as training through TSLC/technical diploma programs.
5. The employment rate is 63 percent, the wage work share is 16 percent, and the nonfarm work share is 35 percent for female training nonrecipients in the trimmed sample.
6. In their evaluation of vouchers for short-term training in Nepal, Bhatta et al. (2017) find that the intervention had significant positive effects on both women and men, and that the effect sizes were similar across gender.
7. More precisely, Card, Kluve, and Weber (2015) find that active labor market programs for women only have larger aggregate effects than programs for men only or those for both genders. Reviewing only experimental evaluations of training programs in low- and middle-income countries, McKenzie (2017) does not find evidence indicative of generally larger effects for women than for men. McKenzie also finds that many of the evaluations do not formally test for gender differences in effects.
8. We are unable to find any studies for Nepal that justify public intervention based on an analysis of failures in the formal training market.

REFERENCES

ADB (Asian Development Bank). 2004. *Nepal: Skills for Employment Project—Report and Recommendations of the President.* Manila: ADB.

——. 2013a. *Nepal: Skills for Employment Project—Completion Report.* Manila: ADB.

——. 2013b. *Nepal: Skills Development Project: Report and Recommendation of the President.* Project Number 38176-015. Manila: ADB.

——. 2015. *Innovative Strategies in Technical and Vocational Education and Training for Accelerated Human Resource Development in South Asia: Nepal.* Manila: ADB.

Bhatta, Saurav Dev, Sangeeta Goyal, Dhiraj Sharma, and Jayakrishna Upadhyay. 2017. "Skills Matter: Impact of Short-Term Training on Labor Market Outcomes in Nepal." Unpublished manuscript.

Blattman, Christopher, Nathan Fiala, and Sebastian Martinez. 2014. "Generating Skilled Self-Employment in Developing Countries: Experimental Evidence from Uganda." *Quarterly Journal of Economics* 129 (2): 697–752.

Brunello, Giorgio, and Maria De Paola. 2009. "Is There Under-Provision of Training?" *Empirical Research in Vocational Education and Training* 1 (1): 1–18.

Card, David, Jochen Kluve, and Andrea Weber. 2015. "What Works? A Meta Analysis of Recent Active Labor Market Program Evaluations." Working Paper 21431, National Bureau of Economic Research, Cambridge, MA.

Chakravarty, Shubha, Mattias K. A. Lundberg, Plamen Nikolov Danchev, and Juliane Zenker. 2015. "The Role of Training Programs for Youth Employment in Nepal: Impact Evaluation Report on the Employment Fund." Policy Research Working Paper 7656, World Bank, Washington, DC.

Crump, Richard K., V. Joseph Hotz, Guido W. Imbens, and Oscar A. Mitnik. 2009. "Dealing with Limited Overlap in Estimation of Average Treatment Effects." *Biometrika* 96 (1): 187–99.

Government of Nepal. 2009. *Nepal Labour Force Survey 2008: Statistical Report*. Kathmandu: Central Bureau of Statistics, Government of Nepal.

——. 2010. *A Profile of Technical and Vocational Education and Training Providers, Nepal*. Kathmandu: Government of Nepal.

——. 2012. *National Population and Housing Census 2011 (National Report)*. Kathmandu: Central Bureau of Statistics, Government of Nepal.

——. 2015a. *National Youth Policy 2072*. Kathmandu: Ministry of Youth and Sports, Government of Nepal.

——. 2015b. *Youth Vision 2025*. Kathmandu: Ministry of Youth and Sports, Government of Nepal.

——. 2017. *14th Plan (FY 2073/74–2075/76)*. Kathmandu: National Planning Commission, Government of Nepal.

Hicks, Joan Hamory, Michael Kremer, Isaac Mbiti, and Edward Miguel. 2015. "Vocational Education in Kenya—A Randomized Evaluation." 3ie Grantee Final Report, International Initiative for Impact Evaluation (3ie), New Delhi.

Imbens, Guido W. 2015. "Matching Methods in Practice: Three Examples." *Journal of Human Resources* 50 (2): 373–419.

Kluve, Jochen, Susana Puerto, David Robalino, Jose Manuel Romero, Friederike Rother, Jonathan Stoterau, Felix Weidenkaff, and Marc Witte. 2016. "Do Youth Employment Programs Improve Labor Market Outcomes? A Systematic Review." IZA Discussion Paper 10263, Institute for the Study of Labor, Bonn.

McKenzie, David. 2017. "How Effective Are Active Labor Market Policies in Developing Countries? A Critical Review of Recent Evidence." Policy Research Working Paper 8011, World Bank, Washington, DC.

Serriere, Nicolas, and CEDA (Centre for Economic Development and Administration). 2014. *Labour Market Transitions of Young Women and Men in Nepal*. Work4Youth Publication Series No. 12. Geneva: International Labour Office.

Tripney, Janice S., and Jorge G. Hombrados. 2013. "Technical and Vocational Education and Training (TVET) for Young People in Low- and Middle-Income Countries: A Systematic Review and Meta-Analysis." *Empirical Research in Vocational Education and Training* 5 (3).

World Bank. 2011. *Nepal: Enhanced Vocational Education and Training Project—Project Appraisal Document*. Washington DC: World Bank.

——. 2017. *Nepal: Enhanced Vocational Education and Training Project II—Project Appraisal Document*. Washington DC: World Bank.